When I awoke, before I had time to speak,
A knocking on the door sounded "Doong, doong!"
They came and told me a messenger from Shang-chou
Had brought a letter,—a single scroll from you!
Up from my pillow I suddenly sprang out of bed,
And threw on my clothes, all topsy-turvy.
I undid the knot and saw the letter within;
A single sheet with thirteen lines of writing.
At the top it told the sorrows of an exile's heart;
At the bottom it described the pains of separation.
The sorrows and pains took up so much space
There was no room left to talk about the weather!

—Po Chu-I
from "The Letter"
translated by Arthur Waley

Pioneer letters:
the letter
as literature

This book constitutes Volume 19, Numbers 1 & 2 of
NORTHWEST REVIEW
ISSN 0029-3423

LIBRARY OF CONGRESS CATALOGING IN PUBLICATION DATA

(Northwest Review, ISSN 0029-3423; v. 19, no. 1-2)
Edited by John Witte
1. American literature—20th century. 2. Epistolary fiction, American.
3. Epistolary poetry, American. 4. Epistolary poetry— History
criticism—Addresses, essays, lectures. 5. Pioneers—
West (U.S.)—Correspondence. I. Witte, John, 1948-   . II. Series.
AP2.N855 vol. 19, no. 1-2 [PS536.2] 81-1903
ISBN 0-918402-05-0 [816'.008] AACR2 081s

ACKNOWLEDGEMENTS

We wish to thank the following individuals, and institutions, for their extraordinary contributions to this project. It would not have been possible without them.

Thanks to Danna Wilner and to Deb Casey for their editorial prowess. Thanks to Kenneth Duckett of the Oregon Collection of the University of Oregon Library, for his permission to use the pioneer letters reprinted here, and to Martin Schmitt, in memoriam, for his invaluable catalogue of these documents. Thanks to Marian Willard Johnson, Dorothy Miller, and the University of Oregon Museum of Art for their permission to reprint the Morris Graves painted letters in their collections, and to Morris Graves himself for his generous encouragement.

Thanks to the staff of *Northwest Review* for their intelligence and energy.

This project is jointly sponsored by grants from the Oregon Arts Commission and from the National Endowment for the Arts, a Federal Agency created by an act of Congress in 1965.

CONTENTS

FICTION

ART

ESSAYS & REVIEWS

CONTRIBUTORS

INTRODUCTION

Literary activity in America, proceeding by its usual fits and starts, has produced in recent years at least one trend of major importance: the extraordinary resurgence in popularity of the letter as a literary form. Many of our most accomplished poets and novelists have chosen the epistle as the vehicle for their new works. John Barth and Richard Hugo, Alan Dugan, Jim Harrison and Richard Howard, to name a few, have written with great originality and authority in the genre. As well, the publication of the actual letters of famous people, usually a seasonal activity, is undergoing a sort of renaissance. The more or less confidential thoughts of Virginia Woolf, Ezra Pound, Sylvia Plath, Anne Sexton, Thomas Merton, Vladimir Nabakov and Ernest Hemingway are among those being made available to eager audiences. And among young writers—especially among young writers—the letter-form seems to exert an unusual magnetism. The invitation to submit work for consideration for this anthology was met with a dazzling richness of new writing, from which was selected, with difficulty, the work presented here.

Why should the letter-form be enjoying such vitality today? Three observations about the epistolary style are useful to answering this question: (1.) the familiarity of the form, (2.) its intimacy and spontaneity, and (3.) the separation it implies.

First, the letter is a familiar form. The letter is, for most of us, the only place we regularly attempt to express thoughts important to us in a clear, written form. The writer utilizing the epistolary style (unlike the writer of sonnets, let's say) may have confidence in reaching his/her audience in a form they will be comfortable with, even practiced at. Further, the letter-form has the appeal of seeming to demystify the activity of the artist.

The letter imparts a feeling of intimacy. The letter is not, strictly speaking, an artform at all, but a private, spontaneous exchange between two people. During a time of continued reaction against "academic" or abstract writing, this spontaneity undoubtedly accounts for much of the form's current popularity. Nothing grandly artistic is being attempted here, at least not ostensibly. In this, the letter-form might be seen as a distillation of confessionalism.

Finally, the letter implies separation, geographical and/or emotional, and this, too, makes it fitting for the literature of our time. Americans are a people in motion, moved and removed from our places of origin. That we suffer separations within ourselves, within our families and communities, is a commonplace. Noteworthy is the ingenuity with which writers have adapted the letter-form to every possible circumstance: letters to oneself, letters from Beauty to the Beast, letters to the dead, letters to God.

"The edge is what I have," the words Theodore Roethke chose to describe his great gift (and burden) remind us that every true artist is a pioneer, someone exploring and exploiting new territory. John Haines, one of our most gifted poets, wrote the letters printed here from his homestead in Alaska: from the outermost edge of America. Like the 19th Century pioneers whose letters compare so remarkably with his own, like the Pilgrims at Plymouth, like Li Po, the T'ang Dynasty poet exiled to the northern provinces of China, Haines' experience is an analogue of the artist as pioneer. In these letters from the wilderness we notice a prototype for current epistolary writing.

As in every time of great disappointment and intolerance there is a moving on, a restlessness felt first by those most sensitive to injustice and insipidity. Now that the last actual wilderness is being parceled out, now that space exploration, expected to open the next frontier, appears unable to capture the popular imagination, we should not be surprised to find our best artists probing the frontiers of psychical possibility. That they should choose the letter-form to convey the sense of their removal from established conventions, and their state of excitement, refreshed as they are by new discoveries about language and about ourselves, seems to me entirely appropriate. And, like the Oregon pioneers before them, they invite us to follow them.

I think the reader of the following letters, epistolary stories, and poems, will feel a gratifying sense of the competence of these pioneers of our culture. Like the territorial pioneers before them, they have an instinct for survival under the most inhospitable circumstances. They have an uncanny sense of direction. They are curious and exuberant and large-hearted.

At last the mail has arrived. There's news from the interior. And the news is good.

JW

Documents

IRA GARDNER

In 1865, Ira Gardner, a woodworker in Oregon, wrote to his sister Avis, in Iowa.

May 14—Year 1865

I this opportunity to inform you that I am well at pres and hope to hear the same from you soon now I will tell you ware I am I am working in port land in oregon working at the painting and finishing of furniture at the furniture machine shop and wages is from three to four dollars a day here now I will tell you something a bout the country oregon it has got thousands froots growing in oregon but the winters here generally warm and wet and rainy and I expect to go to puget sound on the seacosat and if it soots mee there I shall take up a hundred and sixty acres of land there if it soots mee there and if it does soot mee I shall stop there and build a house and secure land plant some froot trees I have seen cherry trees of different kinds loaded cherrys and I could stand on the ground and reach out my hand over the top twig of the tree you can raze in three years plenty of all kinds I can not tell yo mutch about the country now but I will write again soon and I want you Avis Gardner to get Elias Gardner and Henry Gardner to write mee for you and I want to know where William Gardner is or whether he got home a live or not and I want you Avis Gardner to let mee know how you are getting along and where you are alive ing now I would like to see you and talk with you for you sayed if I would come first and see the country and if I liked the country you would come out here with mee what do you think about it now I want to know about your health and whether you are able to come out here or not if you are not able I will come back and try to make you as comfortable as I can and I would like to see Lemuel Smith and old grand father Smith talk with them now about mattes and tings now—tell lemuel smith I would like to hear from him now

May 14 year 1865

I This opper tunity to inform you
that I am well at pres and hope
to hear the same from you soon
now I will tell you ware I am I am
working in pu et land in oregon
working at painting and
finizh ing off furniture at the
furniture mashine shop and
wages is fro thre to four dollars
a day here now I will tell you something
a bout the contry oregon it has
got thousands fruots growing
in oregon but the winters here are
generally warm and wet and rainy
and I expect to go to pufet sound
on the sea cost and if it soot mee
there I shall take up a hundred and
sixty acres of land there if it
soots me there and if it does soot mee
I shall stop there and build a house
and improve land plant some fruot
trees I have sen cherry trees
of different kinds loaded churrys
and I could stand on the ground
and reach out my hand over the
top twig of the tree you can raise fru

July 2, 1865

Avis Gardner my love to you is stil the same and the time seems
to pass away very slow when I cannot see you but if we cannot see
each other for a while wee might have good faith and hope and
love and trust in the lord for the preservation of our lives and
health and strength for we cannot do any thing other than too trust
in the lord and rely on his promises and I hope we may have luck
to live to see each other again but if not on earth let us strive to
meet in heaven where all sorrows are turned into pease and happiness too them that love the lord and rely upon his promises but
I hope that I shall see you and talk with you in this country now
I will tell you something about this country here this country
abounds with froots of all kinds and that of the best kinds cherrys
here are a grate deal larger here than I ever saw in any other
country before and appels of the best quality of all sort and of the
largest and best kinds and pares are so much larger and better
here I have never saw any thig half up to them that I have seen
here and quinces are the largest and the best that I ever saw any
whare else and strawberrys are mutch larger here than they are
in iowa that you would bee surprised to see them and currents and
goosebarys and damson plums and apricots and all kinds of wild
froots such as berrys black berrys psalmon berrys gooseberrys and
a grate menny other kinds of froots grow in abundance here and
you would be astonished too see the abundance of froot that grows
here and of such a superior quality too that you have seen in all
your life and the people here says that if anny one will plant froot
trees here and take care of them that he will have plenty of froot
in three years of his own and we can have froot here all the time
now and at the table whare I bord there is current pys and black
berry pys and appel pys and custard pys and good lite biscuit and
litebread and freash mutten and fresh beef stake and good smoked
pork ham and chicken stew and fresh psalmon and lettuce and
onions radishes of the best green pees and corn bread and potatoes both mashed and baked with the skin onn and this country
beets iowa all together in raising potatoes onions radishes and
pees and beens and in raising wheat it beets iowa and in oats and
barley and buck wheat but iowa can beet this country in raising
corn and what eatables I spoke of on the table was all on the table
at once and the table is set with froots all the time froot is plenty
    I have lots more to write but I have not got time now

WILLIAM S. PRICHARD

William Prichard left Polk County, Iowa in 1852, was in Marysville, California, in 1861, in Union, Oregon in 1865-1867, and Rye Valley, Oregon in 1868-1869. In 1865 he built a toll road from Union to Express Ranch, Oregon, an investment that failed.

F. Desmoines, March 21, 1852.
Dear Sister and Brother:
Once more I take my pen in hand to inform you that I am well at present. I received your letter and was glad to here, from you but was very sorry to find you in so much trubbel about my going to Oregon. I think you ough to be willing for me to go. You know when I take a notion to do enything that I am very apt to do and I don't comprehend Eny danger what Ever and if I did on the planes why I am willing and expect to die Satisfide and I don't never Expect to See you again Dear Sister til I have wander over the Western Countries!

My school is out and I am going to start to Okaloosa day after tomorrow. K. C. Knowlin is there now waiting for me, if the weather will admit we are going to start the first day of April.

Don't Grieve Sister about your Brother I am coming back again and perhaps Sister is the last Letter that you will get from me til I land in Oregon: and perhapes it may be the Last that you will ever get but Dear Sister if I live to get there why then I will Write to you immediately and let you know where I am and all about the Country & Co, you nead not be uneasy about me for I am going with men that I am well acquanted with and all is right on my Side dont fear Sister I know that it does asseam hard for us to part so long but I hope to See you once more on Earth but if we never do why I hope to meet you in the world to Come. I have nothing of interest to Write to you now tell all my inquiring friends that I am well and in good Spirits and going to Oregon.

I would be very glad to See you all once more before I Start but as I am so fare off I cant Come: Dear Sister I must now bid you farewell. I immagine that I have yet hold of your hand now: dont grieve all is well with me now: friendes must part while wandering here below and Some times to meet no more but I trust that the time will Come when you and I will meet again: I want you to forget that you ever had a brother by the name of W.S. So Sister Fare you well I am Coming back again and Cannot ask you to with bare with me eny longer as expect your patience are all ready worn out—

Wm. S. Prichard To Jessy Coleman and Nancy An Coleman.

Dear Brother, I Cant Hardly tell you how I felt when I read you Letter and finding you to be so ancies for me to Come Home. when asking my self the question finding that I was fane the other way, my good Brother you must know that I felt very bad. Dear Brother you must Concider that I am young and that I am like every one else in this World. that is I have awork to do. I am young and Dear Brother I have flattered my self that if I had some means to go on I Could make something out of my self, and I have flattered my self that Oregon is the very place. Now Dear Brother All That I Ask of you is to let me go willingly and give me your well wishes. if I Can take up my whip in the Spring, and bid you all fare well and just think that you are all willing for me to go why Brother it will be the gratest cumfert to me of eny thing you Can do for me. I am well aware Brother that it is a very solemn under taking but if it is my lot to die on the Planes, why I am contented and I think you aught to be too, I expect that the Question will arrise why are you agoing to leave Iowa? Answer, I have nothing particular aganst Iowa eny more than money is very scarse, and is very Cold in Winter. it is aroling Cuntry and general it is dry under foot

Amos Prichard   William S Prichard

WHEN I REFLECT ON THE PAST!
My Dear Brother I All most wish my self Back agane with you again but I think that if life be spared I will have the plasure of seeing you about the Year 1855 I am sure that that is along way off and as we have no Lease of our life Dear Brother I think that there is two Chance for me never to See you where there is one for me too see you, but as we cant tell Enything about it we can onley hope for the future. I want you to Write to me just as soon as this Comes too hand and let me know How you all Com on. I want you to tend to my land. Jessey Coleman has got the Dead, I want you Or Him to pay the Tax on it. you Can Sell it (the Land) if you want too and use the money as you thought best, I beleve, Amos, I would druther you would sell it than not and use the money and if I ever get back why we Can fix it. if you do sell it I want you to keep Coleman and Nancy, because they have avery hard time in this world

Amos D P Wm

Not Much To Write This Time Dear Brother. I will now tell you some thing about my trip to Oregon, I am going With aman who lives at Oskaloosa that is 65 miles from this place. I have no acquaintence of acount Eny more than what his Nabors Say. they give him avery good name. Green Berry Camplen Bowlen talk of going with me, and I think he will be apt to go if he does go why I will just be fixed for Green is afine fellow. Green is Teaching School One hundred miles West of this place. Fishback has left us and we do not know where he is or Eny thing about him, the Peopel of this Cuntry thinks it quite asmall job to go to Oregon they think nuthing of rigging up there teams and starting with there famley,

So, Dear Brother I must Com to aclose. I am geting along well teaching school they think that I am afine scholar and in fact I have the name of being the best Scribe in Polk County Iowa, I have taken one scholar threw the Arithmetic Grammar and Geography. Direct Your Letter To Oskaloos Iowa, I have forgot the County but it will Come with out,

Remember your Unworthy Brother
Amos D. Prichard,   William S. Prichard

Marysville Cal
May 7th 1864

Madam
        Yours of 21st March 1864 enquiring about your brother
Wm S. Pritchard received and contents noted.
        He was in town about two months since and at this present
time is, I am informed at Virginia City in Nevada Territory
mining—
        He was over that way last year with thousands of others
from here
        I presume letters would reach him addressed as above—
Your letter to Mc Daniel or your brother Mc Daniel has been
received—
                                I am
To   Very respectfully
Mrs. Nancy A. Coleman   Yours
Terrue Haute   Wm B. Latham Jr.
Ind.

Walla Walla Washington
Territory July 17th 1865

Dear Brother and Sister
I have neglected to write to you when I left Nevada I am not
located as yet in this country but when I do I will write again: I
leave here today will write soon: I am as ever your
                        Loving brother
                        W.S. Prichard

Union Sept. 16th 1865
Dear Brother & Sister
It has been a long time Since I heard from you but I am to blame.
I brot a Saddle train to Boise City Idaho Territory and am now
in Oregon. I think something of building a tool road in this country
and if I suceed and do well this year I am coming home next year:

I have nothing to write to interest you this is a hard country and I am living a hard life I hope Dear Sister that we may live to See each other yet: but the chances looks hard: I could write you strange things about my   was! old friend! G.C. Bowlin, but will not now I hope to see you in life and if so will tell you about it:

Give my love to all inquiring friends.
Direct your letter to Union P.O. Union County, Oregon.

I am as Ever your Brother

W.S. Prichard

Give my love to Amox ' wife and tell her to write

Union Union County Oregon
17tth of July 66
Miss Marrie A. Coleman.
Dear Niece I have just received two letters from you one of April 24 and the other of June 5th and was glad to hear that you was well and that Sister's health is improving: My health is modrath good at present. I came veary near coming home last Spring one year ago and Sad do I regret the day that I gave up the notion and went into this road speculation: I have built a road 40 miles threw these mountains at a cost of 14000 dollars and the County has gone down so that it has proved almost a complete failure and consiquently leaves me in a bad fix financly. and leaves me as far from the path that leads homeward as I was when I came to the Country. I have had quite a hard time Since I landed in this Country as it is a veary cold and bleak climate. the snow fell Three feet deep in the valley and I have been working from ten to thirty men ever since last August 15. and only lost 7 week last winter. Well Matt I can not think of any thing to write to night so I shall close. I want you to tell me some thing about your country and if there is any thing that a man can do there to make a living as I begin to think that I can not make a living here, if I attempt to stay here much longer I shall have to get married or do something desperit to see if it will not change my luck. I am glad to hear you say that you feel anxious to get an Education as it is better than money to you. dont forget to write. and I will try and not. Give my love to your Father and Mother and all inquiring friends. Your ever loving Uncle

W. S. Prichard

Baker County Oregon Dec 8th 1866
Mrs. N. A. Coleman & Mattie
Terre Haut Indiana

Dear Sister & Niece I received yours of Oct 10th and was glad
to hear that you are all in the land of the liveing. My health is
only modratly good: you wish to know all about my road speculation well it is quick told. I came here about 16 months ago, with
12000 dollars and went in to build a road from Union town to
Express Ranch burnt river. Distance 42 miles. I bot a ranch and
put up a big lot of hay, and maid some money out of it. at the same
time runing a big lot of men on the road. I have put in all my time
ever since. The road is dun and there has been Considseble travel
on it this Season. the totle cost of the Road is 12,543.00. I now
find my Self destitute of a dollar and 1200 dollars in dept with no
prospect of raising the money to pay it off. I Dash below to morrow
morning to see what I can do about raising money to pay off the
dept. if I succeed I may get 1000 dollars or 2000 dollars out of it.
and if not I am with out a cent for the first time since I have been
on the Coast. You dead not write to me here any more untill you
hear from me again I will not neglect to write to you Again and
let you know how I am getting along.

Your Brother as ever
W.S. Prichard

Rye Valley Sept 12th 1868
Well Matte Coleman your letters have come in upon me so
thick and fast for the last month that it compeles me to write I
have received three and am glad to hear that you are all well and
doing well. You still insist on my coming home and seam confident that I am quite able So far as money is Concerned but only
like the disposition. I wish you were wright. I told you of my loss
on the road well my road just lays there and is a totle loss So I
came, in to this little Mining Camp a little over one year ago with
out one Dollar. So I had to Commence with my hands and this is
a hard Country to make a raise in I have managed to live so far
but made nothing as yet, I have just got a letter from my old
partner in California wishing me to come back and go in partners

with him, his name is McDaniel, and if I can rase money anuff to get back on this fall I shall go as California is a better Country than this, I should be veary glad to come back and see you all if I could and to see the Country as I have a veary faint idea of the Country. Yes I spoke of William being in truble about Something. I should be glad to know who William is and what the truble is. You must remember that I have forgoten a grate many persons there and it wil require some explination.

I am working hard and living in a dirt house I am Mining on my own Luck it is a hard and uncertain buisness:

Give my love to all inquiring friends. You have all of my best wishes for your success in your studes I think you deserve greater prase for your success and perseverance in such a good Cause. You can write as often as you please As I am always glad to read if not to write

Yours as Eever
W.S. Prichard

Rye Valley February 7th 1869
My Dear Niece

Your kind letter has just come to hand and I am glad to hear from you and that you are geting along so well I am in sympthy with you Dear Niece for the loss of your Dear Companion, it looks hard to see the young and beautiful taken away so young, but its God's will, and we must submit. Dear Matte I am sorry and heartily ashamed of my last letter to you, but you are so kind hearted I know you will look over my weaken exeseses. And I am determined to be more prompt in writing from this on, I have had a great deal of hard luck but that is no excuse for such conduct, we have had a beautiful winter so far the Sun is Shining like Spring. And every thing is waring an air of Cherfulness to day. I will be glad when spring comes in truth, and I can go to work, for there are no amusements here and time passes off veary Slowly. I think I can get Some little money ahead Next Summer. And then I shall leave the Mines and try my luck at some thing else. I have just been out to Baker City distence 37 miles it is our county seat, and I had Some offeres made me while there to build a Seminary and go to teaching, but my education is so veary limited that I can not think of undertaking it. I could built it by supscription and pay so much yearly and I think it would be a paying institution. I want you in your next letter to give me an out line of your School No. of scholars price of Tueshon and so: Jane Prichard tell me that she has a Daughter going to school in your city I should like to know how she is geting along. You said nothing in your last about your and Molly's Likeness. I should be veary much pleased to receive them and if ever I get in to an other sivelized country I will send you mine. Give my love to my Dear Sister & Brother and all relations.

I wish you to send your letters Direct to Epress Ranch Baker County Oregon, if you can hunt me up an old maid of 18 or 20 it might be some indusement for me to come home for a short time, as old maids of that stripe are rather scarce in this section of the country

Yours as Ever
W.S. Prichard

ALMIRA ADELINE DAVID RAYMOND

Almira Raymond, wife of William W. Raymond, mission farmer, arrived in Oregon in 1849 as part of the mission "re-enforcement." She wrote to her sister in Catskill, N.Y., from the Willamette Mission, and later from Tansy Point, Oregon.

Tansy Point Oregon Feb. 20, 1852

Dear Sister,

I have often thought I would give a few particulars of my history in this country, but time and opportunity has failed untill now. I seem to have a little time. I have a young babe 3 weeks old, my husband has gone up the river to Portland and dayton to attend to his public business and get supplies for the family and I am left with an indian boy and my children sometimes feel a little lonesome as I am not able to work or get about much yet but think I am ganing now. We who rais families in this country have had much to do. We have had 9 children in 13 years in having these I have suffered much. I have never been less than 24 hours in child birth and generally 48. My life has been despaired of a number of times. Twise I have been delivered by artificial means and the children died at both times. My husband has been my only strength and he has done all he could for me. It has been as hard for him as for me. The lord has brought me through trials and difficulties and I could not have believed I could have lasted through but I trust they have been for my good. I am afraid I have much to learn before my patience is perfect but I have seen the goodness of God in delivering from trial many a time and have felt to say the visitations of thy spirit have sustained my life. We have many ups and downs in this country. Sometimes provisions have been dear and scarce and sometimes plenty and cheap. This market with California is very fluctuating. We have had about one month cold weather this winter wich is a long time for us to have freezing weather here. Mr. Jaffelmine stopt with us 3 weeks I gave him the best accomodations my house afforded and questioned him much about you all at home and I am glad to say he gave information I could not get by letter. It was pleasing to see one come from you all. I was glad to hear that most of you are in good circumstances. It would be a greate pleasure to me if I was so situated as to step in and spend a day or an houre with you it would help to aleviate the cares and ills of life and offer rest. But dear sister all these and many other previous priviledges are deneyed me and I must toil every day for my bread but my sister this toil will not always last for there remains a rest for the children of God and that rest I am striving for. May God grant to you and I and all his people is the prayer of your unworthy sister,

Almira Raymond

Astoria Feb. 24

Dear Sister,

I improve a few moments to inform you we are well. I was glad to hear from you but sorry to hear of the war and bloodshed that makes wretched and desolate your once peasful and happy land. I hope you may hear from James. I know his absence must have caused you many a lonesome hour but dear sister after we have done all we can we must leave our children in the hands of God. In a few years we shall have to leave them altogether and go, I hope when the wicked cease from trouble and the weary are at rest. I feel anxious about Ira. I know he has a very responsible situation in the army and in this war many of the Officers have got killed and wounded. Please write and send us the Detroit press that we may know how he is getting along. My children have been to school this winter and have got along vary well. I hope Mother and Aunt Clara are getting along well. I know they must be lonesome without Charly. Give my respect to Ira's family. I want very much to see his children. Ask Adison to write me. You do not write any thing about Mary. I want to hear from her. Jonny I think must be a smart boy to work in the mill and get 9 shillings a day. I think he may yet come to Oregon and make a good farmer. Tell John I think he has forgotten that Almira is in Oregon. For years he has not wrote me a word. Times are hard, goods high, wages low, all the time news from the mines of rich diggings but so many false reports. Many are afraid to go and many are not but are moving to the land of gold. Dear sister how glad I would be to see you and all our friends at home and visit the dear old grave yard and our dear old home stead and also

Clatsop Plains Jan 4, 1880

My Dear Sister

     My health is very poor at present. An Absess in my side that discharges through the bowels as much as a cupful dayly. I am poorer in flesh than when I wrote last and feel much weakness. I had hopes of seeing you in this world but I have given that up now. But we will be sure to meet in heaven. I feel sorry to think you suffer so much. You are feeble as well as I am. I suffer so much at times. My youngest Daughter is staying with us this winter. Nathan my son is Surveying. The Lord is with me. In him I put my trust.

Give my love to all. I wrote to Ira but have received no reply.

Your loving Sister,

Almira A Raymond

DARIUS SMITH

Darius Smith, friend of William Raymond, wrote from San Francisco in 1859, describing that "dashaway town."

Sanfransisco, June 5th 1859

Friend Raymond

According to agreement I occupy a few moments this afternoon in addressing you. We have been in this fast city one week waiting the sailing of the steamer and have enjoyed ourselves very well considering the great contrast between a bustle bustle clear the track, life and a quiet country life among the Pikes in Oregon. Frisco is a dashaway town without doubt. We have been feasting on all kinds of vegetables such as Potatoes Peas Beans Squashes Turnips melons strawberries and in fact there is no use to try to mention evry thing it would take more time and paper than I have got to spare. Suffize it to say that there is every thing to eat drink and wear that you ever thought or heard of. Peddlers as thick as hops. While I am writing they keep annoying me by passing by the window of the hotel yelling out Orenges six for a quarter. We attended church this morning at Dr. Scotts Presbyterian Church where were congregated from a thousand to fifteen hunderd Persons. It was a splendid church, built at an expence I should think of fifty thousand dolars. They have a good choir and an Organ. We have attended no other church since we have been here. We attended last evening an exibition of King Solomon's temple which was grand. We start to morrow on our journey for New York. I have purchased a ticket first cabin on the oposition line. Steamer Uncle Sam. I paid 320 dollars for two tickets. Both steamers will be crowded to overflowing.

I suppose every thing goes off as it use to was did in Forest Grove.

No more to you at this time.

Yours with Respect
Darius Smith

San francisco June 5th 1857

Friend Raymond

According to agreement I occupy a few moments this afternoon in addressing you. We have been in this fast city one week waiting the sailing of the Steamer and have enjoyed ourselves very well considering the great contrast between a bustle bustle clear the track, life and a quiet country life among the Pikes in Oregon. — Frisco is a dashaway town without doubt. We have been feasting on all kinds of vegitables such as Potatoes Peas Beans squashes turnips melons Strawberries and in fact, there is no use to try to mention every thing it would take more time and paper than I have got to spare, suffice it to say that there is every thing to eat drink and wear that you ever thought of or heard of. Peddlers as thick as shops. While I am writing they keep annoying me by passing by the window of the hotel yelling out Oranges six for a quarter

KATE L. ROBBINS

Kate Robbins was born in Cohasset, Massachusetts. About 1854 her husband Abner went to California, where he mined and farmed at Yreka Flats and Indian Creek from 1855 to 1859. In 1859 he returned to Massachusetts and brought Kate back to Indian Creek. In 1868 the couple moved to Ochoco, Oregon, where Abner raised sheep, cattle and horses. They were among the first settlers in the Ochoco region.

St. Nicholas Hotel, N.Y. March 6th, 1859

Dear Brother:

I thought a few lines from here might prove acceptable. We did not leave Boston until 5 O'clock Saturday as the Steamer is delayed on account of Congress or something or other. I do not exactly know what. Got to Fall River about half past eight P.M. Had to sit a long time in the Cars waiting for the boat which connects with the cars, went on board, took supper at 10, had a nice state room. It is one of the handsomest and best boats out (The Empire State), was lots of passengers en route for California. Went to bed and between one and two heard or rather felt a kind of crash as if the boat had struck. I tell you it didn't take Abner long to get his pants on and his California tickets and money into his pockets, and to tell me to get my clothes on, for he did not know what would be to pay, but he soon found we were not damaged but had run into a Schooner called the Knowles, loaded with coal, belonged down east. She sunk immediately, all hands saved, boats picked them up, all but one who had caught a rope. One man jumped into the water near the wheel of the steamboat, one turn would have killed him. There were five. She was loaded very deep and went right down. The coat was for the Bay State Company, the company to which the Empire State belongs. Shall leave here tomorrow. Got in today about 12. Mr. Cozzens of Cohasset is going, the old man. Abner had got his hair cut in style. Don't look like the same man. Am up in the fourth story of a big hotel, one that I saw the painting of at the Panoroma. I also saw the Empire State there and Broadway. They all look natural. Mrs. Tilden is here. Abner says she is here but shan't lay on such a big pillow no way. Write soon. Kiss Eunice. Give this to Amanda when you have a chance. Write soon and tell Sarah to.

Kate L. Robbins

Wednesday, March 16th, 1859

Reached Aspinwall yesterday about $3\frac{1}{2}$ o'clock. Think it quite a pleasant place but warm. Did not have time to go up to Mrs. Johnsons. Abner called and left the papers that Sarah has sent. There are any quantity of natives as black as your hat. Bananas, orange, and other southern fruit trees, left in the cars about 5 for Panama. There were two passenger trains crowded and such a confusion. O dear! Every nation and tongue, women smoking and children naked. A great deal of baggage more than usual they say. Reached Panama about 9 o'clock, and had to wait some time before we could go off to the Ship which was some ways from shore, went off on a steamboat about as much of a rush as I ever saw. The Golden Age is a beautiful Ship, everything in the best style and quality, "nigger waiters" in abundance. We have got to lay here till two or three this afternoon until they can get the mail and baggage on board. The scenery is delightful. Oranges in large quantities, limes and bananas. Boat loads have been off here today, but I do not dare to eat many as they say it is bad while here to eat much fruit. Pineapples, especially. I wish I could send home a bushel. I enjoyed crossing the Isthmus very much. The scenery was so wild and romantic. Negro huts and wild flowers. I should like it if I could go more of the way by land. First Cabin don't dine till $7\frac{1}{2}$ P.M. Lunch at 12.

Thusrday 17th

Very warm. Are getting along finely. Have gone 250 miles in 19 hours. Left Panama yesterday at $4\frac{1}{2}$ o'clock. A beautiful night, clear and a full moon, sea very smooth. There are quite a number of N. Hampshire people on board. General Walker, the Filibuster is on board. A small inferior looking man. There is also one old lady 75 years of age, is as smart as a steel trap. I have nearly blistered my neck by the heat. The captain is from Boston. Watkins by name. A very large, portly man. I don't know what to write and put down any idea that comes along. If you can make English of you are welcome to it. There are 850 passengers in the Steerage, a very small jam, I should think. There are 1200 on board. I tell you the waiters have to run around some. They keep cows on board so as to have milk fresh. They also kill all their meat and fowls on board. Our chest got split but is all nailed and tied up. Tell father I have got so I carry Abner's pistol in my carpet bag. Brought it across the Isthmus. Don't you think I am brave? It is not loaded. I can see a shark along side, the first one I have ever seen. Abner sits here trying to find out what I am writing but he can't do it.

Tuesday 22nd

I have been sick and not able to write since I wrote last. Thought I would try this afternoon. Have not been sea sick at all but took a severe cold and was threatened with a fever, the doctor said. Have a bad sore throat, which does not get much better. It has been very warm but today is a little cooler and will probably be growing cooler every day until we reach San Francisco. We reached Acapulco, Mexico, last night, having been 5 days and a few hours from Panama. The quickest time they have every made. It has been pleasant weather and they have put on steam. Abner says more than they are allowed to, he thinks, Acapulco is their usual stopping place and is 200 miles over half way. They take on coal, water, fowl and fruit, and I heard hogs squealing last night so I guess they took them. It seems funny to hear rooster crowing away out at sea. We took 60 more passengers. It was real fun to see the natives fighting for the passengers to carry them on shore. They brought off shells, coral, bananas, pineapples, oranges, limes, etc. They sell any quantity to the passengers. Abner is sick today, or nearly so with a cold. There is one gentleman on board from Illinois that lost his wife on the passage from n. Orleans, and left him with two little girls about the age of Eunice. There was also another lady that started with two children and died leaving them alone. Abner begins to be discouraged and says he is coming right back with me again, but I think I shall be real well when I get over this and reach cool weather. I want to try a good steady bed once more.

Friday 25th

I guess I shall finish my journal of this trip today. I am bolstered up in bed, and quite sick. The doctor has been to see me twice a day for three days. Mrs. King, the lady that is going to Yreka is very kind indeed and so is the head steward and stewardess. I am not in so much pain as I was yesterday but suffer a great deal. It seems to me as if my throat was filled but of course it is not. The Dr. has examined it twice. Says there is a small passage. I don't think it is going to break, wish it was for it would get well sooner. It is swollen awfully outside. The doctor's name is McNulty of Pa, a middle aged man, very kind, but I know nothing of his skillfulness. They think we shall reach San Francisco Monday night, having a very quick and pleasant voyage. It is getting quite cold again. I am the sickest passenger on board, unless I should except a woman in the steerage who had a baby a few nights ago where the people are as thick as sheep in a pen. She, I hardly think, is an exception. Oh dear, I am dreadful tired.

San Francisco, March 30th

Dear Mother:

Here I am in the "land of gold" all safe and sound. Since I wrote last Friday I have improved fast. I can eat and talk nicely. I never had victuals taste so good in my life as it did last night. Everything so fresh and nice and I seated myself to a good hearty table. I hardly know what to do I was so overjoyed. Since I wrote we have had a very rough time. Abner said "awful rough", so I think it must have been, but I can say I was not frightened, but pitied those who was. I saw one man cry and bid his wife goodbye for the last time, he thought, but he never was on the water before and was not very punky. His wife laughed at him. I believe I have seen big waves now if I never did before. It was not a storm but very high N.W. winds and heavy sea. The doctor did not charge anything, is hired by the company. He was very kind indeed. I don't know what I should have done without him. I am pretty weak, but the air is so clear and bracing it makes me feel quite smart. I believe Abner is as much pleased as myself to get here. He don't seem to know his head from his heels. He is so wild. He thinks I am getting well so fast. We shall leave here tonight. tonight. Reached here yesterday afternoon. I think I shall like it here first rate. Give my love to all and tell them all to write. Tell Eunice I would send her something if I was well enough to go around and find it. I feel dissappointed myself for I want to go over the City and see the pretty place but have to stay in my room so as to be rested so as to start again. I have no fire in my room and am almost froze. I suppose you got my letter from the Isthmus. Write Often.

Kate L. Robbins

Indian Creek, May 31st, 1859

Dear Brother:

As I happen for a rarity to feel just like writing you a little and having nothin of more importance at the present time to claim my attention, I accordingly seat myself at my lettle table with pen, ink and paper and commence scribbling.

I wrote Mother last mail, and have her all particulars concerning my affairs, also those of Abners, excepting what I kept to myself and what he keeps to himself. My hen has done her setting operations and "nary chicken". I expect father will laugh, but Abner would set an even number and I told him we shouldn't have any luck so you see I hit right, no doubt if there had been an odd number, we should have come out right, in the first place she did not like her situation. Expect she was homesick, then again every time she came off after oats Scott would drive her like fury. They have set him to watch oats sometimes, and he, I expect, thought that strange hen was a "poacher" so he made her "get" as the saying here is. All they do is to say "get" to the dogs and they go out doors. Funny, isn't it? I expect you would like to see how we look here tonight, supposing I tell you. Abner is standing back to the fire smoking. Robert is reading Hiawatha by the light of my candle, Mr. Hill is smoking with legs over one of my roundabouts, and last but not least, Scotty is snoring on his wolfskin. It is just about eight o'clock in the evening, the sun does not set until past seven. The trees grow large here. There is a pine close to our door that Abner says is a great deal larger than "grandpa's big tree in the old horse paster" I say it isn't, now for fun, measure rount the butt of that and tell me I will around this. We well have something going on if we are a good ways apart. But will save some paper for next time.

Good Night

Wednesday June 1st

A little more tonight and I guess bye and bye I'll make out a letter. We are all well and everything goes on about the same. I have been out to ride this afternoon, but a first rate ride. They say Mrs. Robbins is a good rider. Can you believe that poor skittish Kate would be seen going two up and two down through the town? She really does do it, but it is very different here from what it is at home. All the women ride, and the horses are used to it, and they usually ride fast, they call it "lopeing" and nobody thinks of trotting a horses all the time. The roads are bad. You know it is right in the mountains, but there is quite a good wagon road through this place. I am going to have a riding dress and hat bye and bye if they praise me so much about riding. I don't know but I shall race with you when I get home. Wonder who would beat! Depend upon the horses a good deal, I expect.

Friday 3rd

Very windy today but warm, feel pretty, Abner and Robert are in good spirits. The claim they thought so much of is a failure. Don't even pay grub as Abner says. it does seem as if they had the worst luck of any body around. They are working another claim now. I hope they will get something. They have lost eight hunderd on their Oregon butter, but they have something left Mrs. Clark's friend, Mrs. Smith has moved, lives about five or six miles from here now. I think of taking a ride over there tomorrow with Mrs. Hill. We do not live in the town of Indian Creek, but a mile and a quarter out on French Gulch. The store that A. and R. used to keep is on the corner of the two places. That is why he used to date his letters from both places. I have measured the tree I spoke of. It is almost twelve foot around. I know it is a great deal taller than the one in the horse pasture, but I think about the same size around. The trees are all very straight and tall. They make fun of me because I send home black sand. You keep it together and bye and bye clean the gold out when you get enough put it in something smooth, say a tin pan, and you can blow the dirt all away from the gold. they have things they call blowers here. Abner says when he gets some money to send you to fix it with, he is going to give you his watch, but he wouldn't let me tell you to take it till he got the money to send you to have it fixed, but I thought I would give you a hint, so that you could be thinking what you was going to have bye and bye. I left it at home in my upper bureau drawer. You had better take care of it for it is all to pieces. It always kept real good time. He has had it since he was 13 years old. Be patient and he will give it to you soon as the money comes in.

Tuesday 7th

I think I will have to close this letter for I can't afford to send much more than a sheet when the letter is heavy. I received letters from home yesterday written the third of May. How does the new road prosper. When Orianne W. is an authoress. Make Eunice learn all she can. Tell her to write me a letter.

Indian Creek
July 16th, 1859

Dear Brother:

I am sitting down to rest a few moments and thought it would do no harm to commence a letter for next mail. Well how do you proceed in old Beechwoods? Does the world move on the same pace and the people all alive and well?

Away up here in the mountains I can see but little difference once in a while an excitement and then still and calm again. Today here is a great rush on the Creek to a political Convention. Perhaps you think there is no politics away up here but you would soon think different to be here today. I couldn't believe there was so many men in all the city of Yreka as have passed here today, and stylish too, dressed up and as nice horses and carriages as our Boston people. O Yreka is a famous city! This is only the American and Anti Secession party. Every party has its own time and candidates electioneer for themselves. I guess the Brewery wagons or rather their owners, will make a pile if they keep politics up. My men are at work as steady as mills, don't follow up the multitude. There has been a Circus Company here the past week but this little house hold had better business. We stay at home all the time. I have calls and invitations in plenty but never been visiting any although there are very nice families around here. I think some of going down to the valley next week to see Mrs. Hill. Abner has been trying to get me started for the past two weeks, and she keeps sending for me, so I'll go and then it will be over with. It is twelve miles from here, but they don't make no more of going twelve here than they do five or six at home. Scotty is here as large as life and twice as cunning. I squeeze him till he grunts sometimes. Haven't been many rides lately. Abner is so busy and I have let Jennie loose, so I can't find her, the horses run on the mountains. We have got 47 chickens and 30 more eggs set. The hens are lent us til Cap. Winson gets back and Abner says it is clear gain if he can make them lay and set all the time. We have plenty of sports over the poor biddy mine that H. Chubbuck gave me, was only 2 Roosters out of 7 and all doing well. The wheat crop is rather poor I believe and flour is 9 cents per lb. has been 8, all is put up on 50 lb. bags and $4.50 worth of flour don't stand us great critters long, have been giving 5 cts per lb. for oats for the Hens. I tell you it costs to live here, but everybody seems to have a plenty of everything with some few exceptions. My next neighbor a Dutchman with a wife and three small children are poor enough and he will not work at $90 per month but is round prospecting. It seems foolish to me. But I must close for this time.

Friday 22nd

O dear I almost cried last night when Robert came in and said

I had got no papers, you said you sent some and I could hardly wait I wanted them so bad for you said Amanda Mary Litchfield etc. had written. I don't see why they didn't come, perhaps they may yet, although it is doubltful. I am going to write Georgianna B. this mail Why don't Amanda and Mercy never write me? Those great Jackasses got into our place where we keep one thing and another last night and destroyed alot of beans and new potatoes that Abner just paid 10 cts. a pound for. I feel provoked. You can't drive them nor nothing else. I am going to heat a lot of water and scald them guess that will make them hop.

Tuesday 26th

I am going to close up this letter today and I want to tell you how I got frightened last night between 12 o'clock and 1 o'clock we was woke up by a bell ringing and some hallooing at the top of their voice. I did not know but the old Nick himself had come. Scot barked and we could not hear what he said but come to find out it was some one from Yreka notifying a political lecture. Was not that a great idea? Had a great cow or dinner bell ringing for dear life and the tone the lobster peddlers put on. "Mr. _____ will lecture in Yreka, Siskiyou County tomorrow at two o'clock." O dear! It makes me laugh to think how funny it sounded come all the way from Yreka to this place and I don't know how much farther. I guess every body in the County knows it by this time whether it was a take off or whether he thought everybody would hear I do not know. Anyway it was comical.

Ochoco, Oregon
29th Jan. 1881

Dear Mother:

Yours of 2nd inst. and directed to Eunice was received yesterday and we were much pleased to get it. Eunice and her father are well and my health is improving. I got worn out in body and the shock to my nervous system was very great. No one knows what he was to me, more to me than the others, dear as he was to them, but he and I were left alone so much that we were all to each other, and he was steady and always so thoughtful for my health and comfort. He told all of us how glad he was that the last thing he did while he was well was to take me to ride. I do not go away from home much and he said one day he would take me to Prineville to do some shopping. He was taken sick coming home and never went out again. I have never been in the buggy since and it does not seem as if I ever could. But it was a great comfort to have him go so contented and happy, every one who talked with him said it was wonderful how he was blessed. He talked more like an old experienced person than a boy who never had said anything about religion or death. I do not think he had an enemy in the world. Everyone liked him and made a great deal of him, especially the old and the little children, during his sickness the elderely men took nearly all the care of him. He seemed to like them best around him. It took two all the time to wait upon him, he suffered so much and needed to be moved so often and so carefully and for five weeks we were never without four men in the house, and some days there would come so many we had to send them off, but they would come from a long distance, some of them and all wanted to be with him as much as they could for the last ten days there were three who never left. He seemed to like to have them handle him best, and they would not leave him, two were old bachelors, the other a widower, one of the kindest hearted men I ever saw Tommie gave him his nice new rifle and equipments of which he always thought a great deal. I have written to Father and Mamie, but there has been so much delay in the mails caused by the storms that they may have been lost. Are Jairus and Sarah Abbie both sick in consumption? I inferred so from what you wrote. What wil become of Elmer's baby if Lucy dies? And who takes care of Mary James little one? Who is Even that you mention in your letters? We received the roll of papers, the "South Shore Advance" interested us as we had never seen one before. Eunice is taking the "New Northwest". She is well acquainted with the Editress, Mrs. Duniway, and is sending them to Ella Bates. Mrs. Duniway put in an obituary notice of Tommies death and I was going to cut it out and send it to you but before I knew it Eunice had rolled it up and sent it, but if Ella gets it you can see it. I hope Mamie will write to me often. Tommy never got the deer skin for Ira as he had never killed one that he thought suitable. I have the horns of the last one he ever killed, also some others, if they were not so cumbersome and hard to pack up I would send you a pair. I think we will manage to send Mamie the little ones I have promised her.

Good bye

Kate L. Robbins

Kate L. Robbins

THE LITTLE BOY THAT DIED

1

I am all alone in my chamber now,
And the midnight hour is near,
And the fagot's crack and the clock's dull tick
Are the only sounds I hear.
And over my soul in it's solitude
Sweet feelings of sadness glide,
For my heart and my eyes are full when I think
Of the little boy that died.

2

I went one night to my father's house—
Went home to the dear ones all—
And softly I opened the garden gate,
And softly the door of the hall.
My mother came out to meet her son—
and kissed me and then she sighed,
And her head fell on my neck and she wept
For the little boy that died.

3

And when I gazed on his innocent face,
As still and cold he lay,
And thought what a lovely child he had been,
And how soon he must decay—
"O Death. thou lovest the beautiful!"
In the woe of my spirit I cried,
For sparkled the eyes and the forehead was fair
Of the little boy that died!

4

Again I will go to my father's house—
Go home to the dear ones all—
And sadly I'll open the garden gate,
And sadly the door to the hall.
I shall meet my mother, but never more
With her darling by her side;
But she'll kiss me and sigh and weep again
For the little boy that died.

5

I shall see his little sister again,
With her playmates about the door,
And I'll watch the children in their sports
As I never did before,
And if in the group I see a child
That's dimpled and laughing-eyed,
I'll look to see if it may not be
The little boy that died.

6

We shall all go home to our Father's house—
To our Father's house in the skies,
Where the hope of our souls shal have no blight,
And our love no broken ties.
We shall roam on the banks of the river of peace
And bathe in it's blissful tide,
And one of the joys of our heaven shall be
The little boy that died.

And, therefore, when I am sitting alone,
And the midnight hour is near,
When the fagots crack and the clock's dull tick
Are the only sounds I hear,
O, sweet o'er my soul in it's solitude
Are the feelings of sadness that glide,
Though my heart and my eyes are full when I think
Of the little boy that died.

SUNRISE IN CAMP

Cast shadows lie along the Eastern slopes,
And on their edges, strange phantoms lurk and cower;
Dim and uncertain shapes, that ever cling
Close to the darkness, and augment it's power.

No hint or hope of cing day seems near;
The tiny star-gleams hurl their little blades,
In fierce encounter with the monster bright—
Then hide their failure in the dusky glades.

Only a waking spirit of unrest,
Troubles the sleeping air, and stirs the leaves
With murmurous intent, that bears no fruit
Save in the deeper hush that silence weaves.

Then, fainter than the faintest starry glow,
And paler than the palest moon-beams ray,
Does the pervassive essence of the dawn,
Steal through the forest like a ghost in gray.

The slumbrous ether palpitates and thrills
With vague, sweet hopes of glory that shall be.
The morning lingers, but the earth is glad,
Because of faith which bids the shadows flee.

The stillness deepens, and all nature waits
Breathless, expectant, for some wonderous word
To break the weird enchantment of the scene.
It comes at last—the twitter of a bird.

And love gives form into the waking air,
With the vibration of those tender notes;
A love so full and perfect, that it wins
Responsive echoes from a hundred throats.

The chorus grows and strengthens voice by voice,
and wild, sweet harmonies arise and swell,
Till forest, field and every little glen
See singing out the message, All is well.

The tinted skies blush like a timid girl,
Who hears her praises by a lover sung.
The dew drops catch the gleam of living light,
Each one a joy-bell waiting to be rung.

All for the coming of the bridegroom waits;
That kingly one whose steps are at the door;
His heralds fling the rosy curtains wide,
And scatter jewels from the royal store.

With flaming banners and with flashing sword,
He wins the world anew—his cherished bride;
His glory fills the earth and paints the sky;
Prince of the perfect day, with us abide!

CRAWFORD ISBELL

Crawford Isbell, of Eugene, Oregon, wrote two letters to his sister and brother about work in the California mines; another letter reports his murder "on the road between Canyon City and Eugene by one Henry Deadmond, who was hanged in this city (The Dalles, Oregon) for the crime on Feb. 7, 1865."

Yreka March the 4 1861

Dear Sister

It is with pleasure that I take my pen in hand to address a few lines to you. I expect you have give up all hopes of hearing from me agane. I neglected writing longer than I aught I know for I haven't had any thing to write. and haven't much now. I am to work mining now on green horne & miles from Yreka. I am getting $50 a month keeping old Hatchler's hall the same as usual. I have had the best of health every since I left home.

The rest of the boys is all well I believe Sam Hawley has left here he is down in the lower Country somewhare I don't know what plase. He left here prety hard up and a little disshonest. He got into me about twenty dollars. The last letter I received from home was one from James I sold him the mashine and Coalt and he owes me $10 and I want mother to have that and yous it for her one benefit as soon as he can pay it. I didn't want to sell that Coalt but as things was I had better do it. I have sold my other horse here for $200. I can get three pur cent pur month for the money and that is better than any thing alls that I know of here.

We have had considerable snow here this winter and I think it will make times a littel better in the mines this spring. It is snowing today. The farmers has got their cropps about all in now. Grain and flower will keep down to a low prise.

As I have nothing more to write this time I shall hafto send you a short letter. You must write as often as you can and not wate for me for you have more time to write than I do.

Crawford Isbell

Scotts Valley April 26 1863

Dear Brother

I received your letter of the 15 in due season it being sometime since I had a letter I was very glad to hear from you and to hear that the folks ware all well. I am well and fare prospect of continuaning so. All those that you are acquainted with here are well I believe. I am very glad to hear from the Boys in the army. I wish them all good luck. I hope they will all be lucky enough to return home safe but I am afrade they won't. My advise to them is to stand to their poste untill no black hearted rebel dare incoureg a Southern Confederate. If they di they di in a good Caws.

I am very sorrey to hear the fate of Niels Miller but there is one concelation. He couldn't have dide in better Caws. It seems a pitty to put as good a man he was against Southern traters but it must be done. This rebellion must be crushed and I am in favor of using every passable means to do it. Tell Jane she has my simpathes as a bereaved wife. She has given one nearest and most dear to hur heart to the support of hur Country. May the lord reward hur for it. I am sorry to hear that I have a Cousen in the rebel army but I supose he has been led astray by southern leaders like a grate many others in the south. If he is a rebel I have no sympathes for him. I shall hafto send you a short letter this time as I have nothing more to write. Send this letter to mother and all the rest of the folks. Give respects to all inquirrers. Write soon.

C.C. Isbell

Scott Valley April 26 1863

Dear Brother

I received your letter of the 15
in due season it being some time since
I had a letter I was very glad to hear
from you and to hear that the folks
ware all well I am well and a prospect
of continuing so all those that you
are acquainted with hee are well I believe
I am very glad to hear from the Boys
in the army I wish them all good
luck I hope they will all be lucky
enough to return home safe but I am
afrade they wont my advise to them
is to stand to there poste untill
no black hearted rebel dare incourey
a Sothern Confedesey if they die
they die in a good Caus
I am very sorrey to hear the fate
of Nick Miller but there is one
Concelation he Couldnt or dide in

Fort Jones Oct 28, 1864

Miss Isbell,

    I take the present opportunity of writing to you..to let you know of your Brother Crafford's death..he was murdered about three weeks a go..his partner also.. he has been up to the Northern Mines this summer..this fall himself & two other men started for Eugene City Oregon..they wore going to Yreka from Eugene..the three of them started together..they camped on their way..to of them went out hunting & left Crafford in camp.. one of the men when out shot the others..& robed him..& then came in to camp & shot your Bother..he was cooking at the time.. he run in to the bushes the man durst not follow him..& of course did not get his money.. the body was found in the Brush..(your Brother's body) he had a Revolver in one hand..& a skillet in the other..he had twelve Hundred dollars arround his body..& also had a pair of saddle baggs..he had money in them it is not known how much.. his partner had about three Thousand dollars..they have caught the man that killed them & he is now in the Dalles city Oregon in Prison..you have my Symphasy & all who ware acquainted with him. Crafford worked for a man that lives here by the name of Fez..he worked for him two years..the letter that brought the sad news was written to him..he did not know your address & requested me to write..I have inquired in to the matter & I am sory to think it is so..I shall make more inquiries about it..& I will write you a gain..his money is in the hands of the citizens of Dalle city..you or your folks had better appoint an Administrator here so that you can get the money..Ichabode Dalley or Sidney Twilegar or any one that you prefer..you shall here from me a gain..

        Yours respectfully,
        Constantine Humphrey

          Address
          Con Humphrey
            Fort Jones
            Siskyou County
            Cal

Crawford Isbell (tintype)

JOHN HAINES

The winters of 1964 and 1965 came toward the end of a period of life that began in the early summer of 1954 when I returned to my homestead at Richardson Alaska after an absence of 5 years. I had come back to take up the work of clearing and building hardly begun during the summers of 1947 and '48 when I first came north and homesteaded the ground. For better or worse, I had come home, and for the next ten years I immersed myself in the wilderness, living very much as I have described it here to Orrin Bly.

Poetry came late during those years, but by 1960 or thereabouts I was writing reasonably well in the time spared from outdoor work. The poems I published from time to time attracted the attention of a few people in the outside world, and a welcome, if sporadic, correspondence grew up with a handful of editors and fellow poets. One of the people I heard from was a young cousin of Robert Bly's who wrote me about a poem of mine he had seen in a magazine. An exchange of letters followed which lasted for two or three years.

As these letters and a few of my poems may show, I have always been divided in myself between a person who loves an active outdoor life, working with his hands and sleeping well at night, and that other person driven to seek out a quiet place in which to think, to ponder the meaning of his life and find words and structures to embody that understanding. Two ways, two disciplines not easy to reconcile. For too many years I resisted being a writer, so that I lived much of the time in opposition to myself. I have only recently been able to come to terms with this and accept that other, stiller self.

Looking back on it, I feel profoundly grateful for those years, with all their hardships, discoveries and promises; grateful for what there has been in me of a love for the land and a determination to live from it as I wanted to. I am in debt more than I can say to people who have been in one way or another a substantial part of the life, either as wives and partners, as neighbors, living and dead, or as correspondents and distant friends.

*While typing these notes I have been aware that I am sitting
in the same place on the closed porch of my old house at Richardson where I wrote to Orrin Bly years ago. Changes have come: a
new highway, built in the 1970s, has cut off part of the view we
once had of the river, and there is more and more traffic on the
road. The homestead buildings have suffered neglect and wear
in the past ten years; the hillside fields above the house that I
worked so hard to clear back in the 50s and 60s are now standing
thick with a new growth of birches, aspens and alders. I myself
am a good deal older, and at times seem hardly to be the same
person who did that work, and wrote the letters and poems.*

*But life at Richardson has not changed much otherwise. The
Tanana is still there, as swift, cold and unpredictable as ever, and
the high, snowy ranges across the valley look the same, be it summer or winter. The same wind blows downriver in the fall, lifting
dust from the dry sandbars and adding to the soil of these hills as
it has done since the ice ages. The big aspen outside the window at
my back is taller and thicker, but the path downhill to the creek
is the same one I cut in the summer of 1948, thick-leaved underfoot from the birches and poplars that shade it. The hawks of
passage still fly through the woods in October, hunting for rabbits
and grouse; there are still moose in the hills, great horned owls
hoot along the creek in the evenings, and for the past several
nights I have heard coyotes singing from one of the islands in the
river.*

*The climate at this latitude seems a little gentler now than it
was in those hard winters of '64 and '65, but you never know;
next year it may all change again. Meanwhile, I have plans for
this winter and next summer: some work on the house and the
greenhouse, a new fence for the garden, new poems and new prose.*

John Haines, October 1980

Jan 5, 1964

Dear Mr. Bly,

I don't know which owl poem you are referring to—I have written a couple of them. I presume you mean the shorter one. Anyway, I thank you for your nice long, newsy letter which we enjoyed. I learned more about Robert and Carol from you than I ordinarily do from Robert's letters.

I will try to answer a few of your questions about our existence here. We live mainly off of what we can grow, catch, shoot, pick, etc. The amount of food that we can afford to buy is usually very small. We have a very intermittent and uncertain income that has averaged about $500 a year. Most of that goes for food, but a certain amount is spent on clothing, gasoline and such things. Most items do cost more here than in the lower states. Kerosene for lamps, for instance, costs $1.00 a gallon. Car gas ,about 55¢ per. Gal. Food has been getting cheaper as compared to the rest of the states, but it is still high. So I think you can see that the biggest problem is getting enough money to live on.

I have no profession or skill that is in demand today. So we just get along from month to month, season to season. My writing brings in a little from time to time, and we get a little money from my family every year. I do trap sometimes. This winter I went out and caught 20 marten and one lynx, which should bring us a decent piece of money if the price is good. Ordinarily I avoid doing such things because it takes time away from writing, and I don't particularly enjoy it. Trapping is one of the hardest ways to earn money you can think of. And one needs a heart of iron.

I kill a moose every year, and catch a lot of fish from the river, for ourselves and for dogfood. I have never shot a bear. I have mostly left them alone as long as they leave me alone. Actually, I'm not much on hunting. I never hunted before in my life until I came here to live, and then had to learn how. I would prefer to live in nature as a naturalist (or poet) observing and letting live. On the other hand, I would prefer to hunt down a wild animal and kill it than raise an animal for slaughter.

We grow potatoes and some vegetables, and have a greenhouse for tomatoes and cucumbers, etc., the only way you can grow such things here. I have no machinery, so everything must be done by hand, and there is a limit to how much you can do that way, so there is seldom anything left over to sell. Actually we are lucky if there is enough even for ourselves. I live for the day when I might win a prize or something that would give me a little freedom from all the work. But I suppose I am just day-dreaming. People are very reluctant to believe that there could be a serious poet, or writer, living in such a place, in such circumstances, and I'm afraid I'll have to reconcile myself to my poverty for a good long time. Especially as I feel there is something new in my poems, and it will take people a long time to get used to that.

Oh yes, most of my hunting is done with a 30.06 Winchester. I have another older rifle I sometimes use, and also a 22. that I shoot an occasional grouse with. I have never used a shotgun.

Since you like to read, there is an excellent book on Alaska wildlife, *A Naturalist in Alaska*, by Adolphe Murie, pub. Deving-Adair, 1961. I don't get many books, which is bad for a writer. But as you can see there is not money for such things very often. Robert sometimes sends me something, and I am much in his debt for those things he has sent, magazines, etc.. I have not read Don Hall's book which you mentioned, though I would like to. I think very highly of Louis Simpson, however, and Robert says he is going to send me a copy of Simpson's new book.

We have neighbors of a sort. The closest is a mile and a half away. They run a roadhouse, but we don't see them very often. We have so much that must be done, and so much else that you want to do. People only take your time, though I enjoy talking to them when we do see them. We are outsiders here for the most part, even though I am an old-timer around here, having first come here in 1947.

We are 68 miles south, or south-east, of Fairbanks, on the north bank of the Tanana River. The locality was once a very well-known mining camp in pre-WWI days, but that was a long time ago, and gold-mining is just about dead.

I formerly had a dog-team, but it was too expensive and time-consuming, considering the use I got out of them. I enjoyed it, but the dogs have died, one by one, and we have only one left. He pulls a sled or carries a pack when he's asked to, and I may get another female if I can find a good pup. But I doubt if I will ever have more than two dogs again. Some day I hope to have one of those motorized sleds that they make today. Something to haul wood, or bring in the moose. Otherwise, we go on foot and pack our gear.

We have a small place, which we keep adding to as we have something to build with. We have two or three other cabins besides the home cabin. We use wood for fuel and that takes a lot of time. We have a small creek where we get water, and when that freezes up we chop ice or melt snow.

I hope this answers some of your questions. One of these days I'm going to write an article or essay on life here, something I've been thinking about for a long time. But I hate to take the time from writing poems, and there is still this book of mine that needs working on. If I can find a publisher.

Best wishes to you and your wife. And if you *do* get the time for a visit to Alaska be sure that you will be as welcome here as we can make you.

Sincerely,
John Haines

Jan. 18-64

Dear Orrin Bly,

Thank you for your kind letter and the offers of help. Believe me, it lit a glow in my heart. We don't often get letters from intelligent and sympathetic people. I sometimes feel that correspondance must be a dying art, people are so busy with their own lives, etc. There are many people, especially other poets, that we would enjoy hearing from, but who can barely manage a post card once a year, or so. You have to live in the isolation we live in for several years before you can really appreciate what a good letter can mean.

I have forgotten what I said to you, but from the tone of yours I must have given an impression of gloom and discouragement. I write out of whatever mood I happen to be in, and my general mood for the fore part of this winter was not good. Now that I have more or less done with the slavery bit and have relaxed, begun to devote more of myself to writing, I am much improved. I go through this every year, about twice a year, going into and coming out of the winter, with much wear and tear on my temper.

I am not exactly hungry for recognition, but I do like to see myself in print. I suppose I have as much, if not more, vanity than most writers. Well, I see so many younger poets coming up, getting their books talked about, winning awards, etc. that I sometimes wonder if the world hasn't just passed me by. Perhaps I'm one of those late—maturing crops that hold up well in storage! At that I may be lucky. At other times I feel, to hell with them all! I'll get through with my life somehow and get my work done, and if there's any lasting value in it, I guess they'll find it. These conflicting moods batter me back and forth.

We'll, I'm rambling here, certainly.

I'm not sure that the 'quietness' you speak of as being present in my poems, is due to my actually living in Nature. I have always lived in Nature in my imagination, for as long as I can remember. Even when I lived in the city I never lost sight of it. But my poems, at least my good ones, are written out of a submerged self that IS quiet, and steady, no matter what this idiot on the outside is doing or thinking about. So I think that quietness, if it is there, would be there no matter where I lived. But this submerged self, as I call it, is not as accessible as I would like it to be. I seem to rather slowly sink into it as other things lose their hold on me. I notice that every winter the writing gets better as the winter comes on to a close, and then I have to break it off. For all practical purposes I do no writing in the summer. I have always envied those people who, like Williams, could turn easily from daily affairs and bang out a poem. Perhaps it is something that has to be learned, I don't know.

I must leave off talking about myself. One of the hazards of living so long in isolation is that you brood so much on yourself and your own problems that you begin to think that you are the only one who has any problems.

You might be interested in how we spend our time these days. We wake up about the time the mailman comes by, around 7:30 in the morning. If he has left anything in the box he usually blows his horn. So we get out of bed, light the lamp and build a fire in the stove. If I think there is any mail I may get dressed and walk up to the box while Jo is fixing breakfast. If there is a lot of interesting mail we may linger over the breakfast table half the morning. Then I usually retreat to my desk and try to get some reluctant poems to stand up and walk around on their four feet. I have a corner on the porch surrounded by mukluks, sewing machine, clothes hamper, and a sack of onions. The floor is cold from there being no fire in the house overnight, so every now and then I get up and walk into the other room and stand by the stove until my feet feel warmer.

In the afternoon I go up the trail behind the house and cut some birch. When I have enough for a couple of loads I get the old freight sled down and harness the one dog to it. He pulls the sled up the hill, and then I turn him loose, load the sled and ride it down myself. When I have a small pile in the yard I saw it up and split and pile it. I usually try and start out the winter with at least half the winter's wood here in the yard. Then I can cut some from time to time to keep the supply far enough ahead so we will have dry wood, since the only wood I can get now is green and frozen. I use my trusty old swede saw (I assume you know what that is), which I keep very sharp. Once I have the wood here in the yard it doesn't take me too long to cut it up. Incidently, I don't want you to do anything so troublesome and expensive as getting me a power saw. I'd love to have one, but that is my problem, and I know you are not a millionaire with money in your pockets and nothing to do with it.

Jo goes down to the creek and chops two or three buckets of ice to melt for water every day, and she usually splits the kindling for next morning's fire. Strong-armed woman I have! About 3 o'clock in the afternoon, when it begins to get dark, we will feed the dog, come in and light the lamp again, and have some coffee. Some-times we put some music on for an hour or so. We have a small phonograph that runs on six flashlight batteries. I paid sixty dol-lars for it a couple of years ago. We couldn't afford it, really, but I don't regret buying it. From time to time we buy some records from a discount house in New York. We couldn't buy many if we had to pay the regular price, but this way we slowly build up a collection of music we enjoy. We are partial to Baroque, and for me music more or less stops around 1800. Though there is some of Beethoven, Shubert, etc, that I like.

We do have a radio, but as you can guess there isn't much on it that we can listen to. We get the news, and on Sunday evening they sometimes play some good classical music. But we have lived without a radio and not missed it very much. The University near Fairbanks has a small FM station, which puts out some good programs, but we don't have FM on our small set. I thought of buy-ing one this winter when I got the money from the furs, but I might spend 30 or 40 dollars for an FM set and find out that we couldn't get the station here, as they have a small transmitter, and I doubt if any other FM stations are within hearing distance.

In the evening I read or write letters, or come back to the poems I always have waiting. Jo writes letters, or reads. Before Xmas she spent a lot of time drawing, making small watercolors for cards. Sometimes late in the evening we get a station in San Fran-cisco where they have people calling up giving their opinions on every subject from civil rights to Cuba.

This is the way the winter goes if all is well, and we are not pinched for groceries or something else that we need. Every now and then when the temperature gets above zero, I will crank up our 22 year old chevrolet and drive 30 miles to the junction for groceries or to mail something. Sometimes we stop on the way and visit with someone.

Before Xmas I was away from home a good part of the time, looking after the traps, and my time at home was spent skining and stretching the furs. If you are going to make anything out of trapping you have to put all you've got into it, which means that you are out climbing the hills, camping in other cabins, and looking for new places to set traps. I made my last trip after Xmas, and last week I went into Fairbanks, and sold the furs. Well, I'm glad that is done with, and we should be able to live the rest of the winter without any privation. We've still got a lot of moose left, and we don't eat so much when we are not active outdoors.

We've had a pretty good winter weatherwise. In November we had a spell of minus 40. In fact the day that Kennedy was shot I caught a ride to the Junction for some fuel and groceries, and had to stand out on the road for some time with the temperature around −45. But since then it has not been bad, and I expect the rest of the winter to be reasonably mild. As long as I don't have to spend a lot of time out in it. I don't care if it is 30 or 35 below, except that it does take a little more wood off the pile. A couple of years ago we had three weeks of minus 50, 60, and 70. Unbelievable how cold it can get here at times, with the air just hanging in one place, stagnant. You think it will never get warm again. We kept using the outhouse, though!

As for books and magazines: I have a subscription to Poetry, which more or less keeps me in touch with what is going on. Frederick Morgan sent me a gift of Hudson Review for a year, for which I was very grateful. Robert from time to time sends me things of interest. And not long ago I wrote a couple of bookshops in New York for a list of some things I am interested in. I had rather read good poetry than anything, but I also read almost anything else that happens to come here. I don't go much for philosophy— all that abstract reasoning bores me after awhile. A thinker like Thoreau, who deals with life as men have to live it from day to day, is far more interesting to me. I like my thinking with its feet on the ground. I read a lot of Natural History, anthropology, ancient history. Anything that is well written. As for novels, well, I like the old ones best. Except for Dr. Zhivago I haven't read a recent novel that impressed me very much. Not long ago I started to read the Bible all the way through, something I have never done before. If you have anything of Jung's I would be very interested in that. I have never read either Jung or Freud. But don't send me any expensive books. What ever you might send I will take good care of it and return it when I'm through.

You mentioned Bach, who is one of my greatest admirations.

But I think we tend to exaggerate the neglect of a man like that from the distance at which we view his life and work. Even though his art was rather old-fashioned in his own day, he was well known and respected, though more as a practicing musician than as a composer. When a man's art is a matter of daily practice, as something by which he makes his living, I don't think recognition as we think of it is very important. If we could imagine Bach having to work as a druggist's clerk in order to afford to practice the organ on Sunday, and devote the rest of his time off to composing his own works, then we would be justified in feeling sorry for him. Though if that had been the case, Bach would not have been able to accomplish very much, and we would very likely not be honoring him as much as we do today. Another case of neglect would be Vivaldi, even more so than Bach. Yet there is evidence that Vivaldi was well-known, even famous in his own time. Also I think we underestimate the part played by faith in those days. Bach and Handel were devout men, and music, apart from being an art which they practiced, was a celebration of religious faith, and offering at the altar. As someone said of Handel, Music was a temple which he sought to make beautiful. It is this, as much as anything, which gives their music such grandeur. We don't have that today, and that is that.

When you come to Alaska you should try to make it in the latter part of the summer, late August or September. At least as far as this part of the country is concerned. Of course you will want to see more of the country than what we have here. It sometimes rains quite a bit in the fall, but at least the mosquitoes are gone. They make it rather difficult to enjoy being out in the early part of the summer. We just endure them. Since you seem to like hunting, you might be around to go out with me looking for a moose, since I have to go. Though perhaps you are not interested in that. In any case, we will be glad to see you, no matter when you come.

It seems I have just been unraveling an old sock here—this letter, I mean! I will make amends for it by including a poem, one I like as well as anything else I've done this winter.

All best wishes,
John Haines

Dear Orrin and Kathryn,

I should have written before this to thank you for the wonderful boxes of food you sent us on Christmas Eve. It really made our Christmas. I was thinking of trussing up a chunk of moose with some kind of dressing, but not very enthusiastic about it. Instead we had ham and wild rice! Because of the cold, we didn't go anywhere, but stayed here and spent a very quiet time. I had much rather do that anyway, but most people think you have to get out and go visit, making merry, etc.. I suppose we are a little selfish. Fortunately the weather spared us from having to refuse a dinner invitation. I managed to get the car started some days before Christmas and made a trip to the grocery store and post-office. I also bought a once-a-year bottle of whiskey. We saved one of your puddings, and just ate it the other night with some ice-cream. In short, we enjoyed it all, and it was very good of you people to go to so much trouble and expense.

Our long cold spell, which stretched from the 25th of November, finally ended last week. Since then we have enjoyed temperatures above zero, and even above freezing for a day. I had to open up the root cellar and start a fire in it to warm up the potatoes. I don't usually have to worry about it freezing until February, but the weather stayed so cold for so long that the frost began creeping into the cellar, even though there are three doors on it. Having warmed it up good, I sealed it again yesterday, and I think it will keep for another two months if we don't get more of that minus 50 degree sort of thing.

Christmas brings a lot of interruptions, and the warm weather brought some more. I had to go to Fairbanks one day last week to straighten out our property tax. That's a long cold trip in our old car, and I'm always holding my breath that I won't have a breakdown and be stranded in a place where I have no friends. Consequently, I seldom make that trip. Jo hardly ever goes with me, and it's just go in and get out again as fast as I can. Anyway, all this has kept me away from writing, but I'm getting started again. I begin by writing a letter or two—hence this one to you!

Don Hall sent me a copy of his new book. Some pretty good things in it I thought. I was rather surprised by it. My book is still hung up at Wesleyan, but I haven't thought much about it.

I've been reading Lewis and Clark's Journals the past few nights. Rather depressing at times, the slaughter of animal life that went on; but there was so much of it I guess they thought it didn't matter. Nature is very wasteful anyway, according to our way of looking at it. Incredible labors that those people went to just to go a few miles. But they didn't know how fortunate they were; despite the hardships, the country was a paradise. We have very much the same situation here today, or at least as it was until a very few years ago. But the wilderness is going, I'm afraid, even here, though it may be many years yet before they've figured out how to subdue some parts of the north country.

I hope you will excuse the delay in this thank you. We really appreciated what you sent more than you can realize. Write soon.

Best wishes for the New Year,
John and Jo

P.S. I'm enclosing some photos of Jo and myself with the moose and his horns last fall—keep them if you want—

MORRIS GRAVES
Painted Letters

Hinterlands
Jan. 27–42

Dear Miss Miller:

Respectfully
P.S.   Morris Graves
   I do not expect a reply
on the above remark on f~~ame~~(?) acclaim(?)
Perhaps it's a crying fault to take oneself so gravely.

Letter to Dorothy Miller (Stone Wings). 1942. tempera on paper. 26½x29"

Rock — Dec.12,46

Dear Marian —

Until then —

Morris

Message, 1946. tempera on paper. 14⅛x14¼″

The Lake — Aug. '77

Dear Marian & Dan

Morris

Message, 1977. tempera on paper. 14½x14⅜
The Five Senses, listed clockwise:
1. Seeing—white
2. Hearing—yellow
3. Tasting—red
4. Touching—green
5. Smelling—blue

Feb.24 1947

Dear Dorothy

Morris

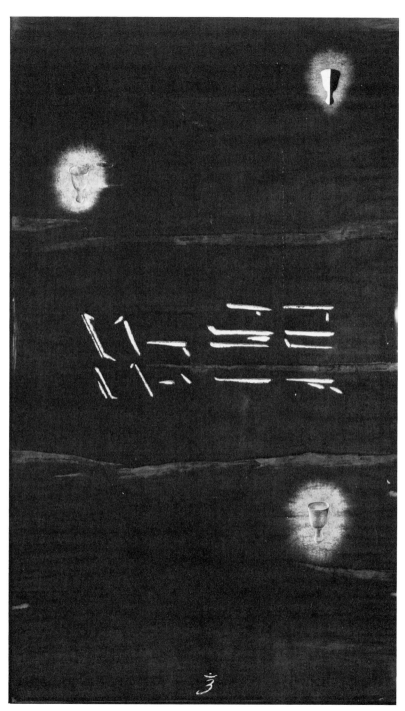

Letter to Dorothy Schumacker. 1946. tempera on paper. 43x25"

Poetry

Regina deCormier-Shekerjian

MICHEL WRITES FROM ROUEN

Maurice, as you requested, I have seen
Françoise. I have brought her flowers. Champagne.
Taken her to dine at Couronne, the restaurant
you recommended here, in old Rouen, and to one
you do not know, out in the country.
She has taken to wearing long chiffon scarves
and scribbles constantly in a truly formidable
looking notebook. Her voice, yes, her voice
has deepened, but she still refuses to wear shoes.
Or her glasses. She explained that it is not
birds, but unseen spirits who rap
the walls of her house all day and long, long
into the night. She prays to Sainte Jeanne
that they are friendly. She reminded me

that Simone is ill, that she has made three
journeys south, since April, for you, reading aloud
to Simone, from her notebook. She asked me to deliver
undeliverable messages, to you. She chants
Aztec hymns to the sun. She embroiders the sun
with threads of gold flecked with vermillion, the deep
pinks of Mexico. And, like Penelope, undoes it all
each night, beginning again when the sun
leaps from the clock tower and flings its net
over the face of her house, over her work

she said. She writes. Every day. And drinks red wine, strong
as blood, the blood of the bull, purchased, cheap
at the corner bistro from the man who was once, just
once, her lover. He has grown fat
but remains charming, she insisted, and gives her

one red rose, each month, on the fourth
Sunday, *un souvenir*, he says. I gave her anemones,
your latest book. As you requested. The cafés

were loud with many tongues. She explained Rouen;
that Rouen has never forgotten its saint, Jeanne d'Arc
with whom she does not compare her own
martyrdom, and the 15th century lives again
in the reconstructed town, in the many circumstances
of changing light and the latter day pilgrims
are good for everyone's table. Except hers.
She refuses to go into the Rue du Gros Horloge
during the pilgrim season and therefore never
has the correct time. The great clock in the tower
is the one she has always
depended upon, refusing to have a clock of her own
that works, one that reminds her of time
disappearing, always, down the rabbit hole. Yes,

she has counted down the hours of too many
unforgiving days, she said. What she wants now
is the sound of bells cracking loose, horses
flying through the trees, climbing the glass mountain,
great shouts of joy echoing down the streets
of her house, a small
celebration. She has finished proof-reading
the second volume of her journal, in which you
loom large, she said, and will begin work soon, hopefully,
on "A Small History of Insignificant Beasts," which
she would not describe. Her editor, Le Blanc, an old
eccentric, rings her daily. He has always
desired her, she said. I called her a conjure woman
and compared her to Colette. She read to me

from an old book, a birthday gift from you:
"Flaubert has left Rouen, at dawn, with a bag
full of words, *les mots justes*. He is headed
south. Southeast. He wears a greatcoat
and a long black scarf, which he does not need,
but which he can pull up across his walrus mustache
and believe that he goes

disguised. He has vowed that he will never shout
his words aloud in his father's house again,
and never again, yes, never again
to see Louise, who besieges him, without mercy.
Yes. He will be particular about everything,
including his chancres
and the cup in which his coffee is served."
Flaubert was a coward, Françoise said, confident
only with women of the brothels, preferably exotic
Eastern brothels. Flaubert, unfortunately, lives
again, she said, in you. At lunch, yesterday

she picked her way through a delicate mousse, pink
copper light burnishing her skin, and wondered
how she would survive the long summer, long evenings
alone, with Victor Hugo, her baby, her adored
monkey, delivering monologues of endless complaint.
She has taken the last jewel
from the chalatan's box, she said, and weeps
in the dark Rouen night. Every night. Alone. Victor

has replaced you, she said. Victor sat in a chair
by the window, keeping his good eye on me. Victor's
head is a brown globe of fur, thick fur, his face
naked. And lugubrious. He ate
the flowers I brought. And the fruit. He stared
resentfully at me all through lunch, and later
as I moved to sit next to Françoise, Victor Hugo
bit me. Yes. He is extremely jealous, she said. Yes,
I agreed, surely one of the truly insignificant
beasts. Françoise
straightened her back and moved with great hauteur
to the door. I left, not knowing what more

I could do. My dear friend, I am no longer
your messenger, apologizer
to old loves who punish me mercilessly for your
unforgivable leave-takings. Yes. She knows
now that you are gone. Forever. And I write now
only to tell you that I did as you requested.
For the last time. The conclusion you draw will
not be the correct one. *Malheureusement.*

Phyllis Koestenbaum

HARMONY

Dear Diane. About "L'Age d'Or" I remember enough.
The woman sucking the toe of an alabaster statue.
A violin kicked like a tin can. Scenes peel.
That flaky. But not tasty as the sesame buns for pork
we order at the Szechwan restaurant we've discovered in Sunnyvale.
A Nazi slaps the face of a woman at a ball
and we see her for several scenes racing by on bicycles
holding a handkerchief to it as to a bullet wound.
It is a bullet wound and the bullet kills a male
of wavering age in a field of tall grasses.
The faces of men in a cave, their dirty tattered clothes,
their unwashed alcohol smell not to be smelled in the movie
I associate with Bowery bums sleeping in doorways
on my way to Eighth Street for piano and harmony
walking fast. Not having practised. No talent.
Dying men hobble to the battle they've been hobbling
to for 50 years. Expecting her father a daughter
finds a cow in her bed. Fun not to have to make sense
of a movie as if the movie was a book.
Are these letters avoidance?
In line in a stylish blazer a girl complained how close
people in line were getting: she was the one getting close.
I had on my old sweater: since it was a bad neighborhood
I might as well be comfortable.
Afterwards to Clement Street for pizza and ice cream.
In bed Peter rubbed my legs.

PICKING THE MOVIES

Dear Diane. You're the name I address letters to.
I pick the movies. Peter gets home late, between 5 and 6,
and I have the movies picked. He brought home pizza for Ian
and we went to "The Devil's Playground."
Peter is beginning to like this going to the city
Saturday night for movies. He doesn't like the neighborhoods
and he hates rushing. I hate leaving Ian alone to eat.
As usual I slept in the car. I usually sleep in the car
unless we're fighting. He listens to music
and the minute it's the hour whether we're in the middle of a Mozart
piano concerto or a Beethoven quartet (it's never a Beethoven
       quartet)
he switches to news and turns the volume up since he has a bad ear.
He hears as well as I do.
The movie is an Australian *Portrait of the Artist.*
How can these boys give up what they don't have yet?
I mean sex.
Their pimply faces reminded me
of my first love, who then I didn't see as young.
I wonder if he's still alive.
The boys must wear trunks in the shower.
The teacher priests shower without.
The priests' bodies shine with repression
like a fire from chemicals.
The priest most insistent that the boys ignore their bodies
sits by a swimming pool where women are swimming
and he imagines the women swimming naked, himself swimming
       naked
with them. I saw the heads of small animals, the heads
of newborn babies. God is pulling. The priest can't take any more.
An opera singer he recites his case against the flesh, a child
he cries that the body always wins.
But he stays a priest so his mind wins, doesn't it?
Peter was relieved there were women in the movie
and I was relieved for Peter.
Again we ate pizza, again we had ice cream.
All fights extend from that one like all roads leading to Rome.

Angela Peckenpaugh

HAM CHAMBERLAYNE TO HIS MOTHER
FROM CAMP WALKER, DEC. 17, 1864
4½ MILES SOUTH OF PETERSBURGH

I forgot to tell
you of the raid
I came near death
in a new unforseen way.

I met a wagon on a narrow
sloping bridge, road
frozen and slippery.

The wagon was still,
room to pass.
Mules started at a trot,
knocked my mare down,
forced my foot thro the stirrup.

Mare scrambled up off me
started at speed,
dragged me over stones,
ran against a slippery bank,
rolled over again,
and I found myself
free and nigh to fainting.

I had no desire to be
a "slovenly unhandsome corse"
so I kept my foot
high in the air
lest it be broken.
All of this was very well

but nothing could have saved
me but her second fall.

Carried on a litter
I escaped with a panoramick view
of the road in all colors
on my body.

Charles Levendosky

4.16.78. (Macon, Georgia)

Dear Theo,

Everyday I go to the mail box looking for some word from you,
but I guess I shall have to wait longer.

Spent yesterday walking through Rose Hill Cemetery with David
Bottoms, a Georgia poet . . . his idea of a good time . . . searching
through the tall grass and crumbling crypts for word of death . . .
the wild lilys along the stream and water snakes undulating in
the clear water . . and gray mausoleums wearing . . . the castiron
fencing stolen or rusting to thin slivers . . . flaking away as the
words on stone gravemarkers:

> the sun sullen in the hazy blue sky
> the ocmulgee river sliding by churning the red clay
> at the banks
> and the railroad tracks silver and quiet
> leading away
>
> we stayed for a few hours.

Nearing dusk
we saw drinking teenagers hiding out near a vandalized crypt
drawn to the side of death,
drawn to the site,
and the Confederate dead.
            Of course that.
Somehow there is a sense of Georgia and the south
in this trek
and I have the feeling that I am about to learn something
    significant
about the south from this.

You see
I try to make new that which others see as insignificant and
the old roses (those grown in this part of the country before 1850)
bloom loudly
on their spindly vines
bloom loudly

in the quiet of the cemetery
          like blood rising to fill a wound.

We are here
and overhead there is a sonic boom
and travelers pass over Georgia,
          over Macon,
without thinking of what is below them.
We are in the cemetery,
        alive and touching
        the effects of death.

Why it occurs to me, does the south have a preoccupation with
   death?

There is a poem here,
       dear Theo,
          should I save it?

love & laughter,

Charles

Gary Gildner

A LETTER FROM MY GOOD HAND

Whenever it rains the four fingers
of my left hand lose themselves
in a sharp confusion of stars, and the ring
my husband gave me flies burning
deep into my ankle.
                  And I hear myself
screaming to make them come back:
but the bright blood pumping into my neighbor's
perfect hedge where I kneel
tells me goodbye, and I realize
—it comes to me as clearly as the caught
notes of a bird's song while riding in the country—
I can only count to six again.
Oh please don't make me stand up
in front of the class and recite!
—and yet, there I was, thirty-five,
calling the whole street to come quick
come help me look for my fingers
under the carved stars of my neighbor's leaves.

One night I dreamt they were leaping
like salmon among the dandelions,
the last two which I sucked as a child
wanting my mouth, and waking up, reaching out
with their purple roots, moaning,
I touched my husband's face.

My husband has the face of a child,
the face of my uncle who tried to find gold
in Colorado, sleeping under the stars with his mule.
Once he said he kicked the mule, and wept,

and then my mother, reading the letter, wept too,
and I cried with her, not knowing why.
But later I understood: he was a fool,
a dreamer, and nothing he touched was worth it,
except maybe the mule, who outlived him.
My husband, a kind, intelligent man,
wakes up early and reads. He reads and smokes,
and when I point out that my ankle has two small stars
he touches me there.
                "I don't ever want the stars
to go away," I say. And yet, one night, he cut them down.
I saw their leaves in the first grainy light, wet with rain,
scattered about my feet and clinging to the fringe of my gown.

What I fear most is drowning, and being unable to cup
the water with both hands under a pump in spring
when I love things more than I understand
and forget—for just that instant—how I am.

I am a woman with two green thumbs
and a sky full of purple martins.
They feed their babies above my asparagus spears
and do not mind my cooing and pruning.
They loop the sun, and dive, clearing the air—
and sometimes I take off my shirt and lie deeply back
in the long grass at the garden's edge,
wanting to start all over, pull a worm to my cheek
and say something witty, intelligent.
But when he takes my hand, kissing the blue
stubs and rubbing my breasts, I feel nothing
—the same nothing I felt when I reached for the branch
caught by the roaring mower, and was pulled under.

We live in a house like all the others on this street,
nice houses with good lawns, and beyond the gardens
most of us keep, children fish in the pond for bluegills.
A week ago I caught dinner; the cat that's going
blind, Illona, sat beside me washing herself.
Not thinking I said, "My grandmother got so fat
the doctor had to cut off her wedding band." Angry,
my husband left the table, and the two small bluegills lay

curled up in their grease till morning, when I ate them.

My mother's small white hands collected stones
—her favorite Petoskey looked like a turtle
and once I borrowed it and lost it.
She also collected stamps until the Navy sent
my father home for good, to carve his ducks.
At dinner no one spoke—we listened to the radio.
But one summer an old crony surprised him,
a large man with a swirling red beard who stamped
his boots in my father's shavings, and reaching out
he picked me up and swung me around,
his green eyes flashing above my father who sat
swinging his chisel and making my mother giggle.
"Do that for me," I said as I knelt in the rain
pushing the cut stars away from my feet,
"do that, do that"—
                              because I wanted to bury
my hands all the way in, deep in that stranger's
rich red beard, and hold him, and make him come back.

Len Roberts

EITHER WAY

Although you're probably out of time by now I want you to know
I go back every year to stand confused and a little amazed at
the grayness of the stone

Some nights when the moon comes flying through the blue windows at the back of my skull I feel your absence fill my throat
my fingers

It's not the kind of situation where I can call and say "hello" so
I thought I'd write and hope there are roots to these words, I
don't know

For three years now I've buried parts of myself and all those fears
you knew about in my wife's stomach and finally I've come to
know some things have to rot in open air

Nick is still alone and quiet in his room talking about investment
and how the weather changes color under the moon

Raymond has left Boston and continually finds himself stopped
somewhere wondering what the hell are stars or cobblestones

Mom's the same never admitting some things actually happen to
people and she's still serving at the Holiday Inn and staring out
windows when she knows some one is looking

Our house is nothing now torn down with row houses built over
those years those rooms and night we touched each other so
much with our separate lives

It's strange how each year I go back everything seems more distant
and I seem to be getting colder although the seasons are milder

Sometimes I swear it's me I visit here once a year and you writing
again sitting in this black chair. Either way we're still together.

Dear Mother

      I know this note is late but I'm sorry for your cold
rooms and seven sisters who never ate steak and potatoes
and I'm sorry for the winter you walked around in your soft shoes.
If I sent this to you would you put on your pink nightgown again
    with the blue butterflies on the sleeves
and move your arms up and down as you walk around the kitchen
    table pretending you were an angel?
Here in Pennsylvania a lone yellow daisy stares at me awkwardly
    hanging over the lip of the rose-colored vase
a gift from my love's daughter
and a purple bird is poised motionless over it
always about to sing or flutter its delicate transparent wings.

Dear Mother

      I am so exhausted I will have to sleep soon
and leave you alone again in the dark with your appendix scar
    and fat white thighs and your stories of St. John's Alley.
I just wanted to say that the willow tree here in Pennsylvania
    is not dripping with sorrow
that its branches are not bent nor broken but rather bowed
    by the excessive waters of winter and spring.

Lyn Lifshin

HOWLAND HOUSE

I am writing you from bed
if you could see this house

it stays night here more than
ever. john has gone to
new bedford and it scares me

Candles on the dark wood,
shadows   each squirrel a
witch's step. there

is nothing
you can. water cuts
like a tourniquet.
i must be less and
less your sister your
eyes there are berries
here that color

and your thin shoulders
blond hair in my
lap the ground a
huge mouth then

Here dying came like
blackbirds (your
shoulders like
birds wings i
thought i could
never leave

we bury our dead
without a moon
black snow stuffed
into mouths
everyone's lips
numb there are
things you
couldn't.

love,

Jody Aliesan

LETTER

the greenhouse works fine
mold growing on the walls
velvet gray, brown, soft black
light yellow patches
at first I thought oh
my shiny white walls but
now I stand and look at them
notice where the mold likes
to grow, next to the barrels
or where the rafters meet the roofbeam

Bill who runs the junkyard
salvaged an oak rocker
out of a demolished hotel
he stripped and oiled it
said it was for the greenhouse
but I couldn't bring myself
to put it there, let it rot
so it's in the bedroom
figure we can use a chair
for the afternoon sun
or to sit by a sickbed in

then Randy found an oak straightback
at an auction, bought it for the store
but Bernie didn't want it
(I think he saw I liked it)
so he gave it to me
it's missing two braces
three slats out the back
but the arm rests curve gently
and it won't mind the mold.

Paul Genega

DEAR SON

I am well and hope you are.
Beryl, Gladys, Naomi, Isabelle, Wynn,
and Minnie Richards played
canasta last night. I served
lovey apple turnovers, so we had
a good time—hoping you are well,
    *   *   *

It is another rainy Sunday.
Dad is in his usual position
and is watching football too.
As you know, I am ironing.
    *   *   *

We had some excitement
at the office on Friday.
A woman jumped
from the 32nd floor.
I suspect she was depressed.
She jumped, took off
her shoes, and went out
the window. Mr. Reisman
is retiring next month.
There will be changes.
    *   *   *

We have not heard
from you. I hope
you are well. I
won't sleep until
you find someone.
Can you meet me
for lunch next
Thursday at noon?
    *   *   *

What an experience!
Someone turned off
the lights in
the ladies room
and I was with
a Negro woman
who was singing.
Can you imagine?
　　　*　*　*

It was nice to see
you on Sunday. I
am enclosing $2
for the incidentals.
　　　*　*　*

Someone at work found
a snake in his toilet.
　　　*　*　*

I am well.
How are you?
How is your work?
Do you continue to see that girl?
Are you eating, at last, a square meal?
　　　*　*　*

What an experience!
Yesterday, after church,
I was hit by a car.
They took me away
to the hospital in Hempstead
where it took four hours
to find out I was well.
　　　*　*　*

Call me on Tuesday.
And tomorrow.
　　　*　*　*

We heard from your sister
yesterday. She is well.
Did I tell you someone
at work found a snake
in his toilet?
I pray for you.
　　　*　*　*

Gladys Flone's niece's
brother-in-law was killed
in a car crash last week.
You never know.
*   *   *
I am enclosing $3 which
you certainly can use.
It's another rainy Sunday.
This would have been
Grandpa's 107th birthday.
Of course I am ironing.
We miss you on days
such as this.
*   *   *
I just want to tell you
that we had a case at work
of a 68 year old lady
who was robbed, raped,
and put in the cellar.
Those people should be hung.
*   *   *
We haven't heard from you
or your sister in a while.
Dad has a cold but
I am getting better.
When are you coming home?

John Quinn

LETTER TO HUGO
FROM BORING

Dear Dick,
I remembered you fat as a basketball,
holding court in your condominium.
Laughing like Satan surrounded by sinners
from the tents across the Deschutes.
Or harmless as a cork bobbing in the pool.
I did belly flops off the high board
to show I knew you don't have to be graceful
to have guts. But you were in the water
for release. I was there to increase
my own embarrassment. Fat is a way
of thinking, and, Dick, goddamnit, girls
are harder than ever at swimming pools.
But then, neither of us is fat like we were.
And I'm back home now, though still lying
low. The desert is a way of thinking too.
Slow to shake. I hope you won't think this
presumptuous. I just wanted to let you
know how good it is to see you here again,
healthy, happy, dangerous as hell.

                    Best,
                    John Quinn

Robert Wrigley

KILLING THEM

Letter to Hugo from McCall

Dear Dick,

Medium trout, dozens. With each catch
I swirl the stringer into sun
looking for the runt: all of them,
none of them. I let go whichever
one seems most likely to grow.

This kind of lake is no uptown bar.
It's a lounge with large-screen TV,
pale paneling and miles
of overstuffed upholstery. Lures fizzle
into the sun like the worst sweet drinks.

I'm killing them, Dick, and it's no fun.
Just once I'd like to feel
slack snap to steel, nylon burn a trough
on the thumb's knuckle. I'd like
to wake to this brassy sun

in this strange, warm place, and raise
a head heavy as the fish of dreams.
I'd like to remember some battle here,
and like the good drunk, inventory my teeth
with a thick, slow tongue before I smile.

Gerard Malanga

SONNET VIII

"The longer you last the less you care."
—Marilyn Monroe
The River of No Return

We say goodbye to an entire decade.
We understand, too, that the skirmish
Goes to sea in the form of a pencil.
Your look illuminates me with spunk.

I think Michael McClure is nothing like
William Bonnie. I come upon you in the line,
"How death is that remedy all singers dream of."

We sit, Peter, you and me, in 8th Street *Riker's*.
We discuss Ben Maddow's poem, "The City"
And my mother working in the "Five & Dime".

Somewhere in my sleep, as a child sorrowfully grave,
I launch a small boat within the phrase,
"It is only the sun that shines once for the mind"
As we stand smiling into the edge of 1964.

It is 2:18 am New York. Dear Allen, hello.

ca. 1963

Jack Driscoll & William Meissner

(These collaborative poems were composed through the mail, be-
tween Minnesota and Michigan, with each author adding two lines.
The period of composition was usually about three months.)

PART OF THE WAKING

In the morning, even before
the dog is awake
I have put on all
my dreaming clothes and walked outside
across the lawn with my shoes
in my hand.
But this will not be enough.
The touch of the grass will taste like green teeth,
and the hammock, stretched between the unpruned apple trees,
can barely hold the day's weight. I must keep saying to myself
lean back, back far enough until you can see
the apples fade from red to pale blue
and feel the ground underneath inhaling,
pulling through the squares of rope
one by one like pieces of sleep.

KEEPING IN TOUCH

Even if no one ever asks me
to talk about wheels
I will live knowing they watch
the spokes in my mouth
and I will pretend to sing
like a bicycle in an attic.

I will write letters to my friends
explaining nothing
and they will reply with empty envelopes
that float to my door like milkweed.
I will phone them, long-distance
and remain silent, letting them guess
whose voice is the stalled engine
on the other end. Before they hang up

I will pour water into the phone
and listen to the sound of them rusting.

FIRST KISS

When he first discovered his dentures
in the garden, he put them
in a glass of cut flowers, watched them
sprout water lilies between the teeth.
Each flower frightened his wife like
a snake asleep in her clay pot.
When he smiled, his gums
were pale roses pressed for years
against the fishbowl of her dreams.
It was always that way between them,
the soft bites underwater, the kisses
that leave a taste for decades in their mouths.

David Walker

SLIPS

(Franz Kafka's last messages were written on "conversation slips" since he was unable any longer to speak aloud. The follow-ing incorporates phrases from these so-called "slips" but is other-wise an imaginary reconstruction.)

Given this: the twelve kinds of fruit
burning me, and every limb
tired as a man after
his whole life;
              given
the lilacs fresher than morning (but
you cut them wrong—
the stems should touch the bowl
only on a slant)
               and given
these pills that stick
like splintered glass, and even the beer
rasping my larynx—

                  I do nothing
and who will pay for it?
What is the prize
for a large swallow, when it's easier
to choke on less?

             Move the lilies
into the sun, if you have a moment. And why
in a vase?

Doctor, are you a connoisseur

of wines, the ones you advise me to take
with a slice of lemon?

       But I'll hold out
another week, such
are the nuances;
      and though my mother
was ill, when she received the good water
she rejoiced. . . .

     Fear again: it's crazy,
they killed the man beside me—
every doctor's little underling
prescribing, until he walked
with fever 106. At the last rites, he had
no time to confess.

       So full of water,
I'm a lake. Which flows nowhere,
no miracles, although the forest
around it is lovely. . . . Memories,
but now we've come too far
from the tavern garden's summer, its blue-black
dragonflies at mating, and enough
flowers for now—
      laburnum, the columbine
too bright to stand with others,
scarlet hawthorn too hidden,
too much in the dark. . . . Yesterday
evening, a late bee drank
the white lilac totally dry!

A little icecream? Rhetorical question,
though the lilac, dying,
drinks its fill—that cannot be
for a man.

I was to go to the Baltic with her once
but was ashamed: my thinness,
misunderstandings. No, not beautiful
but slender, a fine body

which she has kept.

                              Put your hand
              on my forehead. For courage: whose?

              Beer now, instead of lemonade: all
              has become boundless, the way
              the help goes away again
                                        without helping.

Patricia Goedicke

LETTER FROM D.S.

What called to me from it was, when it arrived,
flat as a stomach in its smooth
brown paper envelope with the new poems, travel
announcements of other journeys, what

called to me from the neat grid of gray
typewriter strokes dense as the clean fibers
of an indoor-outdoor rug, the nap close woven, pre-
cise, industrious as ants walking together
in supple single minded columns from

all directions at once raising up like true
and enormous saints a cathedral
that spoke to me, that grabbed my heart
like a rose and flew away with it

Murmuring the fine complicated texture
of the pure and the impure: poetry as the wild
passionately lonely bridge between what is
and what we most desperately and forever

long for, "*What* a romantic!" my friend said but she's
in favor of romance, only the night before
at a talk I'd given on the particular, the letter
of the law, if it were really possible in art to use
the private to commandeer the general, out of the loose

amiable array of the closed, individually shut selves
and meaningless pieces of time to create
those blazing batallions of abstract beauty
that *can* openly bloom in the church blade
even of only a single hieroglyph, she said

"But it's *all* opening and closing, isn't it, the chromosomes
rhythmically bend and twist
in and out like arms, like long ribboned braids," stooping
to tie her sneakers the next day she wondered

"What's he like, your friend?" waving the part of his letter
I'd just given her to read before we left for tennis
as usual, out on the wide, eroded, bare
windy plateau at the foot of the patchwork mountain

with tin shacks, radio jingles blaring,
ricocheting from the canyons,
on the other side the lush green of the club, palm trees
like jewels, luxurious bougainvillea
and, right in the middle of the tennis court,

large wet puddles my friend, small, black haired,
with snub nose and liquid muscles leaped over
quick as a goat but far more sinuous
and silkily graceful but tough, tough as a little
brown nut, how lucky she is, I thought

my other friend's letter said diabetes
just discovered, a worry, but this one has
two children, paints, and not much money,
sometimes the charming nose twitches

nervously, the skin drains
even as she charges the net, growling, picking up
pollen from everywhere, dust, seeds out of the wind
if she hits one she hits them all, she is one

smart woman, my friend who wrote the letter
would surely like her, would know her
for what she is, swinging the tennis racquet wide
open and then swiftly, with great generous force closing
on the ball only to send it springing

round as a little moon spinning
in and out like petals, like the compact
closing and opening single
white athletic leaves of your letter.

92   *Patricia Goedicke*

DON MILLER
Postcard Reassembly

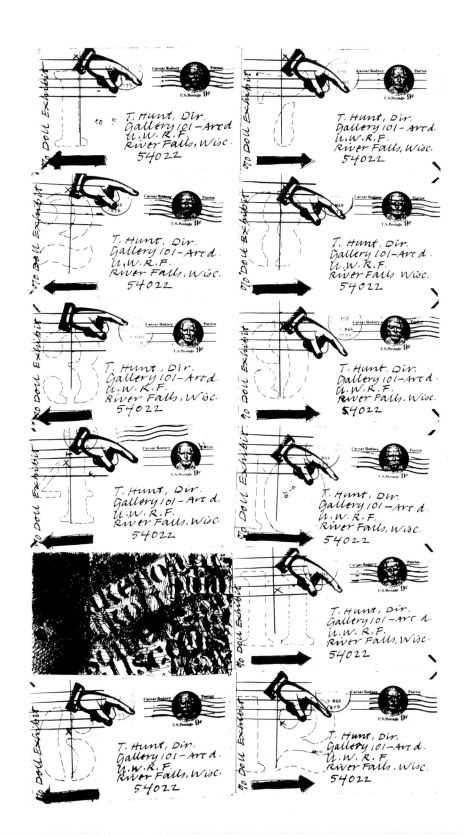

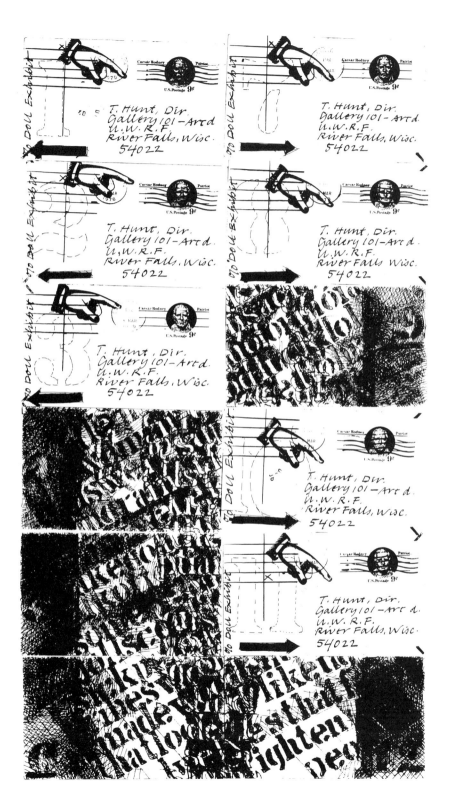

Postcard(#5), actual size. 3¼x5½″

Postcard Assemblage. March 9, 1978. 20x11″

Fiction

Harold Leland Johnson

A WEAVER AND DYER OF PURPLE

Starhill, Kansas,
May 14th, 1865

Dear Cecelia:

What times we live in! Yet, to tell the truth, now that our Nation
has ended its long quarrel with itself, we can at last look toward
the future in spite of the confusions around us. Here in the West,
we are at the very beginning of things; and because we may not
have suffered as much from the turmoil and exhausion of confiict
we can bring to peace more than was wasted in war.

For example, only in charity could this place be called a town,
and yet rumors of railroads are leading it to make bold pretenses.
I hear people talking in that positive tone that my husband uses
when he is selling a mare, and more so if she is in foal. I take this
as a sign that people are beginning to put away the past and turning toward tomorrow. Oh, I know that men still hang upon the
telegraph to learn what Greeley says, or Stanton, yet how much
better informed they might be; they do not understand the import
of the letters we women write to one another. Surely, it is always
we women who must arrange this world so that it is fit to live in.
And we do it. If we did not shape affairs into new orders and relations in our own way, historians would have to be even more
imaginative to reconstruct something from the rubble of events
that men scatter over the land. (Of course, in that respect, the
writers of the Scriptures did a little better.)

Now let there be a confession of what all this has to do with you
and with me. We had only heard about the terrible events in Wash-

ington, and the assasination of our President, when a letter from our cousin Amy arrived telling us of your father's death. To me, all such news comes like a darkness; but I know the world moves and another sun will come to rouse us from it. That is why I ask you now, directly, what is there to keep you there in Lexington now that you are alone? Come and stay here with us. Let this be your home. There is much to do here; all the material needed to create happiness; enough to make one bold enough to undertake an even longer journey than I propose. Now I will close; I shall make things ready; I can provide you whatever you need to come to us. Write to me now, and you will see how well I can do. With love, and in great expectancy,

your cousin,
Lydia Kinsett.

Starhill, Kansas,
June 22nd, 1865.

Dear Amy:

Does anyone ever remember, by the end of spring, how the powder snow sifted in beneath the doorsill in winter? Now the plain is green; the winds blow gently, and no longer is there a crackle of rifles and a grunting of cannon to spread a winter sound through all the seasons. Yet, what happens when we lay our hands upon the bell-rope to ring out the news? Yes, the bell tolls fully; but the clapper must strike both sides; see how, in Washington, our President is slain; and in Lexington, Death also takes one of the dearest of our relatives and friends; John Rowan.

Amy, if I seem to make much of this, it only because a shadow seems to run after us as if it would make only a candle of the faithful sun. Now, we need all of the light for our restoration. When there is such a time, I believe women are the first to know what work is to be done. I admit that I am scornful when I hear men talk about "women's place." Even the Almighty, with a creation under way, saw that nothing could proceed further without us. Usually, our "place" is assigned to us by those who feel ordained to declare that a woman may not prophesy. Who is more practiced at looking into the future than we are? Our foresight comes from much practice, and an urgent need. I do not think we get it from peering into palms or teacups; there are other ways; we may look only into the eyes of those around us, or when alone, inward toward the truth of our dreams.

I have already exchanged letters with Cecelia, as you may know. I do like a certain firmness in the writing from her hand; I see by it that she is independent and self-reliant. This is good country for people like her. Besides, when the girl can teach, an empty schoolhouse here in Kansas should be fancied more than tutor's work in some big house in Boston. After all, I had to teach my own offspring to read and write before the men got around to the building of a schoolhouse. And no sooner was it finished than we lost our schoolmaster to the Northern armies, with my son Mark tagging along in his footsteps. And it was only Mark who returned this Spring. He is now, by prayer and good fortune, well and strong. But what is Victory that overcomes our enemy and sends us either an empty grief or a silent stranger home to us? All I know about his service as a soldier I learned from the only two letters I received while he was gone. One came from somewhere in Pennsylvania, and the second was not even in his own hand. It was written for him while he was in a hospital near Washington by a friend whom he called Whitman.

Now that he is home again, he is too much by himself. He reads and reads some more, as if to find in books the replies to all the questions that the guns did not answer. Forgive me for going on at length about these concerns; it is only that here at home I say nothing of any of it, and try, by keeping my hands busy, to also keep a quiet mind.

Affectionately,
Lydia.

MacDonald, Hempler and MacDonald
Attorneys At Law
Starhill, Kansas.

August 10th, 1914.

Miss Cecelia Dowan,
112 Carl Street,
Bryefield, Kansas.

Dear Miss Cecelia:

I am sending you this letter and enclosures by my son James, who has returned to join us here in law practice, as you see by the added name above. You may remember him from several years ago as one of your pupils in the old Willow Avenue school. I know he is looking forward to seeing you again, and will tell you how pleased we are here to learn that the new high school there in Bryefield is to be named after you. But let me say that your name is always in the recall of so many of us who gained from your years of devotion to our own education as well as that of our children.

The enclosures are from the estate of Lydia Kinsett. As her attorney, I am of course familiar with their contents, excepting the one envelope that is sealed and addressed to you. I hope that nothing in it will add further to the sense of loss that we, too, feel at her passing. She was both a client and dear friend to me.

I will be coming over to the country seat a little later in the year and hope to have the pleasure of calling on you myself. Meanwhile, if you should think of any way in which I might be of help to you, please write and let me know.

With my warmest personal good wishes,
Henry MacDonald.

Starhill, Kansas,

Dear Cecelia:

Right now I am thinking of your visit here with me in this old
house just the summer before last. As we were talking, you said
that the years seem to come along like chinese boxes; open one,
take out the box inside, open it, and there is another a little
smaller, and so on. Since then, I have written this letter. It has taken
me some time. For one thing, I am enclosing another letter, an
old, old one, sealed and addressed to you long ago. This letter I
am writing and the one I send represent the last two boxes in my
world. When you have read this, you will understand why I never
chose to learn what that last "box" contains.

Another thing I have never before mentioned to anyone is this:
all my life, I have been warned in a dream—the same dream,
repeated—of a task I must soon perform. In this dream, it seems
that I am walking in some high forest; a great wind is roaring in
the darkening sky and everywhere the giant limbs are cracking
and branches falling. Yet I pass safely, to awaken suddenly to
daylight in the room.

With consciousness, I know at once how close I am (usually
within the compass of a day) to the whistling scythe of some grim
reality; that the sheaves have fallen, and I must go and bind them.
There has never been a time when they have failed to be there
waiting.

Last night, a distant lightning beyond the horizon of my dream
showed me that I stood alone in an empty field. Plainly, it is I who
will fall, but not until I have shared with you this secret kept for
all the years we have known each other. You see, there was that
certain day, now years past, when I came from that dream of the
forest into the first light of morning. On the table in the hall, just
outside my room, I saw this letter. I took it up; and I saw that it
was addressed to you. But the moment I touched it it came to me,
by my own sure way of knowing, that this letter was an end; a
testament; that it contained the last word that either you or I would
ever hear from my son Mark Kinsett.

Although it has been in my personal keeping all this time, I
have felt no temptation to open and read his letter to you. I re-

member that I thought of destroying it becaues of the pain I was sure it held for you; I have known the ache of wasted hopes, and I was certain that was all that this letter could mean. The months and years have gone by, each adding proof to the insight that was given to me. The truth must now be complete in this explanation of what I have done. But I should also say that it has been like a purple bruise, hidden and painful to me; a thing that has been long in its healing. Yet I now believe that there has been such healing, if you will not grieve for him or for me,

With love,
Lydia.

Sunday, June 17th, 1866.

Dear, dear Cecelia:

When you and I have stood close together in the field as the wind came down to us, rolling in over the newly headed wheat, your eyes would turn from me and look into the distance. And I knew how you felt when you said you remembered the sea. Yet what I saw in my own mind was the green of the valley of the Shenandoah as we came marching and burning. That is really why I am marching again today. It seems nothing will stay my going; all I can do is take my memory of you as a seed to sow in some better earth than this; perhaps the one I go to find. Right now, there is one word in my head: Oregon. If you were to try and say it slowly to yourself, you might come to my understanding of the word "Oregon."

Does it begin with an arching up from the mind like a bridge to the clouds? I seem to hear, reaching into a fulness, the tone of an organ; one that ends with the sound of a voice calling in a dream and a tender ache from the dream left at waking. How can a name be made of the motion of waves on the rocks and the whisper of rain on the sea; or how can a sound rise up like the curve of the sand in the dunes and float like a mist in the tops of the firs and cedars? Its syllables are to my thirst like drops of water shaken onto my lips from the tips of ferns as high as your breasts. Oh, the ferns grow well in a land where winter is only the cold that creeps from the caves above and stands looking over the

valleys, and spring is always in the air where cascades are dancing to rainbows.

Oregon. How many echoes there are in that name! When it is
spoken, even in the language of strangers coming out of their
ships, or by the voices that shout from the wagons high on the
mountain, it is fresh in the mouth like taste of a cloud in the forest.
That is the meaning I hope to read in the mosses and lichens on
the rocks of the passes. Then, I will follow the streams to a place
that will never refuse that man who comes slowly, in silence, with
praise in his eyes; a man who is willing always to keep its seasons.
And, once I am there—oh, Celia, wait for my letter. Please wait
for my letter.

All my poor love,
Mark.

Kevin McIlvoy

From THE SHAKINO GANG

Culvert, Oregon

December, 1970

To Whom It Might Concern:

I'm the one who put all this about Shakino and some of the Shakino gang together.

I'm a foreman for Bende Boxboard, and I keep getting told I got better things to do than all this. But I just had to do it. Now it's over I can work even better I bet. What do you think?

I think when a man gets something as big as this Shakino thing between his ears he's either got to talk about it or just explode into pieces of hair and nose. If some high school teacher could've written *Gone With The Wind* I know I could've. I graduated high school and could've gone to college on a wrestling scholarship. But you might say boxboard is my born evocation. Some people call boxboard "packaging" the way some people call a book "a novel," but to me it's all the same, book or box. See, I was going to sit down and write it up the way my father, Sheriff Alfred, told it. But he just told me a few names and stories about the names before he died. By then talking was like hard labor for him. He was 87 if that explains anything. He never could read or write because he never had education. He grew up in Alicel and worked the Butter Wash Mines for 40 years. I was raised in Grande mostly by mother who died just 10 years ago. Right after she died my father just melted all together like an engine out of oil. He was living with me here in Bende then, but it got to that point where he just shuttling from here to the hospital. When he could at least walk again the Medicare people helped me find a place for him. But I never liked those kind of places. So I brought him back and we waited.

And finally the strangest thing happens. A guy named Mr. High-pockets calls from the Shakino Chamber of Commerce. I thought it was some kind of joke or something because I knew Shakino had been a ghost town for 70 years. But this guy says, "No joke— we got a population of 42—all of us over 65. What do you think?"

I thought it was a joke. But this guy says, "No joke— we'll send you some city information." "Wait." I said. "How do you know about my father?"

"You got a woman in the house?" he said. I said, "Had one." "And you get calls from perfume people and jewelry hawkers?" he wanted to know. I said, "Sure."

Then he said something about how those people call because they know you probably got a woman, and how Shakino calls because they know you probably got an old man in the house. That made sense to me. What do you think?

So a week later we get this letter from a ghost town. Do you believe that? In it it's got things. An old unused postcard from Minnesota that's got a plate of pancakes in the picture. A typed letter from the town mayor, Mr. Dizzey. A paint-by-number handkerchief. And a snapshot of a desert graveyard.

I sent the postcard back asking, "Can you take care of old people?"

Two days later I get a letter saying, "We *are* old people." So I took him there.

Shakino was the best place I've ever been to I think. It really was a ghost town once until some rich woman got a notion about 1972 that it could be a sort of Noah's Ark for every kind of old people. So what she did was she had contractors make over the Hotel Golden there. And then she started choosing people that make a town go. This Highpockets guy was a politician once. Ever wonder what becomes of a guy like that when he retires? Me too. This rich woman, Mrs. Calash, got one of them—and got herself a banker and a librarian and a mayor and a pool shark and a waitress and a good collection of citizens and *gave* them Shakino. Rooms in the Hotel Golden. The Hotel Golden Restaurant. A city government. A graveyard. And bad elements like the pool shark. It was because they needed a sheriff that they were calling people like me and my father. The thing is—they didn't *really* need a sheriff. The bad elements in town just played at being rotten. So what they needed was a pretend sheriff, which as it turned out my father was perfect for. They even found him a deputy.

What do you think? Don't you think it's like someone said, "Just in case there's no heaven—just in case—here's this here ghost town. All yours."

People were happy there. Sure. But you got deaths and funerals as regularly as haircuts. You got no children born there.

Still. In Shakino you got the satisfaction of knowing if you die the town is all of a sudden without a sheriff or a pool shark or whatever you were. I haven't figured out what, but that means something.

Now when the government decided to close down Shakino after 4 years, telling Mrs. Calash it wasn't *healthy* to live there, I thought they were joking. I went into town. I asked around for Mr. Highpockets, President of the Chamber of Commerce. He said, "No joke. You ever eat stadium franks?" I said, "Of course." He said something about how the government found stadium franks could give you cancer and so you'll never see stadium franks again. He said he guessed the government found living in ghost towns must be dangerous so you'll never see that again either. "Same thing." he said. "As stadium franks?" I said. "No joke." he said.

So that's it. They moved them all over and separated even married people according to what Medicare they had.

I took my father to live with me here in Culvert. We're within driving distance of Shakino. My father likes to visit the graveyard there and look at it from the car window. But no one is ever there. Sometimes I think even the dead have been taken away.

Something has happened that is important. I know it. You know what I mean? And I wanted to remember it by writing something. I wrote Shakino's librarian and history man, Little Rick, to ask about the whole mess with the government at the end. He and I knew each other from my visits to Shakino. What I didn't tell him was that I wanted to write something myself.

He wrote me a letter back that gave me an idea. What I thought I'd do is see if I could get a fistful of letters like his and put them together with the letters my father had gotten like some big scrapbook. So I made some calls. Travelled up 97 to 80 to Hood River and found out that my first chapter, Mr. and Mrs. Hairful, had both just passed away. But I got their final effects. It seems they had written letters for a whole year to Mayor Dizzey which were all returned to them in the mail. I found out the reason he didn't get any of those letters was because just after he wrote them a first letter he died. Looks like they lost his letter. I couldn't find it anywhere. They had other letters from Shakino people, but not many. Most of the gang didn't know where everyone had been taken to. I kept the letters to Mayor Dizzey.

For a year I drove from Pendelton to The Dalles to Greenspire and everywhere else to find letters. Little Rick sent me a lot of his from Miss Minnie. I got Slam's letters from Miss Minnie in his final effects. And Miss Minnie who was in a home in The Dalles very kindly gave me all her letters from both men.

I never did find Highpockets and Tenpercent, but I got their letters too from Slam and Little Rick who they wrote to mostly.

But my favorite part is the Christmas cards they all sent my father. He must have asked me to read them to him a hundred times. After a while we even stopped driving to the graveyard. The cards were just as good. I don't know why I didn't think then they were just as good. But what do you think?

With all respect,
Lester

*

LETTER FROM LITTLE RICK

Summer

Dear Lester.

This is the letter. that I promised. about the Shakino wars.

At the party. Miss Minnie said. "If theyrs anything I love. it's the long arma the law. and the big blue eyes and the flat top. and things." Sheriff Alfred. that's who she ment. And every body laughed. out loud. Sheriff Alfred. he laughed too. and shot off a hole roll of caps. The mayor. Mr. Dizzey. punched the bottom outa a paper glass and proclamed and declaired and swore in announcment. a holaday. Shakino V-Day. Sheriff Alfred. his gun smoked. He put in a fresh roll of Sure-Fire caps. Miss Minnie put on a big hat did a toe dance. Highpockets joined her shook his six foot legs. Tenpercent. the town banker. he tried to cut in. Slam. played the tinwhistle. Shakino V-Day. we always celabrated it big.

The Housers, Elimanators, and Well-Fair folks. they began it all. Suits and ties and pencil and paper and eyes like sliding rulers. thats them. Last fall ten years ago. when they first came. walked everywhere. sniff sniff scratch scratch. on a pad.

"Hi."

Howdy. mister.

"You live here?"

Yessir. Town librarian. (I was proud. I guess.).

"Your name?"

Dewey. Folks call me. Little Rick. Never liked that name. Dewey. (Id said too much alredy. I knew that.).

He scratched "Little Rick" on paper. Your name. you get it stuffed between two blue lines. that makes you scared. Miss Minnie. Hairful. Tenpercent. Mr. Dizzey. Highpockets. Slam. Me. Sheriff Alfred.

"Sheriff Alfred." we said. "This means some thing. dont it?"

Deputy Hairful. he said. "Yup."

Mr. Dizzey. he asked. "Well?"

Sheriff Alfred. he said. "Wheill see whut she wll see." (he talks that way!).

Miss Minnie. went "Ooooooh." like a tomcat smoking cigar butts. She liked all of men. Miss Minnie.

And she was the first taken. "Retarded." we know that word. HEWmen. they said it like saying. Dirt. "Old." we knew that word they said it like saying. Mud. Sniff sniff scatch scratch. Then. they came back for more. In the Greenspire Gazette we read. "adult services workers for the state are removing Shakino residents to a Hood River nursing home, other facilities, and a foster home in The Dalles."

Mayor Dizzey. called a town meeting. He asked Sheriff Alfred. "We gotta plan? We gotta plan yet?" "Yup." his deputy said.

"Yup!" Mrs. Clache. she said. but in her mouth. her plastic chappers clakked together. She said. "Iksha good shing xzyes men glike you. bueafhefhul." like a dog drunk and drownding. a religioned woman. But Deputy Hairful. he loves her feircly.

It was about electiontime. Sheriff Alfred. he said. "Thisuz the plan now . . ." He was anomynusly relected from then on. for ten years.

(OVER)

So.

So. the next time five HEWs come to Shakino. one day aheada time. Sheriff Alfred. he put up notices at the tavern and hotel. and library. They read. HEW VISITS SHAKINO. WELCOME HEW.

In a blue van. about 10:30 in the morning. they filed out. Mrs. Clache. Miss Minnie daughter. who glued her teeth in specialy. she waited near. The five men. they looked at her close. "Ooooh." she went. like a rabbit just born. she. (that sentences a mess. sorry.). Mrs. Clache. she winked her glass eye. One man. he went scratch scratch. an other. he looked closer. If her teeth stayed in. we had one front covered. for sure.

(OVER AGAIN)

At lunchtime. under the lamps. Slam. he played pool with a vest and tie type.

Mister. you play thisher game?

"Sometimes I do. Sometimes. old man."

Quarter down buys a rackful. mister.

"After lunch."

Then. after lunch. Slam. and this guy. they play pool a couple hours.

Where we at? Mister. where we at. I mean. in money.

"About 30 bucks. ha! ha! 30 bucks! You got that much?"

Slam. he says. I can go fifty. if you want.

"*Okay*! ha! ha! *Okay*!

Then. Slam. he breaks. Then. drops fifteen. smiling like a hangman.

Vest and tie. his mouth drops like a paira pants.

Slam. he says. Lets seeya pull. a rabbit outa yur hat. mister. Smiling like a stripper.

Vest and tie. "Hey. but."

Slam. Yeesssss. Ear-to-ear smirk.

Sheriff Alfred. he happens into the light. "Thisuz Shakino. aint Portland. No gambling. in Shakino. Slam. you know better."

Slam. smiling like a monday drunk. Yessir.

"Give that stacka fifty back then. Slam."

Yesser. Slam. he counts fifty Monopoly sheets out. gives them back. to vest and tie.

Vest and tie. sweats. pushes the fake fifty and his hand into his vest.

"Your free. Slam. Thats Retrabution. I guess. About you. mister. Deputy Hairful. book him on Gambling."

Vest and tie. "Hey. but." He pulls them Monopoly sheets out. hands them to Sheriff Alfred.

"Deputy Hairful. book him on Bribing An Officer of the Law and Order."

Vest and tie. he looks at them bills. MONOPOLY bills.

"Deputy Hairful. book him on Distrabuting Counter Feet Bribery. Handcuff him." Sheriff Alfred. he says. "Take him to jail."

Vest and tie. pale as dead breath. he says. "Ha! ha! this is funny! a good joke!" slaps Sheriff Alfred on the back. "Ha! ha!" hands to Hairful the handcuffs. "Ha! ha!"

"Deputy Hairful. book him on Asalting An Officer of the Peace and Quiet. book him on Resisting A Rest."

(OVER)

Mayor Dizzey. and Tenpercent. they took two pressed pants. ona tour a the town. talked about real-is-state and profit-marching. and over head. and things. Tenpercent. offered them smokes. he showed them the bank safe. Mayor Dizzey. gave them keys to the city. called them. "gentle men" this. and "gentle men" that. "Gentle men. thisis the Town Hall. thisis Pigeon Park. Gentle men. thats the jailhouse. town tavern. the Hotel Golden. law firma Alfred. Alfred. and Alfred. the library. Those three houses. theyr the town suburb. And. gentle men. thisis the town treasury."

"Unlikely place!" one pressed pants says.

Thother pressed pants. he says. "Sure is! boy!"

Then.

Then. Tenpercent and Mayor Dizzey. they lock them in. Miss Minnie's two room. You could hear the pounding. across town. even in the jail. 2 miles down. Later. just sniff sniff scratch scratch. scratch scratch.

When they was arrested. hour later. Deputy Hairful. he booked them on Breaking and Getting Into.

(OVER)

The fifth stuffed shirt. who me and Highpockets figured to have family. who wore a stupid handsewn tie. The fifth stuffed shirt. he got it the worst. Sheriff Alfred. he told stuffed shirt to leave Shakino. or to meet him in the street at noon. for gun battle.

"Ha! ha!" stuffed shirt.

"Ha! ha!" Sheriff Alfred.

So at noon. Highpockets pulls out two silver capguns. loads them with caps. he says to stuffed shirt. he says. "gentle man. choose your wepon."

"Ha! ha!" stuffed shirt. But the whole town. everybody. has come. lined the street.

"Ha! ha!" Sheriff Alfred.

Noon. twenty paces. and they turn. Sheriff Alfred. raises his hand. Snap! Snap! two caps explode. two more. Sheriff Alfred. he tilts his head back to bi-focus the stuffed shirt. in his glasses. Snap! Snap! Snap! Sheriff Alfred. he drops to the dirt. drops dead.

"Ha! ha!" stuffed shirt.

"Murder murder!" a whole crowd. it closes in. a whole crowd. "Murder! murder!" Deputy Hairful. he weeps over his friend. Sheriff Alfred. Then Hairful. he collars stuffed shsirt. He's dead! he's dead!

"Hey. but."

He *died*. stranger. He's dead.

"But." says stranger. just before they took him to jail.

Sheriff Alfred. he got up. dusted him self off.

In the Hotel Golden. you could hear the scream. like a hundred ducks hitting water. Sheriff Alfred. he ambled towards it. had to rescue Mrs. Clache. Miss Minnie's daughter. whose teeth was just now dropping. Mrs. Clache. who had been im properly and ill legally 'approached.' Sheriff Alfred. he said. "Deputy."

Yup.

"Jail the suspect."

(OVER)

When they was tried. by a jurya there peers. "old." "retarded." they. the five guys. was found innocent. sent back in their van. Sheriff Alfred. he said. "Boys. we got more tricks up our sleeves. than arms. You. send Miss Minnie back. and dont come back with her."

"Hey. but." they said. then. "okay." Nuna them laughed. alla them. they put their pads in their pockets. The end.

Well.

That aint the way it happened. you know that. Miss Minnie. she lives in the Madras Nursing Home. Slam. hes in Dalles. its a foster home. Highpockets. Tenpercent. theyr outa state. I think. Mayor Dizzey. he was in the hospital. last I heard. prostrate. Mrs. Clache. she married Deputy Hairful. they lived happily ever after. not really. (they got seprate rooms. ina home. in Hood River.).

Sheriff Alfred. he died. (of capgun wounds.).

You still tell stories? Its a better story. if you tell it starting with. "At the party."

How oldur your kids now? about 45. 50 I guess. huh? Tell your kids. Mean while,

> Keep it under your hat,
> Little Rick
> Greenspire, Oregon
> Salvation Army Shelter no. 71

Joan Retallack

7·2·77

Pour flavour!, my love; if I may so address you over this exquisite cup of Russian Caravan tea. As Galileo once said (several times, actually), *straight motion seems entirely excluded from nature and her environs*. Perhaps he didn't say, *and her environs*, though you'll agree it's implicit (cf. *Dialogue Concerning the Two Chief World Systems*) and I, who am almost entirely resigned to *her environs*, whether referred to by Galileo or not, reduced to the penultimate indirection of wishing you were here, with me, now, sipping this unparalleled blend of the old Russian Aristocracy . . . I, savouring visions of rainbow hued verbiage alighting on your exquisite brain as lepidoptera upon a thistle, I, in the midst of a lifelong, albeit unpaid, vocation, "I, and the world," as Heidegger said . . . Oh Hell!, I digress, as usual, before I have even begun.

My love, you asked me in your last letter (7.1.77, only two days after remarking in your inimitable style, "I disagree with what you are saying, but I admire your embouchure."). "Can any situation be said to be inherently apolitical?" In full cognizance of the rhetorical nature of such a question, I must attempt to answer it, within the unabashedly seminal conceptual framework of *Gerberhornian Colour Theory*, title of my last book.

Picture the following "slices of life" gleaned from a random sampling of both personal experience and newspaper accounts over a modest but exemplary period of one week:

1. A man spreads peanut butter on a slice of Women's Community Co-op Bakery wholewheat bread.

2. An entire audience coughs in unison during the 2nd move-

ment of the *Eroica.*

3. A woman lobs a dachshund into the face of the visiting Chancellor.

4. A poodle explodes in the micro-wave oven of his widowed mistress who wished only to dry him off. The oven is ruined. The woman suffers a heart attack and dies.

What, if anything, can all of these events be said to have in common? To answer this question, let us "re-describe" them in the terminology of the Gerberhornian calculus:

1G. With the serene ironing of eternal blue, a man spreads . . . .

2G. With the lubricant effulgence of eternal green, an audience coughs . . . .

3G. With the blistering pith of eternal red, a woman lobs . . . .

4G. Within the *Feltanshaung* of yellow, a poodle explodes . . . emitting a fine spray of apricot flecked beige . . . .

We have thus accomplished the simultaneous universalization and particularization of all four events. Darling, I know your perfectly calibrated mind is, as always, racing ahead. You are thinking of the Samurai movie we saw together three weeks ago, the incomparable Takisha Moshikada bursting out of his ambushed coach, demanding, NAME!, REASON!, APOLOGY! only to find that, with his ancestral sword, he has slain his attackers, his driver and his horse through the curtained window, this amalgamating (mettle with metal?) the gratuitous particularity of Life with the unrelenting universality of Death, random chance with necessity, 'botching it up' with reasoned intentionality, etc. You are right, you are right! Of course! It's the same thing! Yes, yes, yes! 1-4, 1G-4G, the Moshikada amalgamation— all come down to the same thing.

To see this clearly, we need only "re-describe" Moshikada's predicament in terms of the Gerberhornian calculus as follows:

blue $+$ red $-$ (green $\times$ yellow) $=$ glurd

Aha, GLURD! Now, let us look at the equation yielded by an algebraic reduction of $1G - 4G$:

blue $+$ red $-$ (green $\times$ yellow) $=$ glurd

The equations (we shall call them a and b) are identical! This might be of only minor interest were it not for the fact that *glurd*

is the Gerberhornian equivalent of *despair*. "How can that be!,"
you exclaim, my little pigeon. I will demonstrate:

First we plug into the Heraclitean calculus (earth, air, fire,
water) by substituting *m* for *gl*. This transforms *glurd* into
murd. Yes, you've guessed right again, my brilliant—etymo-
logical first cousin to the French, *merde*. Divide in accordance
with the r-infinity axiom, giving *merde*—sorry, $\dfrac{murd}{r}$, reducing
to *mud* or, in the vernacular, despair.

Despair is thus seen to be the foundational element in events
1G — 4G and, by the principle of the "return to the original,"
events 1 — 4— mediated, of course, by axioms 303, 305 and 307
of the Gerberhornian calculus, too complex to unpack in this little
billet doux (see my book, *Gerberhornian Colour Theory*, pp. 56-
287). *Despair*, as we all know, is "inherently apolitical," knowing no national, cultural or ideological boundries. Hence, it is
the case that events 1-4, IG-4G and the "M.A" are "inherently
apolitical." Quod erat demonstrandum.

Write soon, my darling, my pigeon, my love. May I call you
"my love?"

As always, from the *environs* . . . .

Audrey Borenstein

LETTER TO A BIOGRAPHER

Dear Ms. Anderson,

You will, I trust, forgive the long interval between your request for my sister's letters to me and this reply. It happens that your self-introduction was unnecessary. Not long before her death, Mona wrote me, "Have appointed Karen Anderson my literature executor and biographer. You will never undestand why, nor will you ever forgive me for setting you free of the burden you must have thought would fall upon you. And I do not ask for understanding or forgiveness, but only for your cooperation. Karen will want you to release my letters. There is nothing she does not know. And she will persevere." In this same letter, Mona went on to chide me: "For eighteen years, we who shared the same parents, the same brothers, who slept in the same bed, we who exchangd our dreams and our illusions, lived as sisters in the flesh. For thirty-five years after that, we kept our vow to write to one another every month that we were separated, until death did us part, you may remember we said, and then to return, each of us, our half of the estate to the other. When the sentence of death was pronounced, I honored my pledge—that very *day*, my sister! That was months ago, months during which you refused to break your silence. This is the last time I shall ask you to send me what belongs to me. You will not hear from me again. But from Karen, again and again."

But, Ms. Anderson, surely you know all this since, as you informed me, Mona began the practice of photocopying her handwritten letters quite some time ago. This must be one of the lot. All the same, it is enclosed in the packet I am sending to you. In the "original," please note. The others I selected for you have all been Xeroxed— an impulsive act, wrathful, most uncharacteristic of me, but what you informed me was a shock from which I have yet to recover. I do not care for relics or for merchandise, and now that I know she made copies of her letters to me, I cannot think what else they might be but one or the other. This is not meant to reproach your undertaking or the art it serves. The packet I am sending you is in quitclaim to what she thought was not my private property, but "material"—in the "public domain."

You ask if Mona intended that her letters to me be published. If she did, I was utterly innocent of knowledge of this. But I do not know if that is a reflection of my naiveté or of my sister's cleverness. Both, it appears, were remarkable. In a handwritten letter dated about a year ago (surely you have the copy?) she wrote, "You are the sort of person whose Februarys always precede her Aprils, and for whom every Tuesday has its proper week. We are so unlike. But I've kept my side of the bargain, my roving and the mess of my life notwithstanding. Can you believe it, your letters are filed in fat brown envelopes, in proper chronology from 1944 to now, and stored in a safety deposit box. I wear the key for it around my neck, as a scapular medal. Can you say as much?" I did not begin to suspect her motive in asking this question.

Of course, just as you say, Mona must have had a literary biographer in mind ever since her spectacular success in 1958. But I supposed she had elected me to that office. I think you ought to know that she made much of the distinction between letters she wrote by hand and those she typed. The latter were either business letters or literary "documents." Those she exchanged with me were acts of love. All this she wrote to me more than once. In fact, I brought up the subject with her just after I read the collected letters of Louise Bogan, a book I read with rapt attention when it was published seven years ago. In 1940, Bogan wrote Morton Zabel of a "great discovery" she made after many days during which she re-read "the complete canon" of Katherine Mansfield's works— namely, that Mansfield was all but major in her letters and her journal, and almost minor in her short stories. And many years later, Bogan wrote Zabel about letters again—this time, his own: those he wrote to her in the late 1930's and early 1940's were, she thought, of his *best period.* In commenting on the collection, I remarked these letters to Zabel, and wondered on paper if Mona had changed her mind about her letters to me. Was it possible, I asked her, that some might be thought "major" and some of her novels "minor?" And what did she think was her "*best period?*" We enjoyed teasing one another like this, so I thought it strange that she never referred to this passage in my letter, and stranger still that she had nothing to say about the collection, for she loved Bogan's poetry as much as I did. Looking backward, I begin to appreciate the eloquence of her silence.

You write that you are keenly aware of how many Monas there were, and that you apprehend that "mine" was a Mona beside which all the others are as ghosts. This sounds quite Mona-esque. Is this Plan A? And did Mona write letters as Bogan did? For there seemed to be a Bogan for Rolfe Humphries and a Bogan for Morton Zabel, a Bogan for Ruth Benedict and quite another for May Sarton. *Who was Mona, what was she?* This is more than a matter of multiple selfhood, the Jungian mandala. You may remember the *Paris Review* interviews, the series entitled "Writers at Work." Mona wrote pages of commentary on some of these to me. But she did not mention the interview with Borges, which held my attention more than all the others. In that interview, Borges told Ronald Christ that when he collaborated with Bioy Casares, they begat a sort of third person. They named this fellow H. Bustos Domecq: Bustos was Borges' great-great grandfather's name, Domecq was Bioy Casares'. Borges made the observation that H. Bustos Domecq is not like either collaborator, that he has his own likes and dislikes, his own style, his own way of making jokes. It so happens that Mona and I begat our own H. Bustos Domecq long, long ago. We created this fantastic author of her letters to me and my letters to her, this being with a life of its own, this androgyne whose name I cannot quite believe she has not revealed to you, yet whose name I am still unprepared to believe she betrayed.

Our correspondence, you see, was not written in the genre you suppose. Perhaps our letters are fragments of a fictional work in progress, a *roman fleuve* if you like. Certainly, they are not "property"—hers *or* mine. I do not mean to perplex you. Remember that I have had thirty-five years to think about these questions, and I am an omnivorous and voracious reader. I have found letters masquerading as entries in a diary, a journal, a memoir. I have admired how deftly they are woven into some autobiographies. Indeed, I found an entire autobiography (Virgilia Peterson's *A Matter of Life and Death*) that was written as a letter to the author's dead mother. We all know of "epistolary novels." But how many of us are aware that an entire correspondence may be a work of fiction? There is an alchemy at work when one is at the writing-desk: we compose letters that are personal essays, letters that are prayers. When one thinks of all the "lost literature," the letters that might have been, were it not for indolence! Edna St. Vincent Millay, you may recall, claimed in more than one letter that she was afflicted with *epistolaphobia*. She wrote that she would rather lay a pipe-line or dig a grave than write a letter. Her affliction is much in evidence in her collected letters; even so, in one of them there is a stunning word-portrait of Brancusi. If Eugene Boissevain had not assumed much of her correspondence to leave her free for her work, we might have more such word-portraits—more poems in the form of letters. Mona, by the way, had possibilities as a poet. Our own H. Bustos Domecq sometimes wrote poetry. I do not mean to whet your appetite, but simply to remind you where you are treading.

You write of the "discoveries" in letters, the "illuminations," the "revelations." I remember reading a letter from Alice B. Toklas to Janet Flanner about a bad dream of Flanner that Toklas had been worried about—a dream that so disturbed her that she wrote of it to Flanner. It is clear from Toklas' letter that Flanner had no patience with dreams (and Toklas said Flanner was right to attack them vigorously.) So I "discovered" quite by accident that neither of them believed in dreams. Is this the sort of illumination you had in mind? Are you a social scientist or a literary person? Will your biography be a "study" or a work of art, that is to say a work of fiction? I would advise you to decide this question before reading my sister's correspondence. That great classic work in Sociology, *The Polish Peasant in Europe and America*, could never have been written if the authors did not take the letters of which it is woven at "face value." Are you after fact or fiction? You may recall that Anais Nin—in the sixth volume of her diary, I believe—wrote letters on behalf of Roger Bloom, who was appealing for parole—letters in which she cited *Bloom's* letters, which she had shown to a psychiatrist who then gave her a favorable opinion of Bloom's character and state of mind. Did you propose to raid Mona's letters to me for clues to her "character?" But how could you find them in a *Rundbriefe*, in a letter addressed to a collective, a public, a "dear reader?" For what else is a letter of which the writer makes a copy? I recommend a passage in Catherine Drinker Bowen's *Adventures of a Biographer* to you. On pages 63-4, Bowen thinks about the meaning of the word "definitive" and about the nature of "evidence." She asks if letters are "the best proof of fact." She asks if something must be written down to be true. Bowen was accustomed to relying on letters. She had based her biography of Tchaikovsky upon letters almost entirely. But she remembered (allow me to quote her exactly) :

> that Tchaikovsky himself had not trusted letters as evidence .... (he wrote to Nadejda von Meck) "It seems to me letters are not perfectly sincere—I am judging by myself. No matter to whom I am writing, I am always conscious of the effect of my letter, not only upon the person to whom it is addressed, but upon any chance reader. Consequently I embroider. . . . apart from letters written at the moment when I am worked upon, I am never quite myself in my correspondence. These letters are to me a source of repentance, and often of agonizing regret. When I read the correspondence of great men, published after their death, I am always disturbed by a vague sense of insincerity and falsehood."

Was Mona afflicted with this sort of conscience? If so, I doubt it was much developed in what I now judge to have been *her* "best period." As for her faithful correspondent, I was shameless. And I remain unrepentant.

Only once, to my recollection, did Mona write to me of the fate of our letters. We had both read Harriet Monroe's autobiography, *A Poet's Life,* when we were both still in high school. In 1958, when her fame was assured, my sister reminded me that Monroe had written that it would be cruel to analyze too carefully, with the "cold wisdom" of seventy years of age, the episolary relationship she once had with Robert Louis Stevenson. "Monroe invented her own RLS," she wrote to me, "just you and I have made one another up through our correspondence. When I think of all that we have brought to life! It is best that we never see one another again. It would kill us—as sisters, as parents. As for our letters, we ought to burn them as soon as they are read." I took this to be an expression of her passion—not for me, you understand, but for that H. Bustos Domecq of ours.

You quote one of Mona's letters to you. "My sister's talent dwarfs my own," she wrote to you—or so you say. "Yet she consigns her literature to oblivion. Like all eldest children, she persuaded herself of the rightness of our parents' judgment, that mine was the gift in the name of which all sacrifices should be made. She would never believe this, but I think now that she had the better part. True Catholics have too much conscience to make fictions of their lives, anyway, and my sister is Catholic in her very marrow." I cannot tell you how much I appreciate Mona's salute to my writing and to my character, and even more her confidence to you about a—if you will pardon me—family matter. But most of all, I appreciate that last line. You found that *arresting*, you say, *insightful*. You ask what I make of it (though we both know what I am meant to make of it.)

This is by way of an answer to your question. In 1942, Ellen Glasgow wrote to Frank Morley that Castine was as lovely as ever, that it appeared that the village was inhabited entirely by old ladies then, but that the war fever was burning there. "Old ladies," she wrote in this letter, "are notoriously militant." Now, this remark contradicts absolutely the impression I have formed about elderly women (whose ranks, by the way, you and I are about to enter.) However, I would hardly have noticed it if one of Glasgow's characters had made it in a novel. If I were a psychologist or sociologist, I would take myself to the library to read polls and questionnaires and surveys and clinical reports in pursuit of the Facts about elderly women's attitudes toward war. Note that I write Facts, not Truth: how can we ever know if people mean what they say and say what they mean? I would research the Facts, fully knowing that a researcher can probably elicit the answer that is desired if the question is put skillfully enough, fully knowing that Fact-finders do find what they are looking for. I would look into what was going on in Castine that year, too, and who these old ladies were. And I would think about why Glasgow wrote that comment to Frank Morley. With all these reservations, I would arrive at a judgment about the astuteness of her observation and the reliability of her statement. All this because the idea that old ladies war-monger as enthusiastically as old men was expressed in a letter! Had it appeared in a short story or a novel, I would have swallowed it whole, even that word "notoriously." How much more vivid, more *lasting*, the image of a pride of septuagenarians, arms linked, briskly strolling across the sands, plotting carnage! I would never take an old lady's smile on faith again, had I read that in a work of fiction—not even the one I glimpse occasionally in the mirror. Look for my conscience, my Catholicism, my marrow in my sister's novels, my dear Ms. Anderson.

They are everywhere to be found in them. The kin of artists are not given a choice in the means by which they will be granted immortality.

Mona told you of my growing blindness. It is growing more slowly than you suppose; when she knew she was dying, Mona gave in to her weakness for exaggeration. I have time before every letter I receive must be read aloud to me by some third person, some interpreter, some translator. I, who have waited all my life with a patience more terrible than a biographer's, know how to take my time with my task. Tell me, for I am a curious creature, what genre would you choose if you were me—a long, meditative essay? a novel? or would you publish the correspondence in all its raw splendor, lest the darkness descend more quickly than you expect? Or would you begin to write an autobiography? The right arrangement of letters may make an autobiography, you know, as well as a biography. And what would you do with all the old habits—the secret salutations and foldings and "complimentary closings?" How many times in my too-long life have I envied those who trust in the instinct to "play it by ear"—face to face, or earphone to receiver, they are deaf to that other voice that makes such mischief in the name of Art!

You remind me that we hear much these days about "lost literature." Do you imply that is what I have written when you say that you want to redeem our correspondence from the drawer literature you imagine would otherwise be its fate? I will tell you why I must refuse your request that I return my letters to Mona along with hers to me. It is not so much that I must save our correspondence from the "cold wisdom" of a biographer's analysis, whether that be yours or mine, for we are both aging. Nor am I ruled by the passion of some avenging angel, as I am certain that you believe. In his *Paris Review* interview, Borges quoted a remark Henry James made to his brother William in a letter. Think for a moment of the odyssey of a single thought expressed in a letter—the transcription from Henry's mind onto the stationary, the posting and delivery of the letter, the care William took to preserve it; eventually, it was gathered into a collection, read by Borges who had the memory and the wit to mention it in the course of an interview with someone who knew how to ask the right questions, someone who then has the interview published in a volume I read and remembered in this letter! All the contingencies upon which the life of a single thought depends! And I have in my "possession," you write, a treasure-trove of these. Only an arch-fiend would deny the world of letters that which rightfully belongs to it.

But the truth is, Ms. Anderson, there is no property which I might bequeath you, there is no "correspondence" to send you. The letters—if that is what they are— are still being written. More precisely, they are writing themselves through the movement of my hand. Of course, they are no longer folded into envelopes and sealed and stamped and posted to my dead sister. Since the year before her death, they have been written on the leaves of a note-book. I suppose that any careful reader would find little difference between those letters and this journal—or is it a work of fiction? —despite the conversion.

Thirty-five years ago, my sister and I began collaboration on a work that she said would be greater—larger—than Art. She changed; I shall never know when. Her arrogance always en-thralled me. My heart races, my blood sings with the memory of the splendor of her vanity. She swore she would "have it all." Do not her complete works attest to the fulfillment of this glorious ambition?

My sister was a cottage industry. I do not envy you your under-taking. I am sending you a packet of dead letters, those I see now I did not truly receive—the typewritten ones sent over the years with the plea for my indulgence of her writer's fatigue, and the "originals" of which you have informed me she made copies. Keep them as insurance against fire, theft and floods. I wish you every success, and assure you that you now have in your possession all that was her portion of our estate. My portion has now become the whole of what we procreated. When it is fully grown—when it is completed—I intend to release it not to my sister's literary estate, but to the world.

Yours faithfully,

Audrey Borenstein

Robert Louthan

SOME UNSOLICITED MANUSCRIPTS

December 12, 1975

Dear Poetry Editor:

For your consideration, I am enclosing three poems: "The Cure For Cancer," "Wet Rivers," and "Haiku Sonnet." I wrote these with *American Quarterly Review* in mind.

Sincerely,
W. T. Hanson

February 20, 1976

Dear Writer:

We regret having to use this form letter. Your poems, however good they may be, do not suit our needs at the present time. We receive too many submissions, and don't like to publish much at all. Good luck.

John Stern, Poetry Editor
American Quarterly Review

February 23, 1976

Dear Mr. Stern:

For your consideration, I am enclosing four poems: "A Cure For Cancer," "Charlie Chan Thinks Things Out," "Good Publicity," and "What The Moon Means." "A Cure For Cancer" has been revised since I sent it to you with the title "The Cure For

Cancer." I'd appreciate any suggestions you might have.

Yours,
W. T. Hanson

June 6, 1976

"*American Quarterly Review* is a rare gem. I could not appraise it too highly."—Louis Pyle, *Pacific Monthly*
"One of the best quarterly reviews around. I even show it to my friends who don't understand literature."—George Truffaut, *Rowboat*
"I couldn't . . . put it down. Everyone interested in contemporary verse should take out a costly subscription to *American Quarterly Review*."—Beth Ingersol, *The Erudite Scholar*

Subscribe to *American Quarterly Review*. $12 for one year. $120 for ten years.

Sorry,
John Stern

June 15, 1976

Dear Mr. Stern:

For your consideration, I am enclosing three poems which I have translated from the Spanish of César García Neruda: "Kisses Or Numerals," "Ode To The Debris," and "TWA Has Better Movies Than Pan Am." Also, I am submitting four poems of my own: "How To Invent The Wheel," "'Death' Is An Anagram For 'The Ad'," "Straight From Mr. Ed's Mouth," and "First The Good News, Then The Bad News."

In case you will want information for a contributor's note, here it is: I have a poem forthcoming in *Leftovers* magazine.

Best,
W. T. Hanson

July 14, 1976

Dear Mr. Hanson:

We liked "First The Good News, Then The Bad News," and César García Neruda is one of our favorite poets, but I'm sorry to say the decision was against publishing these. Send again next month, when we may not have so many submissions from better writers than you.

Cordially,
J. Stern

August 1, 1976

Dear Mr. Stern:

Thank you for your encouraging reply to my recent submission.

For your consideration now, I am enclosing three more poems: "Rough Weather On The Ant Farm," "O.K.," and "Elegy For My Shadow."

In case you will want information for a contributor's note, here it is: I have poems forthcoming in *Leftovers, Medical Monthly*, and *Poetic Learner's Permit*. And, in case you will want to print a photograph of me, I'm enclosing one. The man to my right is Rod McKuen, and to my left is Allen Ginsberg.

Yours,
Wilbur Hanson

February 24, 1977

Dear Mr. Hanson:

"Rough Weather On The Ant Farm" and "Elegy For My Shadow" are both okay, but our favorite is "O.K." We'll consider publishing it if you change the line "Adjustable birds are like high school proms" to read as follows: "I'll never forgive you for this kiss." In any case, we look forward to new poems from you.

Best,
John Stern

February 27, 1977

Dear Mr. Stern:

Thank you for your suggestion for the change in my poem "O.K." I have taken your advice, and am enclosing "O.K." as revised. Also, I am enclosing another copy of the same revision, with what is perhaps a better title: "Adjustable Birds Are Like High School Proms." If you decide to publish the poem, the choice between titles is yours.

Also for your consideration, I am enclosing three poems that are new: "Trouble At Church," "Monogrammed Facial Tissues," and "Yet Another W. T. Hanson Poem."

In case you will want information for a contributor's note, here it is: I have published poems in *Leftovers* and *Medical Monthly*. I have poems forthcoming in *Adult Tricycle, Good Poetry, Poetic Learner's Permit*, et al. I'm studying with Donald Mercy at the Poetry Rehabilitation Center in Iowa City.

By the way, I like your poem in the current issue of *Read This Now*.

Sincerely,
W. T. Hanson

August 22, 1977

Dear Mr. Hanson:

We'll publish your poem with the title "Adjustable Birds Are Like High School Proms" if you change the line "I'll never forgive you for this kiss" to read as follows: "O.K." We also like "Monogrammed Facial Tissues," but the last stanza is too explicit for this family magazine. Your other two poems, "Trouble At Church" and "Yet Another W.T. Hanson Poem," have been thrown out.

Let us know what you're going to do with "Adjustable Birds," and we look forward to other poems.

Sincerely,
John Stern

August 25, 1977

Dear Mr. Stern:

I have revised "Adjustable Birds Are Like High School Proms" as you have requested.

Also for your consideration, I am enclosing my only poem that you have not yet seen: "The Situation Of Robert Pinsky."

In case you will want information for a contributor's note, here it is: I have published poems in *Adult Tricycle, Medical Monthly,* et al. I have poems forthcoming in *Good Poetry, Poetic Learner's Permit,* and *Words To The Wise.* I have an M.F.A. degree from the Poetry Rehabilitation Center.

Yours,
W. Theodore Hanson

April 2, 1978

Dear Mr. Hanson:

Mr. Stern has resigned his position as Poetry Editor. He is being replaced by Gregory Paddle.

I am returning your poems.

Emily Wood, Editorial Assistant
American Quarterly Review

Brian Turner

SELECTED LETTERS FROM *PANICKERS' TRAVELS*

December 18, 1973

> Walter G. Kenner
> 11 Mechanics St.
> Mechanicsville, CT

Dear June Bug,

About an hour ago your bother busted into the house and ran into the bedroom. What a kid, he's lucky I didn't shoot him dead like a thief. Warren G., I said, can't this wait? Dad, he said, I'm flying to London in the morning. London? Up I get, wondering what's going on. I asked him, so what do you want from me? Money?

He said, I've got plenty of money. Then he pulled out a thousand bucks in Travelers' checks. I said, where the hell did you get that, *drugs*? He began to shout, I worked! OK, I said, and down I went into the kitchen to make some coffee. That's when I reminded him he owed me fifty bucks or had he forgotten? Is that why you came, to pay me? He peeled off a fifty dollar check, slapped it on the kitchen counter, and signed it. I never thought I'd see the day, I laughed. This is going to be the most expensive cup of coffee you ever had, I said.

Then he said, dad, I need advice. Well, well, well, I said to myself, after all these years the kid's coming around. I poured him a mug of coffee and said, Warren G., I know what's eating you, you want to skip this London thing, right? Go ahead. You want to marry the girl next door? Be my guest.

I don't want to marry anyone, he said, That's good, I said, so what do you want to go to London for anyway? To see my friends, he said. What friends are these? You mean those Englishmen? Joe and Jeannie? He said very slowly, Garth and Ginger. I love them, he said. Oh no, I thought, has the kid been going both ways? I want to trust people and be trusted, he said. Isn't that what makes life worthwhile?

I don't know, I said. That's when he broke down. What a kid. I never saw him cry, not even when your mother died. I remember him then, all dressed up and dry-eyed like a little mortician. What's the matter, I asked him. Life sucks, he said. This town sucks.

Will you stop telling me what sucks and what doesn't, I said. After a while I added, I don't know how to tell you this without making you feel like the world has ended, but it happens all the time, everyone you see, we all feel the same way, so what's the big deal?

Meanwhile, Junie, the kid didn't touch his coffee, so I drank it. Get this, I said, if you leave home, all the bets are off. Fine by me, he said, and his eyes turned hard. So I backed down a little and said, if you stay, I'll get you a job. He looked up, and I could see he was angry. A job? In the Teamsters? Run some numbers? Forget it, he said. Jesus, I thought, what a kid. The way he looked at me, you'd think I was a scab. He curled his upper lip and walked out on you, on me, on Mechanicsville. From the street he shouted, so long Walter, so long to the town that can't be licked. I was in the driveway, standing in the snow like a jerk in my bathrobe. I couldn't see him anywhere. Warren G., I yelled, don't forget to write, OK? I don't know if he heard me or not. I just stood there watching the snow come down. It was nice.

So I drank the rest of the coffee, and it's kept me on the john for the last two hours. I figured I'd write you while I was at it. I really wish you'd get a phone. Just because the telephone company's a monopoly doesn't mean you have to cut yourself off from the rest of the world. I'll pay if that's the trouble.

Love, Pops.

December 20, 1973

June Kenner
14 Spruce Street
Worcester, Mass.

Dear Walter,

It seems poor Warren hitched up to Worcester after he left you. About one in the morning he rang the doorbell and threw snowballs at my window. He told me everything he was planning, the same old story, his eternal quest for the goodess of the eventful mattress. It was hard for me to listen to him go on. I held his hand, said the things I thought he wanted to hear. True friendship? That's not easy to find, I said, look at me. You haven't even tried, he said. I wanted to throttle him then and there, but instead I said calmly as I could, Warren, people always want what they can't have, and if it's wrong to have it, they want it all the more, I should know.

Oh God, don't I sound wise?

I had so much to tell him. Every day is an effort, every morning seems to cover me in bed like a big grey army blanket I can't shake off. I told Warren we must understand our emotions as we do our friends and be ready for them to betray us even as we betray ourselves, but even as I said it, I swallowed a yawn. I don't think he was listening, which is OK, since none of my ideas ever did me any good.

So here's the bad news. London's just the first stop. He's really going to India. He wants to find his British friends, the ones who went to India, he met them last year. He thinks they're waiting around for him in Benares, the Hindu Holy City. Well, let's hope so, I said. He told me he could find them no matter where they were, and when he found them, he said he'd find some reason to live and love and all the rest. Dear Warren, I said as sympathetically as I could.

He got up and got ready to hitch to New York City. I asked him, is that it, all the stuff you're taking with you? You see he had a backpack and a spring jacket on and these beat-up old work shoes. Sure, he said, I won't need much in India, will I? Oh Warren, I said, I felt so frightened for him. The snow was coming down heavier and heavier, and I watched from the window until he had disappeared.

Frankly, this whole business depresses me, and yet I wish him the best, because he's getting out from under the thumb of the family and his failures. I wish I could do the same.

Merry Christmas. I guess you know by now I won't be coming down. It makes me sad to think of you by yourself, but Christmas makes me sadder, so for my own sake, I'm staying away. O hope you're not too lonely.

By the way, please don't call me June-Bug.
As ever,

June

December 27, 1973

Walter Kenner
11 Mechanics St.
Mechanicsville, CT

Dear June,

I didn't want to believe your letter, so I expected you for Christmas right up to the last minute. I had wrapped your presents as best I could and as I did it, I said to myself, Walter, don't be a sap, she means it, she's not coming. But no, I wouldn't listen to the half of me that has a brain, would I? It made me so angry that I took your nightie and tore it into strips, then tied down the damn TV aerial with it. The reception has been much better, thank you.

What really got to me, though, was the crack about the family. What family is there except me? If you want to insult me, young lady, at least you could come here and do it to my face. Let me say this, I think our generation had reasons to live and work, ideals and morals to live by. If you kids got decent jobs, played more sports, or otherwise settled down and got married, you wouldn't need kicks and weird places to go to. All the experts say so, and while I usually don't give a good goddamn about the experts, in this case I have to agree. You should get a job.

I have one question for you. Just what do you know about family life? Family life is for the long run. What do you know about the long run?

I hope to see you soon, and maybe then we can talk things out once and for all. That'll be the happiest day of my life, what's left of it.

Love, Pops.

December 30th, 1973

June Kenner
14 Spruce Street
Worcester, Mass.

Dear Walter,

Anyone who works for the Teamsters has a nerve telling other people to get decent jobs.

As ever,
June

January 16, 1974

Warren Kenner
D17/14 Bhueshwar
Dasasurmedh
Varanasi, India

Dear Dad,

I'd like to file early for a quick income tax refund. Maybe you can help.

As always, the Internal Revenue Service requires the wage statements from my various jobs. When my employers send them, please save them. There remains the tricky matter of my signature. You'll have to send me some forms to sign. Please, please, whatever you do, don't send the wage statements, because I'll probably never see them again, nor will the Internal Revenue.

You know, Walter it occurs to me how very reasonable we both are as long as we don't have to face each other. Maybe in the future, all sons will be required to deal with fathers only if several continents apart. I mean, letters are perfect! We have to hear each other out. No interruptions or thinly veiled insults. Of course, if you wanted, you could easily toss this letter into the trash. Not knowing any better, I'd probably blame it on the Indian Postal Service, a reputation they deserve and reason enough, to my mind, for you to send one tax form to:

> Warren KENNER
> POSTE RESTANTE
> Head G. P. O.
> Varanasi, U.P., India

Local postmasters hold mail up to a month, sometimes six months. If not collected, this mail is returned to sender. The G.P.O. stands for "General Post Office." One day the postmaster in Benares went on at length to warn us of "rascals who could jolly well make off with your goods, tossing things of value back to accomplices who toss these very same things to other accomplices, so forth and so on, until they have made off with whatever it was you desired to post." Hold on, we're not finished yet, because for a precautionary measure please send a second form to:

> Warren KENNER
> c/o AMERICAN EXPRESS
> Connaught Circus
> New Delhi, India

I hope the rascals who make off with things of value won't be allowed in the American Express. In any case, please keep a few extra copies of the tax forms on hand for emergencies.

As for my role, I plan to come across at least one of these tax forms in the course of my travels. While the law of averages does not necessarily apply to India, I refuse to believe the Indian Postal Service can lose both of these parcels. When I get either or both of them, I'll sign them and send them back to you. You in turn will affix the wage statements (which you have kept safely in your drawer next to the revolver and bottle of Jim Beam) and mail it all to the Internal Revenue Service. Some months later, when the refund arrives, forward it to me by international money order to whatever city I happen to occupy. I can't thank you enough. I hope to hear from you soon.

> Respectfully, Warren G.

P.S. On second thought, maybe you'd better send a third tax form
to:

> Warren KENNER
> POSTE RESTANTE
> Head G.P.O.
> Panjim, Goa

> Thanx, W.

February 21, 1974

> Warren Kenner
> Poste Restante
> Head G.P.O.
> Bombany, India

Dear June,

The night before I left you asked me why I felt it necessary to
leave home and leave Walter and you. It was the last day in the
life of my vintage Fury. The slant-six engine had frozen up. The
odometer registered 147,653 miles in black, white, and red numerals. I sat there stupidly in the dead car and stared at the numbers, and I realized that fifteen years from now, if that odometer
exists in some junkyard of rusting, ruined cars, it'll read exactly
the same right down to the tenth. So, I asked myself, well Mr.
Know-It-All, how many times could this car have traveled around
the world or to the moon and back, et cetera?

The next day I found my answer in the World Atlas. Six times
around the world, and something like half-way between here and
the moon. Now, this impressed me, and yet it also left me unim-
pressed. All those miles, yet my Fury slowly falls apart beside
Route 131, an uninteresting road. Junie, don't you see, I want to
get the most for my mileage. I don't want my heart to seize up
after sixty-five years of strolling to the corner store for coffee and
paper. That's preciesely when I decided I had to leave.

As for why I do the things I do, I don't know really, except that
I've never done them before, or at least not quite in the same way.
I seek out my friends because I don't want to be alone, that's
sensible enough. I try to help them because I want to make myself

indispensible. I write letters to convince myself I've got something to say, and I try to make money to convince myself I know what I'm doing. Yet I can't get the letters right, what makes me think I can make a killing? This letter to you takes on a shape I never planned. To Walter I write that letters are perfect, and yet I don't believe it for one moment. What lies should I tell you, Junie?

My letters are too stupid and inadequate to say what must be said. I think I'll go outside and watch the wedding procession making its noisy way beneath my window. I know I won't be thrilled, no matter how exotic it all sounds. Instead, I'll be frightened. I feel this more and more, the fright. Something else is happening here, and to tell you the truth, June, I haven't the faintest idea what it is.

> I miss you,
> Warren.

March 2, 1974

> Walter G. Kenner
> 11 Mechanics St.
> Mechanicsville, CT

Dear Warren,

No income tax stuff yet. Here's the latest speech though. Aren't you a lucky guy?

As usual, who puts his name on the dotted line? Naturally, me. You want an example, sure. I'll give you an example. I deposited $500 in an account at American Express to cover your claim for the refunds, but I'll be damned, when I called New York City, the AMEXO officer said, sorry, we had to confiscate the money. Holy cow, I said, every cent? He said, you'll be getting a bill for the balance. He said your checks had been cashed in Pakistan or Iran or somewhere out there. He said, they had a signature which according to our records resembles your son's. So, you're definitely a suspect, kid, but of course I'm waiting to hear your side of the story before I pass sentence.

Concerning the tax stuff, don't worry. I'm an old hand at this. I've been saving thousands for the Union thanks to tax breaks I've initaled Next week the books get a going over by federal auditors, justice department guys. They want to nail us, as usual, but that's their problem not ours. We're closing up the Union offices and going to New York City to have some fun, the staff that is, while the auditors snoop around. Maybe they're from the Treasury Department, I don't know. Who cares? We're going to get ourselves a few chippies, have a few tall frosties in Times Square. Then, get this, we'll chalk it all up to business expenses. The American way is best, and if you don't believe me by the time you get back from India . . . , hey, you are coming back aren't you? March 12, 1974

> Keep your nose clean, Pops.

> Warren Kenner
> c/o American Express
> Connaught Place
> New Delhi, India

Dear June,

I swear to you and to Walter, I don't know what happened to those checks, had nothing to do with them, apart from losing them. Does this sound desperate? Let me put it this way, whatever is going on, Garth calls it "the panic." Nobody can explain it away or ignore it, he says. By denying it, the panic that is, I might as well admit that it sits on my shoulder. "Panic wanna cracker?" Garth always clowns around and makes like a parrot when I begin to complain. Please June, impress upon Walter that everything I do, I do because I have no other choice. I believe that my friends need my help even if they don't approve how I go about my business. Tell Walter I have the feeling I haven't been all I should, never really had the chance, now time is short.

It's not as if I'm having a dull time here. I just hitch-hiked over one thousand miles in about ten days. At the start of the trip, I tried to board a train out of Bombay, when all at once I was thrown forward by a crowd against the carriage. The doors were open, and the Indians trampled all over me. They caught me up, knocked me down. As I tried to crawl away, I imagined bodies falling through space, don't ask me why, a bruise spreading across entire cities, the same damned panic. Typhoons lashing palm trees, some movie we once saw, knives dicing kidneys, all the same to me. Tell Walter I said hello. Surely June, you see why I chose to write you, not Walter.

Once I got up from the station floor, you can imagine my surprise—the way was clear after all. Why this push and shove, you guys? I boarded the train. All the seats were taken, and more people spread out against the walls. Still more people boarded and then, when it seemed there was no more room, we all pressed together. I thought I was drowning. I recalled Garth's idea that "panic" was in fact nothing less the human condition. Can you drown in the human condition? He cited as evidence a certain travel agency in New Delhi, a booth here (where I am, sipping a coffee special) at the Indian Coffee House. It's name: Panickers' Travels.

Shortly before we parted, I asked Garth to be more specific, but he only laughed, puffing on his bidi as he whittled a stick. I turned toward the jungle beyond the beach. Secretly, I wanted his knife to slip and knick his thumb. Goddamn him, he's gotten under my skin. How was I to take his little who sir, me sir, what sir riddles? How could I have known who robbed me and why? Tell that to American Express, will you June? Tell them there was no more room, and yet more Indians crammed into that train. I was there, the sweat dripping down my face, my clothes soaked up to my armpits. More people boarded. Impossible, someone cried out. Silly, I thought. They formed a wedge of human beings that bulged over the rails. They pushed and shoved until our carriage let out a collective groan, a universal *ahh*, the thing I have been looking for everywhere. I don't want to make too much out of this, but at that moment I thought I knew every single one of us shared the same dialect of misery. If you asked me, but you didn't ask, so why am I bothering? Everything's fine. Wish you were here. Wait, I'll tell you why I bother, because you must tell Walter what I cannot, that I love him as any son would love a father, which is to say I detest him too. I am miserable, but he must not know. I have to tell someone, but not him. When the train started from Bombay, dozens of people less fortunate than me tumbled from the wedge of arms and legs grappling at the door. Car after car shuttled north. At one point, I thought we were suspended in mid-air above the blue harbor, and yet beneath us the elevated rails clack-

clacked. Then a landmass rushed by, and I counted all the shanties littering the peninsula, and the families huddling there amounted to more than all the days in either of our lives. The families huddled by fires and watched us pass, our carriage full of lucky ones, my fellow sardines.

Someone cried, "Impossible. I can't breath."

June, it was me, and I was disgusted to hear me crack like that, some hysterical kid from America, mi, mi, mi, oh beautiful for spacious skies, you bet. If I had said anything, it should have been that *ahh*, which says nothing and everything all at once. Instead, I let go, went limp, lodged among Indians, and I knew I shouldn't care, and yet I did care. Unlike you, June, I've never been west of West Virginia, and yet for hours, I hungered for prairies, anything and everything flat, the endless and empty, God help us all.

I'm ashamed. I'm ashamed of this letter. I'll write again, try again, honest. Tell Walter what you wish, but only what makes sense. Then again, tell him nothing.

> Love,
> Warren

March 23, 1974

> June Kenner
> 14 Spruce Street
> Worcester, Mass.

Dear Warren G.,

India sounds icky, especially for women, and I wouldn't go there unless you paid me, but since you're broke, you need not bother. Things are pretty bad here too, because the other day a gang of alcoholics on a streetcorner started laughing at me, saying in a stupid sort of way, hey baby, did you leave your tits at home. I threw them the finger. To tell the truth, when I do stuff like that, I feel lousy as if I'm not rising above the worst in men but becoming as bad as them and macho. But wait until you hear what happened the next time it snowed! I called Streets & Engineering to come and tow my car. I pay taxes after all, sometimes. The man who came made me shovel off the car first, and while I was bending over he put his slimy hand up my back. It felt like a fish, cold and wet, so I whacked him across his puss with the shovel. I'm not getting weird with you, I said, so why are you getting weird with me? The car's still there, of course, buried deeper than ever, we've had so much snow this winter, you're lucky. The police kept putting tickets on it, the car, a big joke downtown, I bet, so I told them I'd never, never pay, not in a million years, not a million dollars. So far, I owe only a hundred. Well, if they want it, they can come and get me.

Gee, don't I sound tough?

Here's the latest bad news. Walter has been accused of engineering illegal tax dodges for the Teamsters and God knows what else. He sends me all the clippings as if it's something to be proud of, though they are always careful to call him the "alleged" embezzler, and he always underlines the "alleged" as if that does any good.

Walter will get off, I'm sure. They all do. And me? I get harassed for not paying parking tickets, a conspiracy I bet between Streets & Engineering and the police. Well, fuck them. That's the way the whole world's arranged, it seems, and as long as everyone's willing to go along with it, nothing will change.

Oh God, will you listen to me talk big? Whatever have I done to change the world? What a hypocrite. What's worse, I can't even manage a family reunion of two without making a mess. Oh Warren, I know you're going to hate me more than ever, but to be perfectly honest, I've got to tell you, I sent your letter, the weird one, to Walter. Not just some of it, but all of it. I'm sorry, but I must have wanted to hold it up to him like a mirror. I felt somehow justified then ,though I can't imagine what I was thinking of.

Maybe Walter was right. Maybe I did leave my brains on Route 131.

Sorry,
June.

March 29, 1974

Walter Kenner
11 Mechanics St.
Mechanicsville, CT

Dear Warren,

I've blamed myself for years, made myself sick raising you kids the way your mother would have wanted, books, schools, the works. Now it seems no matter what you do, no matter how rotten a father I am, June and you will screw up a few jobs, blow a few marriages, crack up a few cars anyway.

Sure, whatever you and June are today, I can take some credit. I can't be blamed for everything, can I? You are what you are, and I am what I am, for better or worse and never the train shall we meet until death do us part, amen. The Lord works in strange and devious ways, in case you never noticed.

Who needs a kid in India without a passport or a daughter in Worcester without a telephone? What's this I read in these weird letters? You're fooling around with pregnant divorcees? You're smuggling rubles into London? Listen pal, someday you'll realize there's no easy money, no girls like the girl that married you know who. The world is screwy, sure, and people screw each other whenever they can. That's the big picture of a bunch of small people. Ten years from now you'll kick yourself for not listening to me. It's small comfort, but I know that when you see things my way, at least, you'll be able to say it better. You're like your mother, sharp about some things and thick about others. You know, I never won a single scrabble game from that woman. Yet I listened to her talk for hours and never understood a thing she said. People will listen to you too, even your own kids. (I should be so lucky!) Your kids won't think you're an asshole forever, and if I can just get that kind of respect before I pass on, by God I'd be happy.

Love,
Pops

April 7, 1974

Warren Kenner
Pokhora Valley
Nepal

Dear Walter,

I don't understand why people like June always feel it's their God given duty to drub the noses of others in the "truth" so called. Sure, I believe in honesty and loyalty, but there's a limit to which these fine and noble ideas can be applied in practical terms. In the name of honesty, for example, dear June sent you letters, letters I had asked her to hold, and even though she might call it loyalty to you, she's been disloyal to me no matter how you look at it.

So much for the sermon. Here comes the lecture. As you so correctly said, there's no easy money, certainly not in India or Nepal. If I didn't know what I was up against before, I sure do now. What motivates me, I think, is an urge to set things right, but where do you start in a place like Asia, maybe some sort of business? Travel? A travel business, now there's an idea. I met this guy in New Delhi, Mr. Ravindra Prakash. He's the reason I plan to go back to Panickers' Travels, his booth where you should address all mail and those elusive tax forms.

What follows is for your information. Rubies are precious or semiprecious stones depending on their quality or cut. Rupees are Indian money. Rubles are Russian money. Whatever gave you the idea, Walter, that I was buying Russian money? I swear to you I did not buy rubles, nor did I buy rubies either. A rube, by the way, is someone who cannot tell an offcut from a stone that's OK. Like me.

This is such a petty, squalid little letter. Look, I didn't choose you. You didn't choose me. I must love you anyway, because I'm extremely upset you're in trouble with the Teamsters. I told you all along, but of course what did I know, I'm just a kid. Can you believe that I care? Does that make you feel any better? If I could zip back there right now, you know I would do it. Then again, if I truly wanted to find a way back, I guess I'd manage one way or another, maybe in a time machine.

Good God, some poor old ravaged woman with a goiter the size of a canteloupe just brought me my tea.

Wish me luck,
Warren

April 21, 1974

Warren Kenner
Jomsom Valley
Nepal

Dear June,

From Jomosom it's a week's walk to Pokhora. From Pokhora it's a day's bus journey to Katmandu, where it's another day to Birganj-Raxaul on the border of India. The quickest train to New Delhi takes at least two days. Another day by train from New Delhi to Amritsar on the Pakistani border, then three days crossing Pakistan. I hear it takes a week to cross Afganistan by bus, longer by the southern route, watch out for bandits. The bus to Teheran takes a single day and is air-conditioned, welcome to the modernity of oil-rich Iran. The Istanbul Express takes three days or more to cross Turkey. Istanbul to Greece, a day or two by ferry and train. At this point we can begin to hitch-hike with some assurance of safety. Myrna Stein said it took her a week to hitch from Yugoslavia to Amsterdam. Of course, I'm not taking into consideration time to eat and sleep, but when you're traveling, you can't have everything, can you? Especially, if you only want to go home. I'm not saying I do, though I've entertained the notion, as this letter reveals. Where was I? Ah, Amsterdam. The ferry to England and the train to London takes a full day, though I'll not be allowed into England if I don't have my income tax refund, so Amsterdam may be as far as I get. Let's say, just for the sake of this letter, I do get my refund, and it's so substantial that I can even fly to New York. Eight hours. There was a time when if I thought it would do any good I'd start walking home right now. If I can remember why that was once true, I'll be in New York before you can say grand jury indictment. That's a despicable joke, but it'll give you an idea how low I've sunk. Gurgle, gurgle. Back in New York, walking down 42nd St. to the Port Authority, from where it's a three hour ride up I-95 to New Haven, then onto the Connecticut Turnpike to Rt. 131 and Mechanicsville, the town that can't be licked. What a thought. I can see Walter now, standing over the sink in his bathrobe, eating his customary bologna sandwich without the bread.

But I'm not coming home, not now anyway. I'll give this letter to the postman, a sturdy fellow who will beat me back to Pokhora by four days even if we both start right now. From Pokhora I'll be on my way directly to New Delhi. Address all future mail to Warren Kenner c/o Panickers' Travels, Indian Coffee House, Connaught Place, New Delhi, India.

Bye, bye,
Warren

P.S. Damn your eyes for letting Walter read that letter. You might as well show him this one too. From now on I think I'll save myself the trouble of writing you two separately, and instead I'll write you together.

XXXOOO
W.

Julia Thacker

FURTHER ADVENTURES OF BEAUTY AND THE BEAST

"Beast was disappeared, and she saw, at her feet, one of the love-liest princes that eyes ever beheld. Though the prince was worth all her attention, she could not forbear asking where Beast was . . . . The fairy gave a stroke with her wand and in a moment they were transported into the prince's dominions; his subjects received him with joy."

Dear Beast,

How I wait in the evenings for you to lie on the lumpy mattress stuffed with the chicken feathers I comb each morning from your hair; for only when you are sleeping may I address you in this way: my love, Beast. And yet it is at these times, your profile lovely as a maiden's and peppered with beard, Youngest in the royal family, Third in line to the throne, these times when I realize most fully that I will never again feel your elephant skin against my thigh, your snout at my breast, nor the ivory finger-nails draw blood from my cheek.

There is responsibility in any magic, you told me, when I confessed my longing for what you once were. As princess, I would take my place as wife of a foreign student in an excellent English Department of a midwestern university, so that we might return to our small country, polished as brass door handles, and encourage our people in western ways of sanitation and contraception. But, darling Beast, my concern is no longer with the gray rags being ground into the village streets, nor with the wombs of our virgins, white as clean sheets of rice paper. Instead, it is my wont to remind you of, no, actually, to defend our nightmares. You do not yet know the danger of these cornfields in the moonlight! It is then our International House opens its secrets. After we have sat around the oak table in our plaid, flannel shirts for the evening meal of hamburgers and beans, conversing in clipped English, then the lights go out in this house on the plains and we, who have each a different name for "water," become most ourselves. Often, then, I slip down the hallway to the bathroom, the bare bulb swinging, and press my face against the radiator vent to hear the various languages in each room, to smell curry and jasmine from the hotplates.

Perhaps the proprietor in the drugstore today saw the midnights in my eyes, or was it merely that we are dark, come to erase the blonde hair and blue eyes of his childrens' children? He took us ahead of the other customers to get us out soon, so that we would not handle the glass bottles and jars; but I could see your assurance that this man knew of your title. His voice rose and everyone in the store looked at us.

"Please, we have Professor Felp's permission, from the university, to charge this on account," you said.

"I think these two better sign, don't you, Jim?" the man asked the other clerk.

And you, in your confusion, forgot the correct English words and left the signature on the wrong line. I could do nothing, only, on the bus ride home, rub your arms with my mittens, because you still grow so cold without fur.

Playing lacrosse on the lawn in your American blue jeans, accustomed to massive beast muscles, you perpetually toss the ball short of goal. Ben, with his wire rimmed glasses and rope sandals, makes great sport of this failing and you both laugh. I may tell you now, I do not trust Ben. In the letter introducing him as our adviser he was described as a most intelligent fellow, but his judgements are not always apt. For instance, I feel sure the boys in the fraternity organizations across the yard are worthy of our acquaintance. From our bay window I have watched them wrapping birch trees in pink and green toilet tissue, in celebration. Ben is incorrect, too, about television. While you were attending the introductory seminars on Shakespeare and Chaucer, after I had been through the town's one museum, I found a color set in the basement of the Hillel House. My love, in America the soap sings!

This is all a surprise? You perhaps think I spend all my time with our creatures? My revelations are only beginning. As you can see, I even now refer to *them* as creatures. I did not invent a name for them as you suggested; for the beauty of the ugly things, their small cat bodies and parrot feathers, heads feline with beaks, the beauty is that they were born beyond definition. They will never yield to scholars or even poets, those namers of islands. Tomorrow night at the party, you will see that they do not yield ...

Beast, you have been kind about my creatures, complaining only when they leave green droppings on your academic papers. When Ben came to ask about the strange noises, you cracked the door and said we were listening to recodings of Noh plays, then helped me puree the catfood livers in apricot juice and drop the mixture down their shivering beaks. Their hideous cry of hunger is somewhat like a cat's mating screech, but higher pitched. I realize they are difficult to handle; the thin necks seem to have no muscles and the heads loll from side to side, especially the fourth, which, we speculate, may not have a brain. It has the smallest body of all, the one most like a bird's, wings limp, and the head very much too large. The eyes never open, even when I force the food onto its hairy, yellow tongue. You think I should stop feeding this one; but, darling, this is the one I most love, with its awkwardness in our world. Have you forgotten already trying to fit the dining silver into your paws, only to please me, or attempting a waltz you had neither the physique or patience for? Now you have fashioned a cardboard box for my creatures, from which they rarely venture. You permit them, as long as they do not leave this room, beyond which you give them little notice, regarding them simply as my pacifiers. Have you, too, forgotten the potential of ugliness? After the tabby gave birth to them in our closet, she clawed the door to get out. Each time I sat her down beside them, she sprang away, frantic to escape the room. Beast, you feign disinterest as to how they were conceived. Listen!

We had assumed our magic had worn off like a callous, but no, on one of our first days here, while you were registering for classes, I, too timid to venture out, wandered from room to room, pillaging the drawers and closets of this House. At the bottom of one trunk I found a silk slipper with sand in the toe. In the Chinese boy's room, the one with acne covering his face, who never speaks, there were erotic etchings browned with age, wrapped in cotton handkershiefs, of delicately robed men and women engaging in contortionist sexual practices. It was in the Hindu boy's quarters that I found the parrot in a bamboo cage. The bird seemed drawn to me, so I unlatched the cage. The parrot perched on my arm, remaining there as I moved through the House. You will recall the young blonde, the biological scientist, who owns the yellow tabby. Under the parrot's constant gaze, the cat was somewhat reticent, but the bird's head shifted jerkily as the tabby circled the room. When I brought them back to our quarters, it was still only in my mind to feed them some sweet morsel. Imagine my astonishment when the parrot leapt upon the cat's back, its green and yellow wings spread. At first the tabby tried to break away and then leapt up against the wall, attempting to get a grip with her claws, while the bird flapped his wings. As I watched them copulate, the long scatches on the wallpaper revealed a faded layer of reddish cowboys and lariats underneath, and behind a deep rose wood.

Had you imagined the creatures' history; for instance, when you scooted their cardboard box so casually away with your foot, searching for your wing tipped shoes? You were so very excited about the gathering tomorrow evening. At this minute, I am seated on the clothing you laid out, the linen shirt and black dinner jacket. No one will notice these wrinkles, darling, I promise you. The signs on campus, tacked to telephone poles and in the Student Union, are green with white hands outstretched, "Lend a Hand to a Foreign Student," and, indeed, the student population is invited to a party, where they will claim us as friends. I understand that they will receive a small payment for their advice and company in this special program. The girls in matching sweaters and skirts, their hair flipped at the ends, will arrive to choose from among us, seated on folding chairs, balancing little, frosted cakes on our laps. So, Ben has appointed you Foreign Co-ordinator. Does this not make us different, then? After hearing your speech, which was composed after many crumpled notes, won't the girls for whom everything is monogrammed, desire us for their own?

For your few words, a distinguished professor from your department has said he may attend. I tell you now, this gentleman will not be disappointed in our spectacle, because I, too, have been planning. For, love, here is at last a revelation: I have been teaching our poor, brainless creature, the one so like its father, to fly! After you are sleeping, I carry it to the mowed-down cornfield in the back of this House. Initially, I believed the wingspread would be inadequate to lift the body, but when I tossed it out of my hands, it sailed, remaining aloft for several moments. Many times since, we have practiced and the creature soars higher without ever opening its eyes. Like a bat, it dodges trees, yet falls after a time, sometimes landing in bushes or scruffs and I must pick the dry corn husks from its feathers.

Have you guessed, darling? When you stand to deliver your speech—then I will emerge with my creature. Just as the young girls are brushing crumbs from their skirts, I will release the greenish thing. Perhaps, sensing the stale air indoors, the creature will momentarily flap upward and perch on the creaking rafters. Will someone scream as it again takes flight, the small cat paws clawing the air, perhaps aimed at a fedora or sorrel wig? Beast, from the podium, your eyes will be most on it. Whatever you think of this act, view it well, the cat head lolling on the winged creature; then look at me in the chiffon party dress, let the creature be the standard by which you judge, the contrast by which I am again

Your
Beauty

Leslie-Beth Berger

A MATTER OF CONSCIENCE

> Ivan Petrovich Medvedyev
> Compartment IV, Moscow-Athens run
> Athens Train Station

4 August 1975

Dear——,

You were right. It was a matter of conscience. I did not forget that. I am leaving this note taped here where I am sure you will find it. Please do not be mad at me. If I told you you would have gotten in trouble. It is better this way. You can see I do not use anyone's name and this way you should not worry about being suspected.

—Ivan Petrovich Medvedyev

****

> I. Petrovich Medvedyev
> Conductor's Quarters, Moscow-Athens
> 1 January 1974

Sophie Aleksandrovna Medvedyeva
74 Zatsepa St., Apt. 67
Moscow 11765

My dear Sophie,

Please do not be mad with me. But before we got to Hungary I ate all the tort. And did not share any with Sergei. I should be grateful I know. He did not have to get me this job. Well next time I will share. Sergei said they searched the train in the middle of the night in Hungary and I was sleeping. Some conductor I will make. Asleep the first night. I will see you in a week my dear. Please kiss Misha for me. Are you wearing your underwear? I hope you will not be sorry you wanted me to take this job. Did you order the carpet? I remembered to get Sarkinin's permission for it *before* I left. Did you see the receipt? I put it next to Misha's books. I am getting very sleepy. Sergei wants me to be awake by the time we get to Yugoslavia. I love you. Kiss Misha.

—Ivan

I. Petrovich Medvedyev
Conductor's Quarters, Athens-Moscow
5 January 1974

Sophie Aleksandrovna Medvedyeva
74 Zatsepa St., Apt. 67
Moscow 11765

My dear Sophie,

I forgot to tell you something. When we got some mail finally only Sergei got unopened letters. And he says that is because his wife marked it Conductor's Quarters and not just the train. Do that yes? And make sure you show it to Cousin Lyudya. It is good to keep her a little jealous. Are you still letting Misha stay with her during the day? I hope you were able to postpone the factory trip to Kiev. When we passed into Yugoslavia there was a couple at it right there by the train track. A kiss for both of you. I will see you very very soon. And I miss you.

—Ivan

Sophie
6 January 1974

My dear Ivan,

I am so sorry I will not be home when you arive. (I hope you find this note—I am sorry the cookie can is empty). At the last minute Krashin felt that a female engineer should go on the factory tour. It is not my decision. You know I love you. Misha is with Lyuda and misses you terribly. Did you remember to purchase some postcards of Athens for him? Ivan, you know I wanted to be with you for your first return. Please do not worry, my little bird, we will have plenty of time before your next run to try again. Ever since Sergei got you that job, Krashin has noticed me. (Yes, I brought my underwear with me. Really, Ivan, you worry too much. I would not dare leave them home for you to find and fret about for days and days). I do not think I will be allowed to call, so I give you my kisses and pinches now.

My heart,

S—

—Oh, Ivan! You *did not* leave the receipt of permission for the carpet.

Ivan
6 January 1974

My dear Sophie,

I am not smart like you and I did not know where to leave this note. I hope you open the cookie can. Already I hate this job. Sophie Sophie what are we to do like this? I am in Greece then Hungary and you in Kiev talking about buildings they will never build. Sophie let me take my old job back. I think I could do better now booking tickets. At least we could see each other. But pigeon can we not leave Misha with someone else? Sophie I was sitting here eating icing and our Misha came with his nose bleeding from Cousin Lyudya's house. That Valery of hers. Sophie if she cannot control him do you think it is wise to let Misha stay there? I told Misha about the dogs at the border crossing and I think he will now play border control with Valery. I miss you. I was thinking how nice it would be to take a nap with you and then maybe go shopping for some cucumbers or even lettuce. Try to bring back some vegetables from Kiev. I am sure they will feed you well. Oh lettuce. I love you. I will try to get some postcards of Athens. But how? You know I cannot leave the train. Oh Sophie I am afraid to talk to the foreigners and that is how the last conductor lost his job. I am not clever like you and Sergei watches me. I think he wants a stereo.

—Ivan

Sopie dear I do not have the carpet receipt. Misha must have it in his schoolbooks. Come home soon.

Galya Ivanovna Mirnitskaya
8 Lomonosovsky, Apt. 4
Moscow 11877
25 January 1974

Sergei Gregorovich Mirnitsky
Conductor's Quarters, Moscow-Athens

Sergei—
  Sarkinin's bonus for you finally was approved today. Now we can order that refrigerator. It is about time. He knows a good worker when he sees one, Sergei. Now are you not glad I told you to recommend that little Ivan? You never listen to me. I will put the refrigerator by the couch. Sarkinin says he will rush the order through so we will have it before summer.
                                Galya

                                Sophie
                                5 February 1974

My dear Ivan,
  Oh, Ivan, I am so sorry again to have missed you. I was awarded the privilege of conducting a special training course but it means being apart from you and Misha. I had no choice, you know that. Please rest, Ivan. On your next tour home will be a *very* good time for me. I hope I can arrange it. Do not worry about Misha and Valery. Be patient, my dear. Valery just needs a father. Oh, Ivan, I do miss you. I will close, my sweet, but please try to find the carpet receipt. Sarkinin is on vacation and he is the only one who can authorize and permit such a purchase. Ivan, I will be terribly embarrassed to tell your boss that you lost it.
                                My heart,
                                S—

                                I. Petrovich Medvedyev
                                Conductor's Quarters, Moscow-Athens
                                10 March 1974

Sophie Aleksandrovna Medvedyeva
74 Zatsepa St., Apt. 67
Moscow 11765

My dear Sophie,
   The days home with you were so perfect my Sophie. And Misha is wonderful. I will try to get postcards. Well my sexy wife with the xxxxx. You have tired me out. Please have Misha look harder for the receipt. All my love. All. All. All. Next time can we bake a tort?
                    —Ivan

                    I. Petrovich Medvedyev
                    Conductor's Quarters, Athens-Moscow
                    16 March 1974

Sophie Aleksandrovna Medvedyeva
74 Zatsepa St., Apt. 67
Moscow 11765

My dear Sophie,
   Great news my Sophie. I found the carpet receipt in my coat pocket. I will send it soon. And what else? I got some postcards from some Norwegians on the train. You should see them. I look at the Parthenon every night but I do not understand why it is so great in its planning. The Norwegians tried to explain it. They were very friendly and I would never gotten up the courage but every morning they were standing out of their compartment IV in the hall just talking with everyone even Sergei. So I did not see the danger. I think I am doing well on this job. I am not so gloomy these days. It is wonderful what a few days with you can do. I love you.
                    —Ivan

Sophie Aleksandrovna Medvedyeva
Science Center, Novosibrisk
20 April 1974

I. Petrovich Medvedyev
Conductor's Quarters, Moscow-Athens

My dearest Ivan,

Oh, Ivan, I am so thrilled. My dearest, I am pregnant, but it does not seem fair to have to tell you this in a letter. I wish you were here. Just keep sending letters home, and in one of them you simply must enclose the carpet receipt. I hope the baby has your smile.

My heart,
S—

Ivan
Conductor's Quarters, Moscow-Athens
15 May 1974

Dear —————,

Do I pick a name for you? I never kept a journal before. I will try Fortochka. My window vent. So Fortochka I am to be a father again if my lovely wife and I can ever be together. I wish I could find my Parthenon. Now that was a building. Oh Sophie I am so sad. And have you noticed we have been writing less and less. Oh my dearest it is times like this being so far away and getting such brief notes from you and speaking to Americans and Norwegians and even Armenians that I think oh Sophie forgive me that I think should we really let this baby come?
—I.

Y. A. Sarkinin
Travel Bureau, Metropole Hotel
30 May 1974

Sergei Gregorovich Mirnitsky
Conductor's Quarters

Sergei Gregorovich:
   Permit this office to congratulate you on the management of your line. We expect no more difficulty. We give you and Ivan Petrovich 3 out of 5. Congratulations on passing your first review.
                                        Y. A. Sarkinin

                              Sophie Aleksandrovna Medvedyeva
                              74 Zatsepa St. Apt. 67
                              Moscow 11765
                              16 June 1974

I. Petrovich Medvedyev
Condouctor's Quarters, Moscow-Athens

My dearest Ivan,
   Ivan, what is wrong? I have not received a letter from you in weeks. I worry about your silences, Ivan. Are you doing well? I saw Galya yesterday quite by accident and she said that you got 3 out of 5. Ivan, that is wonderful to pass your first review. Please write, Ivan. My dear, I got a promotion and we are getting our new apartment in a *very* short while. Or, Ivan, so many marvelous things have happened since you took that job. I could not be happier anywhere else, I am sure. And I do love you, only please send the carpet receipt. Write, Ivan, we need you very much now. I want you to feel by belly.
                              My heart,
                              S—

                              I. Petrovich Medvedyev
                              Conductor's Quarters, Athens-Moscow
                              2 July 1974

Sophie Aleksandrovna Medvedyeva
74 Zatsepa St., Apt. 67
Moscow 11765

My dear Sophie,

Oh how my spirits lifted to get your letter. I even mailed the carpet receipt. Sophie Sophie I feel so ashamed. I have just been very irritable lately. I am so glad for us my dear. Do you know what I learned today? You will be shocked Sophie. We are playing bowling wrong. You are not supposed to throw the ball. Remember how dented the floor was at the bowling place at Park Kulturi? Well you are supposed to *roll* it. Oh Sophie your Ivan is very confused. Another thing. In America I could still be an engineer. Still. This couple said they do not take your degree away from you if you do not use it and there is no such thing as expiring. Do you think it is true? I love you very much you know.

—Ivan

Galya Ivanovna Mirnitskaya
8 Lomonsovsky, Apt. 4
Moscow 11877
3 July 1974

Sergei Gregorovich Mirnitsky
Conductor's Quarters, Moscow-Athens

Sergei—

I have been waiting for your explanation. 3 out of 5! I hope you are not pleased with that. That Sophie is pregnant and has been approved for a two-bedroom. That child is not even born yet and we still have a two-bedroom for all of us. I am not complaining (you just ask those Americans if they *really* have a room for each child. You just ask them). Supervise more seriously Sergei and I am sure Sarkinin will help with the stereo we need.

Galya

Ivan
Conductor's Quarters, Moscow-Athens
2 August 1974

Dear Fortochka,

I cannot find you or my Parthenon so I will start over. Do you think Sergei found you? One day after we were drinking a lot

Sergei was staring out the train window at Yugoslavia eating crackers all over him. I asked him if he ever thought even once of jumping off the train. But he told me he had a family and privileges like the good school for his daughter. I think he has good bonuses too. It was a matter of conscience he said and he especially loved his daughter and it is too bad in a way that he has her to care about. I miss Sophie and Misha so much. I hope I will feel better. Did I mail the carpet receipt?

—I.

Lyudya Nikolaievna Korotskaya
71 Zatsepa St., Apt. 14
Moscow 11765
3 August 1974

I. Petrovich Medvedyev
Conductor's Quarters, Moscow-Athens

Ivan,

Misha asked me to write. Your carpet arrived. Since you are away I did not think you would mind if I used it. When you return you must spend more time with Misha. He is becoming wild and insists on playing a game where he imitates a border guard. It is a vile game and I cannot imagine how he learned such a thing.

Lyudya

Galya Ivanovna Mirnitskaya
8 Lomonosovsky, Apt 4
Moscow 11877
3 August 1974

Sergei Gregorovich Mirnitsky
Conductor's Quarters, Moscow-Athens

Sergei—

I am so mad that I simply must write. Sophie got her new carpet —in a pattern *we* were told was discontinued. You must talk to Sarkinin.

Galya

Y. A. Sarkinin
Travel Bureau, Metropole Hotel
4 August 1974

I. Petrovich Medvedyev
Conductor's Quarters, Moscow-Athens

Ivan Petrovich:
This afternoon at four o'clock on Leninsky Prospect a driver
of a cabbage truck lost control of his vehicle and killed your wife
and son. Your wife was pregnant and the baby of course could
not be saved. Report to this office.
                    Y. A. Sarkinin

Y. A. Sarkinin
Travel Bureau, Metropole Hotel
8 August 1974

I. Petrovich Medvedyev
74 Zatsepa St., Apt. 67
Moscow 11765

Ivan Petrovich:
Our regrets. You have been reassigned to the ticket counter at
the Metropole. You will receive a bonus and of course will be
eligible for your previous position as soon as you re-establish a
family.
                    Y. A. Sarkinin

Ivan
74 Zatsepa St., Apt. 67
10 September 1974

Dear Fortochka,
    I do not believe it.
                    —I.

Ivan
74 Zatsepa St., Apt. 67
20 September 1974

Dear Fortochka,

I still do not believe it. Last night I dreamed I was in Kiev trying to make a call to Sophie and I did not have enough kopeck
pieces. I can hear their voices. Even smell my Sophie. Even smell
her and it seems like yesterday and so real.

—I.

Ivan
74 Zatsepa St., Apt. 67
10 October 1974

Dear Fortochka,

It is me again. I cannot sleep. What's wrong with me? I yell at
everyone at work and today I just grabbed my stomach and
doubled over. It lasted a second or two but it was very sharp and
if I cry out I will surely lose this job. It is hard to stand here all
day and help people who are going places.

—I.

Lyudya Nikolaievna Korotskaya
71 Zatsepa St., Apt. 14
Moscow 11765
11 October 1974

I. Petrovich Medvedyev
74 Zatsepa St., Apt. 67
Moscow 11765

So you have made me write you. Do not forget me. I am still
family you know. I am coming to see you at work soon. This time
I will get in. I must ask you something.

Lyudya

Ivan
74 Zatsepa St., Apt. 67
21 October 1974

Dear Fortochka,

It is worse. These pangs are coming more often and I cannot seem to be kind to anyone. Today Cousin Lyudya came in. Carpet carpet she said. Who cares about a carpet. Why should she have it? Why should she have anything? Oh Sophie I am sorry but I never liked her. If only we had a few more times together before such a thing had to happen to you or our Misha. It is my fault my Sophie I know it now. We could still be together somewhere working if only I did not let my degree expire. Somewhere and a few more days together. That is all.

—I.

Ivan
74 Zatsepa St., Apt. 67
23 October 1974

Dear Fortochka,

Some Yugoslavian couple came in and I thought of those people in Yugoslavia screwing by the train tracks. Forgive me my Sophie. Cousin Lyudya stopped in. I said I would watch Valery and I thought it would help but Valery is not Misha.

—I.

Ivan
74 Zatsepa St., Apt. 67
7 November 1974

Dear Fortochka,

Today is the anniversary of the Russian Revolution. So what? Oh my Sophie listen to me. Just listen to me. I am going crazy.

—I.

Ivan
74 Zatsepa St., Apt. 67
8 November 1974

Dear Fortochka,

Oh Sophie I am. I am going crazy. Last night I was walking around this big apartment for me and I looked at myself in the window and I saw that I was walking the way you walk. That certain rise in your step that you have. Had. See. See what I mean. It is like I still do not believe it. Oh Sophie I am so mean these days especially to Cousin Lyudya. She calls and calls and I hang up because she is bothering me about dating her friend. Oh Sophie who would have me?

—I.

Lyudya Nikolaievna Korotskaya
71 Zatsepa St., Apt. 14
Moscow 11765
12 November 1974

I. Petrovich Medvedyev
74 Zatsepa St., Apt. 67
Moscow 11765

It is ridiculous for neighbors to write. You are going with friends and me New Year's at Red Square. I know you do not have plans. It is not good, Ivan, to stay inside all the time. I am mailing another letter like this one to you at work.

Lyudya

Ivan
74 Zatsepa St., Apt. 67
28 December 1974

Dear Fortochka,

I was not going to write you. I am still superstitutious but I am feeling better. My hands stopped shaking a few days ago and I am able to sleep and eat. Oh eating. There is an American tour here and I love seeing them and making out their plans. There was one goodlooking one in the line with red hair and big blue eyes and breasts. Sophie I love you but I am lonely. I was just looking. She said engineering was a good job in America.

—I.

Ivan
74 Zatsepa St., Apt. 67
1 January 1975

Dear Fortochka,

Something is happening to me again. I went to Red Square with Cousin Lyudya and I am not proud of the way I acted. Misha would be shocked to see his father carry on that way. I do not drink Sophie you know that. But I do not think I hit Cousin Lyudya very hard.

—I.

Ivan
74 Zatsepa St., Apt. 67
1 February 1975

Dear Fortochka,

Tonight I read back what I have here. I am feeling better. No more pangs and New Year's seems a long time ago. I behaved so badly but Cousin Lyudya does not think so.

—I.

Ivan
74 Zatsepa St., Apt. 67
13 March 1975

Dear Fortochka,

The worst is over now. Do I believe I wrote those things? I have some peace now and a good plan for myself. I know what to do now. I am not crazy my Sophie. I am not. I have a plan and it has been here all along this opportunity. I will never forget that talk I had with Sergei that day on the train. Soon.

—I.

Ivan
74 Zatsepa St., Apt. 67
21 March 1975

Dear Fortochka,

It is the first day of spring and it is very cold and dark but I am sleeping well. It is slow in the office these days because of the weather. A few Poles and Georgians. Those Georgians. They would screw *on* the tracks. Cousin Lyudya and I had lunch again today and my plan is going well.

—I.

Ivan
Conductor's Quarters, Moscow-Athens
5 June 1975

Dear Fortochka,

Today is one of the happiest ones in my new life. I feel like I am home again. Sergei is the same as ever and he was surprised to see me so soon. Very surprised. Good. I will stay out of any trouble. I brought my engineering texts with me to keep busy. I do not think I forgot so much. I have peace now my Sophie and I thank you every day for making it so possible. But it is sad that we could never do it together.

—I.

Lyudya Nikolaievna Medvedyeva
7 Lenin Hills
Moscow 11102
6 June 1975

I. Petrovich Medvedyev
Conductor's Quarters, Moscow-Athens

Dear Ivan,

Today was our first morning apart in almost two months. Valery wants postcards of Athens. He will not let you back in the apartment without them. I ordered the bookshelves and desk today. I decided they will look good in Valery's room. He promised to study this year. I am decorating our new apartment very nicely. The carpet looks most attractive. I bought Valery that jeans outfit with the extra bonus. We did not need that new lamp anyway.

L.

Lyudya Nikolaievna Medvedyeva
7 Lenin Hills
Moscow 11102
11 June 1975

I. Petrovich Medvedyev
Conductor's Quarters, Moscow-Athens

Dear Ivan,

I wish you had not been so tired last night. You will have to make better use of your times home. I am aware that it was your first day, but we had many things to accomplish, Ivan. Now I will surely have to select a new kitchen table all by myself. Try to get postcards. I heard they gave my apartment away to a dancer from the Bolshoi. A whole apartment for one person. Well, I have no complaints.

L.

Lyudya Nikolaievna Medvedyeva
7 Lenin Hills
Moscow 11102
4 July 1975

I. Petrovich Medvedyev
Conductor's Quarters, Moscow-Athens

Ivan,

Why do you not write? How much time could your studying take? Valery is feeling better. You did not ask for him, but he is doing fine. *He would feel a lot better if his father could remember to bring him some postcards.*

L.

Lyudya Nikolaievna Medvedyeva
7 Lenin Hills
Moscow 11102
17 July 1975

I. Petrovich Medvedyev
Conductor's Quarters, Moscow-Athens

Ivan,

I did not expect you to be home while I was in Leningrad. You did not tell me your schedule. I will try to coordinate with yours, but this engagement in Leningrad was an honor for me. It is not often that one gets to substitute for her factory boss. I hope you are happy. My boss said you should be duly proud of me. I bought myself a hat for the occasion so the funds are short this month.

L.

Ivan
Conductor's Quarters, Moscow-Athens
29 July 1975

Dear Fortochka,

Duly proud of her. Oh Fortochka spare me. Patience Ivan.

Ivan
Conductor's Quarters, Moscow-Athens
3 August 1975

My dear little Fortochka,

I may not have room for you so I will say good-bye now just in case you cannot come. I am nervous but I am ready. Finally there are some Americans who will help me. They speak good Russian and they are very proud of me. They do not think I am mean or nasty and I feel better having them say that. Well maybe I exaggerated a little about Cousin Lyudya. But not about Valery. Not about him. I have truly made a good decision and I am very lucky that Cousin Lyudya and Valery are in Sophie's family. Thank you Sophie. Thank you for this gift you do not even know you gave. I am sure no great harm will come to them after I leave.

They will lose the apartment and some privileges for sure. But it is the only way for me and I kiss you a hundred times my Sophie. This American couple will leave my note for Sergei taped to the window of their compartment. I know he will find it. They are helping me get to the American Embassy and maybe can give me some American dollars. Well good-bye friend. Thank you Sophie thank you.

—I.

Carla Hoffman

FOR THE FORSAKEN, THERE IS NO SONG

Aldo Moro's letters were published by the Italian press. They are, in the terminology of the press, "pathetic" and "humiliating" epistles. My story is based loosely on these letters.

C.H.

March 16, 1979
Dear colleague,

   You already know the details of my abduction. There were witnesses. I saw them, watching, from various balconies in my neighborhood (we were not far from my home when the terrorists struck). The witnesses: a schoolgirl with a sprinkling-can, intent on watering her azaleas; a man arrested midshave in his white underwear, razor still poised beneath his chin, hairy arms like raw meat in a market stall; a woman. She was the one, I believe. Oh I know you've heard about the blonde woman, the terrorist with the guttural Italian, acting authoritative as a policewoman. I saw her, partially obscured by the sun gleaming on the chrome of the car, saw her above a band of light as though she were enclosed in steel. She held a submachine gun and shouted at me, at my fallen men, at the people on the balconies.

   But not that woman. The one on the balcony. I saw her most clearly, as though one real face had surfaced from a dream. She was slim and stood very still, without expresion (everyone else had an abundance of that). She wore a dark gown, I don't know whether it was a dark green or a burgundy, the two colors seemed to flash together. Her hair was black and pulled away from her face just at the jawline. Her nose and chin were pointed giving her a birdlike appearance.

How did I look so long? It was as though I had seen her all my life, as though she silently assessed the situation, as though she alone had power over it.

The situation: my kidnapping, of course. I have not been drugged or tortured. I am kept in a small room with no windows. They have given me paper and pen and told me to write my colleagues. What they want is an exchange, your leader for theirs. It should all be simple to arrange. I am to write and explain. But first, this letter. It is what I might say if I could. What I must send, in actuality, will be something roughly dictated—or at least approved—by them. These are the thoughts you may never see. These are the letters they must never read. I will secure them in my inner coat pocket till I am released to you, on that day to which I turn constantly, hopefully, that sunny spring morning when I will be riding through northern Rome in my motorcade, when the journey will be unobstructed, and I will arrive, on this day, at my destination of this morning and my life will go on as though nothing had happened, the cycle will be complete.

The bodyguard? The driver? The armed guards in the second car? You ask me how their lives may resume? I saw the curious puncture wounds in the windshield of the car, heard a series of thuds, how did my driver get out the door and start across the green lawn? These are strange moments, without coherency. I still try to piece things together. But, if you will recall, above the spot where the driver fell, where he fell face-down onto the earth as though in supplication, above him was the balcony and the woman. Did she look at him? Did she give him any sign? No, she did not. She simply accepted his sacrifice. I don't believe in pagan gods, I am a Christian of course. But if I were to believe in such things, I would think she was a pagan goddess calmly accepting our lives. Our lives? Am I to include my own? Certainly not! In a matter of moments, seconds, hours, days?, I will be driven to some spot where you will collect me and take me, weeping I suppose, home.

My warmest greetings.

March 21, 1979

Dear colleague,

I have sent you the letter with their terms. I am confident you can meet them. The world will obviously support you in what must be done. This is war, of course, as they have pointed out to me. So an exchange of prisoners is perfectly proper, as in war, approved by the state. What I really want to tell you is this—I know where I am! They have tried to keep my whereabouts secret, from you, even from me, but how foolish of them! To think I would not recognize the seashore! At first, you understand, it was intuition. I can't remember asking myself, quite rationally: Now where exactly am I? The situation has such loose links with reality, one just assumes it is some dream landscape. But it is, in fact, a real place!

The second day I was here I could smell salt, you know the sort which mingles with seabreezes. It was sharp in my nostrils, it was clean and clear. I nearly hyperventilated, breathing it in all day. It kept me from hysteria. And, later, I could hear waves breaking on a beach. Could I hear the boats far out on the water? Of course not, they are much too quiet. But I could sense them! You have no idea how one's senses become acute in such a situation, how the slightest movement miles away sends reverberations through the air. I could *feel* the ships passing, the outlines, their shapes, were drawn inside my eyes as though my eye had an inner screen for the viewing of such spiritual passages.

No, no, they have given me no drugs. The food is by no means even passable, but one must eat to stay alive. And there is much to live for, of course. The exchange should be arranged as soon as you receive the letter. These things can be done expeditiously, and I know you will see to it personally. A high officer of state cannot be left to count passing ships, struggling to maintain sanity. I have done much for the country. My wife and children need me. The morning I left, my wife kissed me at the door. You don't believe me? You suspected that we quarreled? You imagine there is no sex life after sixty? Ha, you should have a wife like mine! But I am dreaming. The woman on the balcony appears in my mind again, she rides a ship, there is a sunset. How do I know that? There are no windows here. But in captivity, in prison as my captors prefer to call it, one is aware of much. It is the disruption of routine, the arrest of the biological clock. They wake me in the night, and then allow me to sleep late into the morning. They come in the darkness, hooded like agents of death or graverobbers. But I am not dead, and they have stolen nothing from me, have barely touched me. Sometimes I wish they would punch their fists into me. Why? It would settle, once and for all, the question of their substance, of mine.

My warmest regards.

March 31, 1979
My colleague,

Your word has reached me here! What! Refuse! How can you refuse to negotiate for my release? They brought me a copy of *Il Tempo*; at first I did not believe it. I held the paper in my hand, but I could not believe it was real. Then I considered it was a placebo newspaper, one they printed at much expense to themselves, in order to trick me. What made me believe it? I have no choice. This is not a real world I am kept in, and this communication from your world is not real. If it is, then it has to be a lie! I have been condemned to death unless you make the exchange. I have been tried in their people's court for crimes, my crimes, your crimes, the crimes of the whole state! And for this, you would let me die.

Beyond comprehension.

Word will come in time. But I have waited so long already. They tell me what day, what month, what year, what hour, it is. But here this has no meaning. If only the woman would sing. I can hear them outside my door, speaking in low whispers, sometimes arguing in loud voices, occasionally someone laughs. But song. There is none. And there is the woman. I have never known a woman who did not sing. My wife, for instance, singing as she dressed for dinner. When we were young and walked the streets of Trento, her laughter was a song. My daughters, rocking their dolls, skipping stairs. And my mother, singing as she danced on the balcony (with my father?). She sang till her face went stone-white. Then she lost all expression. What did that mean? The end of the song? The end of the dance? She still sings and dances in my mind.

Expectantly,

April 3, 1979
Dear colleague,

I can now prove I am kept at the beach! Sand! I unrolled my pantscuff and sand poured onto the floor! When they come in now, they no longer pass like phantoms. I can hear the sand grinding beneath their feet. They cannot keep me here when summer comes. The beach bars will open their doors, vacationers will cross the wooden floors, sand grinding beneath their feet.

It was a long drive from Rome to Ostia Lido, beneath umbrella-shaped trees which towered like Roman legions. A journey through a green tunnel which carried me round and round and deposited me here, in this small, windowless, cold room. It is also damp.

They say you will not negotiate, but I don't believe them. Surely you would not leave me here much longer. Surely the day is at hand when the wooden door will open and I will walk through deep sand, blinking in sunlight.

Surely you will send word.

In truth, I feel abandoned by you. You are so far away.

My best regards.

April 5, 1979
My colleague,

You see what risks I take writing to you! She saw my letter, they took it from my coat with the others and, although she has never entered this room, hooded or otherwise, they showed the things to her! And what do you think? Instead of receiving a visit from her, instead of hearing her lighter female foot setting into this room, I have received a written reply. She wrote me a letter! Here I attach it. Read it, my colleague, when you have recovered me and my writings. She says:

"Il presidente,

You wonder why I do not sing. I wonder how anyone can sing while our country is contaminated by the putrification of your regime. I am a soldier, not a woman, and soldiers do not sing. We are involved in an armed struggle with you, our foe. We have tried you and found you guilty in the people's court. You are condemned to die. Your fellow conspirators refuse to reverse the sentence by making a humane exchange of prisoners. You have been condemned by your own. When the time comes, the sentence will be carried out. Until then, you must understand this is war. A song is out of the question.

Comrade Monika Schall."

I hold her letter in my hand, fold it, press it out flat. It is the first real communication I have had. I look at the words, the erratic lines of her handwriting as though she were unsteady, the incorrect grammar (as you guessed, as it said in *Il Tempo*, this woman is not Italian!).

And yet, her words. They have to them a certain substance. I keep her letter, attached to my own. Black veins on white skin; nightbirds flayed across white snow. You take life by the roots and shake it, and from the tree falls paper, white blossoms falling from the tree. Will you read this after I've died? Will you find anything of me in it?

I am already gone.

Regards.

April 16, 1979

Dear colleague,

A dream. She comes in the night and tries to seduce me. But I am pure, purged of desire. My body does not exist. I am cool. I feel nothing. She climbs over me as though I were a mound of earth. Her black hair is loose now and falls over my face, blinds me so I cannot see her body, forming sudden as snow. Light creeps in between the slats. The wind rises.

Her gown is satin, which accounts for its changing color. It holds both light and shadow. Green, dark as a forest, teasing with a flash of sunlight.

She's not the woman I hear outside. This woman speaks perfect Italian, has a lilting voice. Perhaps she comes to comfort me, but I am not comforted. She has made me miserable.

The building has been moved closer to the sea somehow. The sounds come more easily, I do not strain to hear them. Images of the passing ships come more freely too.

Who said it? Everything returns to the sea.

Greetings.

April 18, 1979

My colleague,

You condemn me to die. And yet I have not given up.

I hear the carbinieri drive down a nearby road, their vans plowing through gravel, an occasional crack of a pistol fired into the air. They are so close they will stumble over me. And when they find me, I will be led out. The beach will be glittering in moonlight.

You still might reconsider. You might recall that I am a man, purified, with a desire for nothing except life.

Regards.

April 21, 1979.
Dear colleague,

Still no word! Is it possible?

Yesterday there was a new voice outside, an old woman who shrieked and admonished my captors. Why? I listened carefully, caught some of what was said. Her anger made her incoherent, but the comrades were cool. *Si signora*, said one, politely, reassuringly, as he has never addressed me. *Si, si, va bene.*

What happened? They put their trash out on the wrong side of the doorway. The women in the area are furious with this breach of custom. The man who collects the trash has not collected ours for weeks. They complain of the stench.

Why did I not cry out?

I ponder this all day (or is it night?). I should have cried out, but no. They would simply have shot the woman. Escape is futile. I had worked a slat loose, but they caught me. They threatened to keep me handcuffed, to take my pen and paper away. I must not offend them. To do so would be foolish, an abstraction. I will write nothing to offend them now, say nothing about the woman who does not enter my room or the men who do. The food comes irregularly and I am hungry. At times I am too faint to write. But when I see the paper, here, on this table, I am lost in its permanence, the endurance of paper, books bound and shelved, cataloged.

My warmest greetings.

April 23, 1979
My dear colleague,

They brought more paper today and told me to write. My head, suddenly clear. I wrote as they dictated. They helped me organize my thoughts. I begged, pleaded, demanded my life. A simple prisoner exchange. If you refuse now, you are murderers. I hereby expose your selfishness, your obstinacy, your blindness to my suffering. Do as they say! Make the exchange! Have the courage to act now! You must free your leader from these chains.

Surely the woman with the complaint about the trash will say something. When she calls the carabinieri, they will buckle on their white helmets and come for me. You will be sorry then. If you are too stupid and obstinate to release me, the carabinieri will do it. They remember my service to this land.

But first the woman must squawk her way home, chew over her dinner with toothless gums, ruffling, then in the blind eye of her mind shall come the flash of insight. She will gobble out my story, the words I willed her as she stood outside the door. She will tell someone about the trash placed, significantly, to the left side of the door. It was a sign.

But I dream. The hag is too stupid. She will spill every story which revolves in the whirlpool of her mind except this one.

And you are worse, my colleague, sitting there with a mind well-ordered like a computer bank.

April 30, 1979
My colleague,

They say the time has come. We are almost at the zero hour: it is more a question of seconds than minutes. We are at the moment of execution.

My funeral stretches, a black road in the future. You are not there. My wife and children stand in the rain. Why rain? It is only tears. At funerals, they fall freely. It rained last night, the drops splattered on the roof, marked the sand. Much was washed into the sea.

And still it is not too late. They have given one reprieve. They may give another. Only a word from you.

They are angry like neighborhood bullies when the other gang has gone scared and run off. They are not angry with me: it is you. I am merely the vehicle of their wrath.

Still, I write my farewell letters. They have promised to post them. The Italian postal system is so inefficient. A postman gathers mail in the morning, stops at a bar. If the conversation is especially good, no mail will be delivered from that point. He gulps burning whiskey. At night he flattens his woman like a reed beneath him, pushes her into an intricate weave, dark reds and greens, woven like flowers so that he may be born, may live and die against her white fabric.

There is so little time left. You must rise from the warmth of your woman and restore me to mine.

Greetings.

May 6, 1979

Dear colleague,

So it is summer anyway, and morning. For the first time it has nothing to do with me. No sun burns for me, no fire.

This is the last time I will write. The moment has passed. I have written also to my love ones, my wife. The nights spin by, the days evaporate. I am slipping, and catch myself, and slip again.

Do not think I have always been passive. I have tried to escape. The walls would not give in, the men came still pulling the hoods over their faces, I caught a glimpse of one: he had a nose and a mouth, but was without eyes. They have not seen my suffering. I have wept.

I imagine death. The opening of the door, the guns pointed like fingers, accusing. I am ashamed. My fears are bared. Perhaps this is a little bit like rape. I want to stand. I am afraid I will cower. It would be easy to go woman-soft. I do not want their blows, their fury, and yet I will explode with the force of it.

She will come then, with the glow of sleep about her, her skirt flowered now and unfolding on the floor. She will wrap me in her arms and rock me, springsong dying on her lips, in the morning.

Robert Wexelblatt

JEU D'ESPRIT

Dear Z.,

It's the hospital I'm writing from. I've had a narrow escape, and it's as they say: best to suppose things could not have happened otherwise. The surgeon, who has just now left and who has given me permission to write this letter, showed me the two bullets he removed from me last night. He seemed almost proud of them, as if they were babies. The bullets looked tremendous, and far more real than the mere designation "38-calibre" might suggest. Still, they had spared me. My thigh and abdomen are heavily bandaged: one of the three bullets which struck me passed right through my leg. The doctor could only deliver twins, not triplets. It's interesting that the missing bullet—the one which pierced me twice and made double the number of wounds—also did only half the damage of the other two. But this is too much like speculative self-pity. Anyway, in an hour or so the police will be back to pose some serious questions, and I shall have to decide what, if anything, to tell them. I have had the idea that writing to you (I know, an unprecedented thing, but so is being shot), that this might help me make up my mind what to tell the detectives. The fact that we have not seen each other for over six years now will also, I imagine, make it easier for me to avoid being elliptical. Of course, you will understand this.

For almost a year I took every opportunity to convince X., with whom I used to share an office at the College, to free himself from the oppressive and impossibly restraining conditions of his life. Apart from certain general principles of mine, of which you are aware, I told him that to free himself from his marriage, his children, his house, his mother, and his job was hardly less than a duty imposed on him by his talent for writing. I confess that I was not thoroughly convinced of his talent, but I did not see that this much mattered. After all, a part of the point I was making with him was that he must discover the extent and magnitude of his talent, and that in order to do so he must . . . and so forth and so on. Only a traducer jumping wholesale to conclusions could claim that I indulged in these suggestions either experimentally or, worse yet, out of misplaced envy. On the contrary, I hid nothing from him of the "other side"; for instance, I openly confessed to him my own shortcomings and various failures of nerve. Yet I was also aware of having become for him an example. As you may know now, bachelors are almost always regarded as examples by married men; and then it was only too clear that if he did not precisely look up to me, he still favored me with all sorts of confidences, especially his ceaseless and sordid domestic complaints. It would, I am sure, have been sufficiently plain to anyone that X. was a cruelly frustrated man, but one whose frustration was not wholly due to his own nature. To give only one instance, there was his marvelous predilection for guilt. While, as you can imagine, perpetual self-laceration in an office-mate is despicable in itself (and especially so for me, perhaps), in the case of X. one could perceive that this tendency might, in the form of extreme scrupulousness, say, have helped his work—would have given it a special stamp and character. Instead, guilt was a stumbling-block from what he told me in all innocence—I mean at those times when he felt no malice—that those around him, not excluding his two little daughters, were fearfully adept at manipulating him through his overblown sense of personal guilt. Even I would have been able to manipulate him in the same fashion, had I wanted.

I was extremely fond of putting to him, on all sorts of occasions and in tones both serious and not, that favorite rhetorical question of mine, which I am sure you can recall: When do you feel most like yourself? But instead of answering it with irony, X. invariably replied with the most pathetic seriousness and, toward the end, almost with desperation: "When I'm writing," moaned he.

One fall afternoon I told him the exemplary and true story of how my mother had fallen ill during the previous summer, my painting-season. I told him how she had phoned me long-distance, something she knew I disliked and had even forbidden, in what tones she begged me to come to her. "Just a day," she'd said, "only an hour. I may never see you again!" X. concealed his shock (but registered no disgust) when I told him that I had unconditionally refused to go. I told him too how one of her neighbors actually called me up later in the week to renew the pleas and add reproach. But I had not given in, and, as usual, my mother recovered.

By no means was I on a crusade, though. It was really always he who brought these subjects up. I was never certain as to why he did so; that is, whether it was because he wished to chafe the cooled comfort of a fantasy or to suffer the refined lacerations of the possibilities I represented both to and for him. Looking back on it, I believe what he was really after was determination, antecedents, courage, and resolution.

From time to time X. brought me samples of his work—in what spirit I'm not certain. Of course, they were all either fragmentary or very brief pieces, and as such they became at once texts for new homilies. How was one to accomplish any sustained work . . . etc.

At last, in the Spring, just before the end of the semester, X. came to visit me in my loft. He came there only rarely, by the way—probably because I had made him so acutely aware of my immense regard for my own privacy—but when he did, we had long, splendid talks on the good old subjects of his work, my work, liberation and the various connections we could see among the three. He came unusually late on that night and, as was unheard-of in his case, without calling in advance. He stayed only a short while.

That night X. announced (it really was a kind of formal pronunciamento; you could tell that he had it prepared)—X. announced that I had entirely convinced him, that he had at last decided to desert his family, abandon his mortgage, leave his car, quit his job, forget his two daughters. His new freedom had, of course, to be quite total—if only to make up for his former servility—and he intended to go about achieving this freedom meticulously and in secret. He would eradicate every trace of himself, change his name, move to another part of the country, taking with him all his savings to sustain his work. (Well, his wife could manage alone if she had to, and this would be a liberation for her as well.) And then he would, naturally, write. Write what? A novel, perhaps; but in any case something weighty, significant, and complete; something too which would do what all his puny collection of snippets and fragments had not—express his nature fully, especially those most human aspects of himself which had been obscured and occulted by the miasma of his life's conditions and commitments. The great work, in short, was to express (of this he spoke feverishly) the very freedom which would make its creation possible.

I must hurry. Already I have lingered too much over these details—details which you certainly could have surmised anyway. But I have been remembering them as I write.

Neither I nor anyone heard anything more from X. His disappearance apparently began a moment after he submitted—on a single sheet of paper, I discovered—both his final grades and his resignation. I did not trouble to find out what became of his family. For one thing, it was now painting-season again; for another, I wasn't interested.

But two weeks ago I received a letter. It was very long. I have already destroyed it, so that it may be difficult to give you a clear idea of its contents. This, again, will depend on how much I can recall as I write.

The postmark was from out West, someplace I'd never heard of. The letter itself was unsigned, but it was beyond doubt from X. The fact that the letter had been typed made deciding how it had been written difficult to ascertain—that is, to know the state of mind of the writer. Such a letter could have been a joke, a function of a peculiar pathology, or (as I have reason to believe) quite impersonally in earnest, while without ceasing to be jokingly pathological at the same time.

X.'s letter had an ordinary, almost a banal beginning. X. compiled for me a sort of tourist's itinerary of his travels, which had tended errantly westward. He described little, but there was one rather finely visual paragraph about the sunbaked town on the edge of a desert in which he had settled.

In Part Two, so to speak, he wrote generally about his work, recalling at odd points our old conversational habit of comparing the verbal and the plastic in art. He gave a dreadful account of many false starts—suggesting there may have been literally hundreds of them—complete with crumpled papers, cigarette butts, and occasionally immolated manuscripts. He wrote of a dozen completed short stories that he hadn't been able to peddle.

Part Three, which began with a sudden expression of pure joy, brought him to what he called his "real work"—a genuine and long novel which had the working-title "Jeu D'Esprit." He decried his own gallicism, but said that probably he would change the title in time—that it was, "like the rest, provisional." X. reminded me of his words, his vow, when we'd last spoken: that his book was to express the absolute freedom which brought it into existence and on which it depended. Following upon this detail was a lengthy disquisition—an admixture of the theoretical and the craftsmanlike—concerning the manifold relationships between form and content, literature and life, freedom and necessity, novelty and recurrence, lines and cycles, originality and rediscovery —a whole range of increasingly abstruse dualities which he somehow claimed to be just on the verge of resolving. This third part of the letter ended by sounding like the ravings of an alchemist who is entirely convinced that he has found the philosopher's stone.

"Jeu D'Esprit," he went on to say, would bear a dedication to none other than myself, as I had played a singular and unique role in the composition of the book. For epigraph the novel would have the question, also from me: "When do you feel most like yourself?"

X. then concluded his letter with an attempt to explain the "notion" of the novel, as he termed it. The book was to be a sort of inside-out, polysemous, and layered murder-mystery. In order to fulfill, in the strictest fashion, its purpose of expressing the freedom on which it was based, the novel would recapitulate the story of a teacher who is convinced by a colleague to throw over his entire mode of life in order to write a book of which he comes to believe himself capable. This theme is presented contrapuntally, with the motif of "feeling like oneself" recurring, under various guises, throughout—even in the long fourth section of the book which would, according to X., "have the ring of a biography." The simultaneous climax and peripeteia of the plot would involve a thoroughly shattering recognition on the part of the protagonist: that after all it is not, as he had deluded himself, "writing" which makes him feel most like himself. On the contrary, writing has from the first been his greatest affectation; his only "real ambition" had ever been to *be* a writer, never actually to *write*. Nevertheless, instead of finding in this hard truth a merely vulgar sense of betrayal and self-disgust, he discovers that the very acts he has committed *in order to* write his book are the ones in which he has felt most true to his own nature. Upon dispassionate examination of these acts, he judges them all to be essentially destructive, iconoclastic, sacrificial, egotistical, and even criminal. The form of his freedom, in short, has been as wholly negative as its consequences. Yet he still aspires to redeem even this suddenly blank freedom by seeking for it its fullest expression equally in words and in action, in art and in life, etc. His plan is relatively simple, inevitable in fact: he will write a book about a man in circumstances exactly like his own, who had been persuaded to throw over his previous life in order to obtain the freedom requisite for artistic expression, who conceives a book which he provisionally calls "Jeu D'Esprit," which will in turn be founded upon terrifying discoveries precisely the same as his own. The one element which holds back the completion of the whole enterprise, however, is the selection of the protagonist's crime. Murder, to be sure— but the murder of whom? Certainly the killing must stop short of suicide, for that would frustrate the purpose of completing the book as well as betraying the true character of the destructive liberation it was meant to express. No, the victim must of course be the office-mate, the friend, model, originator, mentor, prophet and precursor. The last liberation must be from the liberator himself. In short, of course, the victim was to be myself.

My hands were cold when I read that. And they are colder now, as I write this to you, my dear. That is because I have lost a good deal of blood. The police will be here any minute. I don't yet know what I shall tell them; for there is one last astounding thing

I have not told you. At the very end of his letter, in a postscript, X. confessed that he was still uncertain about the opening and closing scenes of his novel. They would ("of course," he wrote) mirror each other in order that the overarching structure of the book might be properly "cyclic." He had three alternatives. In one version the book would begin with the discovery of my body and end with him firing the fatal shots. In the second version, the book would begin with a failed attempt on my life and end with a gruesomely successful one. But in the third version (which he said he favored, "awaiting the outcome of events"), the novel would both begin and end with me, wounded, lying in a hospital bed, writing down these facts, unable to decide what to tell the soon-to-arrive police investigators, uncertain too if another attempt would be made on my life. If this version proved feasible, X. concluded, then I should myself be made the narrator of "Jeau D'Esprit."

As ever,
Your estranged husband,
Y.

HAROLD ADLER
Letters to Helen

Querida Helenita te escriba a usted a ti porque su esposo no tiene mucho tiempo porque esta muy ocupado con su trabajo y como, y como, y como, y como. Wed., April 16, 1969, he mailed letter number one to Lima, Hotel Crillion. Did you get letter forwarded to you in Quito from Mrs. Hicks? Harold had to make a rush delivery to the photographers today, inviting the designer Jose Ferro along. Jose wanted a soda so we stopped at Brown's on the way back. Brown's hasn't changed one bit, even the same waitresses. This was the first hot fudge nut sundae Jose ever tasted. He liked it. Esther Gospe invited Harold for dinner next Wednesday. She does give you notice. Grace Snow phoned saying she was writing to you, did Harold want to say anything, yes, he sends his love. He worked tonight. Received your card from Panama. Thursday, April 17. He had dinner at Joe and Barbara's. Low heat cooking is great. Friday, April 18, Helen Wexler invited him to Mark Taper Theater but both you & Harold saw the play and besides he got home late. Your minestrone soup is great. You should have left more. Sat, April 19. He woke me up real early getting to work at 5:45 a.m. working a full day. I noticed this is the first time he watered the entire yard & he sprayed me twice doing so. Please tell that bastard to throw away the canned pet food and feed me the real McCoy fresh off the steer's back. Your communication number three arrived today. Sunday, Ap. 20. He again awakened me out of the garage rafters and tried to palm off that lousy cottage cheese on me with an egg. It's not for me. He danced out of here to play golf leaving me to watch those two coyote pups frisk about. I hope they don't get too close. He invited Michael Levine to play golf with him as his guest. Michael was very appreciative. He is a nice boy. Three o'clock he comes traipsing home with some shopping including Knudsen's. This time—just give me the red raw meat and forget the rest. That's about all for the present. The weather has been very warm & not too smoggy. Con amor por usted bueno amigo, Blanquito, el gato, y Harold con amor Buenos dias.

South American Letter from Helen's Cat "Blanquito" with Cat's Combing on End of Tail. April 1969. 11x17"

Helen Adler enters Moscow October Fourteenth

October fifteenth Napoleon Bonaparte flees in retreat

Letter to Moscow. September 1972. 18x24″

DEAR HELEN CONGRATULATIONS ON OUR THIRTY SIXTH ANNIVERSARY? LONDON IS A SMASHING PLACE TO CELEBRATE OUR ANNIVERSARY SO TAKE THAT BELATED EXCURSION TO KEW GARDENS AND HAMPTON COURT ITS ON THE HOUSE

I SEE YOU HAD A NINE I SHOULD SAY FIVE AM DEPARTURE YESTERDAY. THERMOS SHOULD BE VERY HANDY. HOW ARE YOU GOING TO GET POTS IN YOUR SUITCASE ISFEHAN BESIDES THE CARPETS WED. OCT 4/ MARK HAD A BRUISED BIG TOE FOR THE PAST WEEK AND HE HADNT ATTENDED TO IT AS THE DOCTOR PRESCRIBED SATURDAY BARBARA TOOK HIM TO THE EMERGENCY CLINIC. THE PAST THREE DAYS SHE HAS TAKE OFF WORK TO TAKE HIM TO THE DOCTOR FOR TREATMENT. IT BECAME BADLY SWOLLEN AND INFECTED NO SCHOOL FOR 3 HIM FOR SEVERAL DAYS BUT HIS

Letter to London, October 1972. 18x24"

I forgot to mention to you that the telescopic lens (135 mm) is not automatic to your EE Miranda camera. From what I was told you find the lens opening with automatic setting in EE position. Then set the opening of the 135 mm lens with the camera's reading. What I can't remember, is whether if you then put camera on manual or not. I would guess it wouldn't be necessary to put it on manual but I'm not sure. If there is a camera store handy you might inquire. The instructions in your manual are on page 19. Monday, July 30 a.m./ I just phoned the Miranda distributor. 1. You take the meter reading set on EE with the standard lens on camera. 2. Set the 135 mm lens to reading. 3. replace lenses. 4. Put camera on manual. 5. Shoot. Just saw Dr. Lin, some improvement. Less decaffinated coffee. 3-4 cups daily two cigars per day, less wine. She's trying to adno medication to regulate the heartbeat, as the side effects on a slow heart beat even slow it up more. I return in six weeks. Hope to trust you are well & having a Queens time. It is now 2 p.m. So am going to the post office to get this letter off. Love Harold and Blanquito el gato,

Letter to London. July 1973. 18x19"

HELEN
DEAR HELE
DEAR HELENDEA
DEAR HELENDEA
DEAR HELENDE
DEAR HELENDEAR H
DEAR HELENDEAR H
DEAR HELENDEAR HEL
DEAR HELENDEAR HELE

Saturday, March 9, 1974 / Went to post office at 9 a.m.
and mailed letter to Mexico City. Pick up is at 10:15 p.m.
Did some odd shopping. The gasoline lines are not so bad
considering it is a Saturday. Your check from strs was in this
morning's mail also a check from Ninet-Gely, the OTR. I decided
to wash the ceiling and walls in my bathroom this afternoon. As I removed the glass light fixture over the sink I dropped the thumb screw into
the sink and it went down the drain. By now I'm real sorry I started this project.
Never having removed a drain goose I phoned Mayne for information, he instructed
me. I hesitantly started but didn't have the proper wrench to work in such tight quarters.
After struggling for more than an hour I finally got it off, recovered the screw, re-assembled
the goose neck and guess what - no leaks. Did you know there were several brands of hair shampoo and
colognes colognes and an elastic & zerox under the sink, besides misc. other items. The sink cabinet
needed dusting & cleaning anyway. I finally washed the ceiling and walls. Twice today I've cleaned up
the driveway, the remains of gophers or rabbits, no wonder the cat hasn't bothered me to eat. I have patiently tried
to give him petro malt with just fair success. Cooked rice again, this time it was successful, had it with lamb leg
bag from Ann. Watched part of Its a Mad Mad World on TV. Saul's titles are great. It's now 10:30 p.m. I was hoping
to receive a phone call from you. Sunday, March 10 / The day is overcast, showers forecast for tonight. Played golf with Maury
at Hansen Dam 10:15 time. On the way home only saw two gas stations open and they were jammed. Tonight Marsha had a surprise birthday party for Dave at Joans Blue Room. I was invited. Besides Dave, Ida, Marsha, myself - Marshas friend Elliott was
also there. The party was very pleasant, with usual cake and the entire staff around our table singing happy birthday. Ida said the
Saturday workshop was very good. A weaver from Modesto who also a surgical nurse demonstrated. She said quote, you don't realize how
difficult it is to thread twelve needles without wetting the ends of the threads. Dave has been nominated for an Emmy award for
his contribution to the Ellsberg case TV reporting. Spoke to Jim Hall this evening and felt relieved that you both have been heard from. The
mail evidently is very slow. Monday, March 11 / No showers are in sight as predicted. Work has been moderate busy, everything rush, I am occupied.
Got the roll of film back. The pictures you took came out fine, so did the Marks, the shots he took upstairs with the flash. The shots I took on thanksgiving with the flash
were all blanks. I give up. Today Ventura county went on the odd and even gas sales system. When I got home this evening I was delighted to find your letter and
post card number two in the mail from you. To celebrate I poured my
self a glass of sherry and lit a cigar and then opened the mail. Your
letters are most descriptive & in such detail. It was lucky meeting
Srs. Cruz & Gil. We will have to try their restaurant upon your return.
I hope you get the accommodations at Chichen Itza. Are you taking
chances eating ice-cream. You sound like things are going fine
and. I do hope you both keep well. Things here are the same, we
are both fine and miss you. Had dog biy from Jeans for dinner tonight. I am going to mail this letter first thing in the morning
at the post office. I wonder if I allowed enough time for this
letter to reach you in time in Merida. Where does your cat
disappear in the afternoons. Much love, Hank & y Blankinstor

Letter to Yucatan, Mexico. 1974. 17x20"

Letter to Conway, Wales on Walking Trip. May 29, 1979. 19x24″

Welcoming Home Wife from Trip to Great Britain. September 1973. 19x24″

Essays & Reviews

Rose Kamel

"REACH HAG HANDS AND HAUL ME IN"
MATROPHOBIA
IN THE LETTERS OF SYLVIA PLATH

Between 1950 when she entered Smith College and 1963, the year she committed suicide, Sylvia Plath wrote her mother nearly a thousand letters many of which Aurelia Plath published in *Letters Home*. Ostensibly meant for her mother's ears alone, Plath's letters throb with an almost daily account of her growth and development as a writer. Their cumulative effect is that of an autobiography with a beginning, a middle, and an implied end. It can be read as an attempt, at times desperate, to delimit where Aurelia ends and Sylvia begins.

We have little evidence of how Aurelia Plath responded to the letters. A self-supporting widow, she consistently supported her daughter's ambitions to write, teach, marry, bear children— ambitions reflecting not only the compartmentalization of women's lives in the 1950's, but the way Aurelia had structured her own life. Furthermore, Plath's letters project little of the hate she vented against her father and Ted Hughes in her brilliant final poems. Her statement that the root of her childhood trauma lay in her father's death invites a Freudian interpretation of her writing that is distortive because it minimizes Aurelia's role in their relationship:

And this is how it stiffens, my vision of that seaside childhood. My father died, we moved inland. Wheron those nine first years of my life sealed themselves off like a ship in a bottle—beautiful, inaccessible, obsolete, a fine white flying myth.[1]

Understandably, critics are reluctant to delve more deeply into Plath's relationship with her mother, who in the aftermath of her daughter's suicide has certainly suffered enough. We cannot, however, overlook Plath's perception of her mother as an anti-self she feared, yet deeply loved and identified with.[2] An anxious tone permeates the exuberance of most of the letters signed "Sivvy," and their careful reading suggests that Plath perceived her mother as a Doppelgänger, a double, undermining her sense of herself as a separate being. It is this perception that charges the epistolary I-You dialectic with ontological tension rooted in matrophobia, defined by Adrienne Rich in another context as:

the fear not of one's mother or of motherhood but of *becoming one's mother* .... Matrophobia can be seen as a womanly splitting of the self, in the desire to become purged once and for all of our mother's bondage, become individuated and free. The mother stands for the victim in ourselves, the unfree woman, the martyr. Our personalities seem dangerously to blur and overlap with our mothers' ....[3]

Although Plath needed to believe herself an "inaccessible" ... "white flying myth," the narrative progression of her letters indicates that she internalized her mother's experiences, made of them analogues for a mythic dramatization of herself as Horatio Alger's virtuous novice starting humbly and obscurely, moving steadily upward to achieve fortune and fame. Plath's mythologizing of her childhood experiences have their counterparts in her mother's reminiscences of her own early life.

Aurelia recalls that growing up near the sea in a household where her parents spoke German, she often felt isolated from her playmates. A highly intelligent child, she was doubly promoted in school and moved from the first to the third grade, "a great boon for me, for I left behind those who had made such sport of my early mispronunciations." Nonetheless, she was again ostracized during World War One when, because of her German-Austrian backround, the other children called her "spy-face."[4] Aurelia turned to books. She became an avid reader and her fare included "every one of Horatio Alger's stories." She read as if in a dream world. "Fortunately, my mother was most sympathetic and when I was in college read my literature books too, saying cheerily, 'More than one person can get a college education on one tuition.' (I remembered that vividly when my daughter went to Smith and I, through her, broadened my horizons further in modern literature and art)" (*LH*, p. 5).

In high school an "inspirational English teacher" improved

her taste and probably fostered her hopes of some day teaching in a liberal arts college. Her father, however, insisted that she go to business school and her first job was relentlessly dull—"a grim experience I vowed no child of mine would ever have to endure." She managed to persuade him to let her study two additional years at the Boston University College of Practical Arts and Letters so that she could teach English and German at the high school level. Then a secretarial job with an M.I.T. professor, "a true genius in both the arts and the sciences" motivated her to prepare lists of reading material to improve her mind: Greek drama, Russian literature, Hesse, Rilke." "It was the beginning of my dream for the ideal education of the children I hoped someday to have" (*LH*, p. 6).

At Boston University Aurelia Schober met Otto Plath, a scientist who became her instructor in Middle High German. The son of a skilled worker, he had emigrated from Germany and was twenty years older than she. Aurelia got her master's degree; they married. Adhering to his wish that she stop working and become a faculty wife, she typed his dissertation and bore his children in accordance with his schedule.[5] Together they read manuals on infant development and decided that their babies would be "rocked, cuddled, sung to, recited to, and picked up when they cried." "At the end of my first year of marriage, I realized that if I wanted a peaceful home—and I did—I would simply have to become more submissive, *although it was not in my nature to be so*" (*LH*, pp. 12-13, italics, mine).

She subdued her nature throughout Otto Plath's long illness until he died of diabetes milletus. Her stoicism exacted its price: a duodenal ulcer plagued her for years. Sylvia, who was not allowed to attend her father's funeral, felt betrayed.[6] Sylvia's grief and rage were to remain unvoiced for years, as did her perception of what Aurelia's silence probably concealed: *her* rage that Otto, for whom she had denied herself, had left her and his two small children to struggle against economic and emotional penury.

Necessity forced Aurelia to find a teaching job. It paid well but her focus was no longer on self-advancement. Wellesley offered more for her children, so she decided to move there, selling the house in Winthrop by the sea mythologized years later by her poet-daughter. In Wellesley she undertook an innovative, but poorly paid job developing a course in medical secretarial procedures at Boston University: "I vowed that I would make the course interesting, yes fascinating by presenting the stenographic skills as only the first step up the ladder."[7] To step up the ladder entailed her working hard on a tight budget in order to secure the social advantages that living in Wellesley offered her children. Edward Butcher's biography of Plath records that Aurelia sent Sylvia and her brother Warren to "summer camps, scouting, sailing, piano and violin lessons, dance 'assemblies' . . . . She cannot be faulted for neglecting any activity which she felt would emotionally and intellectually enhance the best future prospects of her offspring. They seemed destined to have everything the mother lacked as a child."[8]

Outwardly, they accepted her ambition for them to make good. Aurelia writes:

Throughout her high school years, Sylvia was very uncritical of me. The remark I treasured most and wrote in my journal was made by Sylvia when she was fifteen. "When I am a mother I want to bring up my children just as you have us." (*LH*, p. 37)

Aurelia Schober Plath was no waif passively awaiting a prince to make her dreams come true. Energy and hard work made her, like a Horatio Alger protagonist, pull herself up by the bootstraps, not for self-actualization, but to vindicate through the achievements of her golden children, her own loss of the American Dream. Nevertheless, despite the Alger-like components of her prose style—cliché-ridden, aphoristic, sentimental—she is deeply responsive to language, at times excited by its power enough to affect Sylvia profoundly.[9] Her capitulation to *kitsch*, then, is not the Alger-like stance of a man secure in the aggressive energy that propels *him* up the ladder. It is the defeat of the woman taught by her father and inadvertently, perhaps, by her hausfrau mother to be agreeable at all costs, even though "Grammy" Schober genuinely encouraged Aurelia's intellectual proclivity; it is the renunciation of a woman conditioned by the genteel milieu in which she was raised to conceal her competitive drives, to disguise the underside of her creativity by adopting a rigid perfectionism. Thus, she could only assume the virtuous posture of an Alger hero without availing herself of the unbridled energy that makes of this posture a palatable game.

Sylvia's aggressiveness likewise lay dormant. Her rage self-centered, its manifestation self-punitive, her letters project the persona of a Barbie Doll with brains. Her early letters reveal that the pain surfacing occasionally from the welter of Dale Carnegie declaratives was infused with fear. To her brother she writes:

One thing I hope is that you will make your own breakfasts in the a.m. so mother won't have to lift a finger. That is the main thing that seems to bother her. You know, as I do, and it is a frightening thing, that mother would actually Kill herself for us. She is an abnormally altruistic person, and I have realized lately that we have to fight against her selflessness as we would fight against a deadly disease. (*LH*, p. 112).

Seldom did she fight her mother openly. The narrative flow of the letters reflect the internalization of her mother's concerns. Obsessed with the dollar value of every prize and scholarship she won, like Aurelia she worked at menial part-time and summer job's to supplement the family income. Often fatigued to the point of exhaustion, prone to sinus and flu attacks, occasionally needing surgery, she armed herself with the will to overcome these vicissitudes and, like a Horatio Alger hero, push on. Even her resolve to be more playful is undermined by the uneasy purposefulness she brings to this effort:

I am really regrettably unoriginal, conventional, and puritanical basically, but I needed to practice a certain healthy bohemianism for a while to swing away from the gray-clad, basically dressed, brown-haired, clock regulated, responsible, salad-eating, water-drinking, bed-going, economical, practical girl I had become—and that's why I needed to associate with people who were very different from myself . . . . I know how to have happy gay times when I really want to (*LH*, p. 144).

Letters Home delineates obvious mother-daughter parallels. Somewhat lonely as a child, Sylvia was exceptionally studious. She read and overread the right books and was good about winning prizes for her stories and poems even before she entered Smith. Like Aurelia she appeared overawed by a prestigious campus "resplendant with colors, medals, emblems . . . I can't believe I'm a SMITH GIRL!" (*LH*, p. 46), and about being in the presence of celebrities. Although time modified this freshman euphoria, she was later as overwhelmed about being a Cambridge girl in the presence of David Daiches, John Lehmann and C. P. Snow as she had been studying in the "illustrious" presence of Alfred Kazin during her undergraduate years.

Tailoring her studies to conform to the expectations of successful women patrons such as Olive Higgins Prouty and Mary Ellen Chase obliged Plath to monitor her behavior and inhibit her hostility. For the most part the glossy, superficial poems and stories she wrote as an undergraduate masked an undercurrent of anger that would be revealed in *The Bell Jar*. Occasionally, an awareness that her conformity was depleting her poetic creativity made her pause in her relentless drive to perfect every aspect of her life. For instance, during her instructorship at Smith after her marriage to Ted Hughes, she recoiled from the demands made on her time and energy and even more from the anemic and alienating quality of campus life, fearing that it would mean "death to writing."[10] Despite the prestigious rewards—the Glascock, Cheltenham, Fulbright and Saxon prizes, despite the encouragement of gifted women scholars like Chase and Dorothea Krook at Cambridge, Plath became increasingly aware that writing and having babies tapped a deeper drive to become reborn as a poet. Eventually she gave up the security of teaching to live with Hughes in England.

Ironically, however, this departure from the Alger format also paralleled Aurelia's career. Like her mother, Sylvia had married a foreigner, the son of a Yorkshire working man. Impressed with his physical strength, height, intellectual precocity, she married someone she believed she could serve. Like her mother, she subordinated her own ambition to further Hughes' fame though it was "not her nature to do so."[11] In part through Plath's publishing contacts Hughes' poems were printed in *The Atlantic Monthly* and *Harpers*. After they moved to England she typed revisions of his manuscripts, organized them painstakingly, sent them out unfailingly. Ecstatic when *Hawk in the Rain* was accepted for publication, she wrote:

I am more happy than if it was my book *The Colossus* published! I have worked so closely on these poems of Ted's and typed them so many countless times through revision after revision . . . . I am so happy *his* book is accepted *first*. It will make it so much easier for me when mine is accepted . . . . I can rejoice much more, knowing Ted is ahead of me.[12]

Contrary to her doubt that she "could never be either a complete scholar or a complete housewife or a complete writer," but "must combine a little of all, and thereby be imperfect in all," she kept house efficiently and cooked gourmet meals (*LH*, p. 219).

Like her mother she first bore a daughter, Frieda (whom she shakily described on a transatlantic phone call to Aurelia an hour after the baby was born as "Ein Wunderkind" (*LH*, p. 373); and within two years she bore a son. The Hughes' moved to Devon where Plath alternated intense periods of writing with housework, gardening, beekeeping—combining the domestic rituals of her mother and her grandmother with her father's work with bees.

At this time her letters express a desire for closeness with Aurelia based on their common experiences as mothers who also write. She anticipates her childrens' creativity and wants to provide them with cultural advantages. She asks about recipes and wants all the back issues of *The Ladies Home Journal* (LH, p. 433). She even urges her mother to write, as she herself has done, for the slicks:

> You could do it . . . You might start with someone resembling yourself . . . . What do you think? Make use of the old adage you taught me: "Get your hero/heroine up a tree, fling stones at him/her, then have him extricate himself." People "identify" with people in trouble, people wrestling with problems! Get to it mummy! (*LH*, p. 393).

Reveling in "newsy pink letters from home," hers abound in domestic images: crackling fires, red curtains, rabbit stews, "the daily ration of soup plates of hot oatmeal (something you and Grammy taught me." Even the landscape has become housebound: "the merest dusting of snow on everything, china-blue skies, rosy hilltops, new lambs in the fields" (*LH*, pp. 440-441). Somewhere in this pastoral background, Hughes is affably adjunctive, gardening, helping with the babies.

In allying herself to and identifying with her mother as a purveyor of the *Ladies Home Journal* mystique, Plath probably increased her deep-seated fear of artistic mediocrity personified not only by Aurelia but by her lifelong mentor, Olive Higgins Prouty, whose *Stella Dallas* resonated with the kind of sacrifice Aurelia had made on her daughter's behalf.[13] More than that: Plath's compulsion to get published in slicks from *Mademoiselle* to *Vogue* warred with her apprehension that the "plushy air-conditioned offices" of these journals peopled with stenographers like her mother whose skills she could never master, oppressed women writers. By remote control, men ran those offices eroding women's creative vitality, turning them into consumers. This apprehension had helped foster her earlier suicidal breakdown in

1953.

Mediocrity is linked to a stenographer's life experiences. Of *The Bell Jar* Marjorie Perloff observes: "Typing and shorthand; her mother's domain become the symbols of male oppression: she rejects her mother's practical notion that 'an English major who knew shorthand . . . would be in demand among all the up-and-coming young men and she would transcribe letter after thrilling letter.'"[14] For Plath, mediocrity was that which abstracted the poet from the wellspring of her creativity, which is why she had found her science courses at Smith repellant:

I really am in a state of complete and horrible panic . . . . I can't reconcile the memory and rote with my philosophy of a creative education. Science is to me, useless drudgery for *no purpose*. A vague superficial understanding of molecules and atoms . . . (*LH*, pp. 98-99).

It is not imaginative science she fears, but applied technology, second hand abstraction, formulaic solutions, the world of Otto Plath translated by Aurelia Plath.

The excerpt from *The Bell Jar* quoted above links mediocrity to rote skills, unproductive work, conventional courtship, packaged relationships. And it terrified Plath that even while repudiating *The Ladies Home Journal* "blither about birdies going tweet tweet and happy marriages," even after Hughes had left her, she was still attracted to these conventions (*LH*, p. 473). Her last letters reveal her ambivalence about becoming a successful poet no longer in Hughes' shadow, yet unable to overcome the puritanical rigidity that did not allow her to envision intimacies other than those found in marriage and motherhood. Husbandless, with two young children to support, she ironically recapitulates her mother's former predicament. Helpless, ill, in desperate need of Aurelia's financial and emotional support, she fears its price— the incorporating of her mother's values which made of the failed marriage a failed self:

I am writing with my old fever of 101 alternating with chills back. I must have someone with me for the next two months to mind the babies while I get my health back and try to write . . . I need help very much just now. Home is impossible. I can go nowhere with the children, and I am ill, and it would be psychologically the worst thing to see you now or to go home . . . (*LH*, p. 468).

Letters Home suggests that "with his vast fund of knowledge and understanding: not facts or quotes of second hand knowledge, but an organic, digested comprehension which enhances his every word," Hughes strongly influenced Plath's growing strategies that drew upon the animistic forces "inherent in the world of nature" in her *Ariel* poems (*LH*, p. 256). While there is little overlap between the demonic persona embodied in "Lady Lazarus" and the dutiful daughter sending cheery messages to New England, a tonal shift near the close of her epistolary narrative expresses, perhaps, Aurelia's creative influence on Sylvia's poetic powers:

I shall be one of the few women poets in the world who is a fully rejoicing woman . . . I am a woman and glad of it, and my songs will be of fertility of the earth . . . (*LH*, p. 450).

I think having babies is really the happiest experience of my life . . . . I am enjoying my slender foothold in my study in the morning again . . . the feeling that nothing else but writing and thinking is done there . . . I have the queerest feeling of having been reborn with Frieda—it's as if my real, rich happy life started just about then . . . I hope I shall always be a "young" mother like you . . . (*LH*, p. 450).

Despite Plath's tendency to mimic her mother's ladylike prose, rendering people and landscapes as if she were painting teacups, overusing intensifiers and adjectives, e.g., "beautiful." "nice," "charming," "dear," the excerpts above indicate more than a response to Aurelia's gifts of pewter and copperware. They demonstrate Plath's awe of the engendering powers of language linked to childbirth[15]—her perception that a symbiotic bond existed between biological and literary motherhood during the time when she was writing "at about four in the morning—that still blue, almost eternal hour before the baby's cry, before the glassy music of the milkman, settling his bottles."[16]

Unfortunately, these epistolary fragments fail to shed light on the final explosive poems, that distanced her sufficiently from her mother. Instead, *Letters Home* tells us that while Plath feared the Doppelgänger staring back "from the mercury-backed glass" with "hag hands waiting to haul [her] in,"[17] she was drawn to those hands as she was to the great mother ocean in which she "could swim forever straight into the sea and sun and never be able to swallow more than a gulp or two of the water and swim on" (*LH*, p. 130). This attraction, reenforced when Hughes' abandonment of her recapitulated the death of her father, could not help but make Plath acutely conscious of Aurelia's self-negation. Fearing the risk individuation would impose on her, the poet chose in 1963 the self-extinction she had evaded in 1953 when "only by returning to the womb in the shape of the basement crawl space at her mother's house . . .does she hope to find the 'dark . . . thick as velvet' which is the dark of death."[18]

NOTES

[1.] Sylvia Plath, "Ocean 1212-W," in *The Art of Sylvia Plath: A Symposium*, ed. Charles Newman (Bloomington: Indiana University Press, 1971), p. 272.

[2.] Plath's most savage caricature of Aurelia appears in *The Bell Jar*. Some poems also reflect her hostility. In an analysis of Plath's poems on motherhood, Margaret Uroff observes that in "The Disquieting Muses" the mother's middle-class platitudes cannot protect her daughter from physical and psychological danger. See Margaret Uroff, "Sylvia Plath on Motherhood," in *The Midwest Quarterly*, 15 (October, 1973), p. 73.

[3.] Adrienne Rich, *Of Woman Born: Motherhood as Experience and Institution* (New York: W. W. Norton, 1976), pp. 235-236.

[4.] *Letters Home by Sylvia Plath: Correspondence 1950-1963*, ed. Aurelia Schober Plath (New York: Harper and Row, 1975), pp. 3, 32. All further references will be cited as *LH* and appear in the text.

[5.] Otto Plath planned his son's arrival two and a half years after Sylvia's birth and so it came to pass.

[6.] Aurelia writes: "What I intended as an exercise in courage for the sake of my children was interpreted years later by my daughter as indifference. 'My mother never had time to mourn my father's death.' I . . . remembered a time when I was a little child, seeing my mother weep in my presence and feeling my whole personal world was collapsing. *Mother*, the tower of strength, my one refuge *crying*! It was this recollection that compelled me to withhold my tears until I was alone in bed at night" (*LH*, pp. 25, 28).

[7.] To the projected course outline she also added "a brief history of the evolution of medicine itself as it emerged from witchcraft, superstition and religious practices" (*LH*, p. 29). Sylvia also compiled and added to her reading lists during her terms at Smith and at Cambridge.

[8.] Edward Butscher, *Sylvia Plath, Method and Madness* (New York: The Seabury Press, 1976), p. 21. Butscher's Freudian bias expressed too often in sexist terms tends to contradict the evidence he has amassed from interviews, tapes, and letters that "Sylvia knew with a kind of instinctive wisdom and dread that Mrs. Plath was essential, the great mother-sea without whom she could not survive, but with whom she could never achieve independent sanity" (Butscher, p. 121).

[9.] Reading Arnold's "The Forsaken Merman" aloud to Sylvia, Aurelia inflamed *her* as well: "A spark flew off Arnold and shook me, like a child I wanted to cry; I felt very odd. I had fallen into a new way of being happy." Quoted by Mrs. Plath, *LH*, p. 32.

[10.] Interestingly, the possibility of an instructorship for Plath occured about the time her mother was appointed Associate Professor at Boston University (See *LH*, p. 313).

[11.] Cf. Introduction to *Letters Home*, p. 13.

[12.] Aurelia comments: "From the time Sylvia was a very little girl, she catered to the male of any age so as to bolster his sense of superiority" (*LH*, p. 297).

[13.] The novel deals with a mother who sacrifices her relationship with her daughter in order to secure for her a prestigious marriage to a wealthy man. Plath probably saw thematic parallels in her own mother's life.

[14.] Quoted by Marjorie Perloff in "A Ritual for Being Born Twice," Sylvia Plath's *The Bell Jar*," *Contemporary Literature*, 13 (1972), p. 517.

[15.] Hughes' encouraging Plath to delve deeper into herself renewed her interest in German, the language of her parents.

[16.] Quoted by A. Alvarez in *The Art of Sylvia Plath*, pp. 58, 59.

[17.] Sylvia Plath, "All the Dead Dears," in *The Colossus and Other Poems* (New York: Alfred A. Knopf, 1967), p. 30. Adrienne Rich, writing of Plath's effort to let Aurelia know that "her struggles and sacrifices to rear her daughter had been vindicated," indicates the psychic pain of that osmosis. See *Of Woman Born*, p. 230.

[18.] Marjorie Perloff, "A Ritual For Being Born Twice," *CL*, p. 511.

Steven Weiland

THE MAKING OF A METHOD:
MARGARET MEAD IN HER LETTERS

*The natives say: "Kor e palit"—that is, the place is full of spirits
and it behooves all men to walk warily.*

*Although these are supposed to be primitive Papuans, they have a
fair number of our institutions—the family, the brain, the kiss,
the chain.*

—Letters from the Field

With respect to their poems, novels and plays, the letters of
great creative artists are an important allied from. In writers as
different as Keats and Flannery O'Connor, letters are often a
means of recording reactions to other writers and explaining the
background and intentions of their own work. Though we also read
letters for biographical information, they are primarily interesting for their compact remarks about writing itself. Letters, of
course, vary in style as much as the standard genres. And as Erik
Erikson has noted recently, "correspondence is a form of com-
muncation which varies in intensity and meaning with personality
and culture." One could add, of course, the critical factors, purpose and audience. Letters which have earned the permanent
interest of the literary community reflect, therefore, some of the
same stylistic achievements characteristic of the traditional genres. We read letters for pleasure and instruction but also for their
informality, the opportunity they provide for getting behind the
scenes and closer to the sources of creative expression.

Letters written by social scientists have not generally merited
such critical interest. Freud's are perhaps the best known, especially his letters to his medical colleague Wilhelm Fliess, written as
he was developing some of the early principles of psychoanalysis.
They are valuable evidence of the ways in which Freud converted

his neurobiological background into a new theory of mind and nascent method of therapy. For Margaret Mead, letters provided a similar opportunity in anthropology. She admitted when a selection from her correspondence was published as *Letters from the Field 1925-1975* (1977), that "When I started to write these letters, I had no sense that I was discussing the making of a method." Her letters, she acknowledged freely, were a form of dissipation," relief from the difficulties of fieldwork. The audience for her letters, essentially family and college friends, was a non- professional one and the letters a means, from Mead's point of view, of maintaining some perspective on the uses and importance of anthropology. "One must somehow maintain the delicate balance," she said, "between emphatic participation and self-awareness, on which the whole research process depends." Mead's letters are important chiefly for the insight they provide into the inner life of fieldwork as it was developing as a research technique. In her hands it was artistic as well. The meaning and uses of her letters, therefore, derive from the same frame of mind which informs the Balinese shadow play as Mead herself described it in a 1936 letter: "The Balinese have no sense of a greenroom at all; putting on the make up of dancers, tying the last flowers of a headdress, tuning a musical instrument, putting up decorations, unpacking the puppet box, all are part of the show to be commented on, criticized and enjoyed." So, too, Mead's method, including the fieldwork reported in her letters, is fully revealed to her audience, the record of a mind too vigorous to ignore even the slightest experiences and too honest to deny the strong personal feeling which shape their expression.

The key to Mead's method as an anthropologist as it is revealed in her letters is her insistence on the utility of qualitative data and the importance of the interests and attitudes of the field worker. In a brief comment on "methodology" appended to her first and still best known book, *Coming of Age in Samoa* (1928), she compares her work to medicine and psychoanalysis, their concentration on cases, and inability to prove beyond refutation the truth of their theses. "So the student of the more intangible and psychological aspects of human behavior is forced to illuminate rather than demonstrate a thesis." Further, she admits that "the conclusions (in *Coming of Age in Samoa*) are also all subject to the limitations of the personal equation." It is, however, part of the appeal of Mead's method that this "limitation" becomes in reality a primary virtue. Mead's attitudes toward her discipline and particular areas of research, and her role in the lives of those she studied, became for her important subjects in their own right. Her epistolary style, as it developed as part of her fieldwork, illustrates the inevitablility of "the personal equation" as well as a talent for observation and a taste for form which make her best letters examples of epistolary art in the service of social science.

Mead's first letters, written after she left the United States in the summer of 1925, reveal very little about her actual professional circumstances. A letter written from Pago Pago to Franz Boaz, the founder of anthropology as an academic discipline in the United States and her teacher at Columbia, is properly deferential—it asks for advice and is reassuring about a young and inexperienced woman's ability to survive in the wilds of the South Pacific—but barely suggests the doubts with which Mead undertook her field tasks. "How much checking should you consider it necessary and legitimate for me to do?" she asks after reporting that her early informants were mainly tribal chiefs and apparently "well-informed." That kind of question, and its apparent methodological innocence, confirms the memory of her departure for Samoa that Mead included in her autobiography *Blackberry Winter* (1972): "When I sailed for Samoa, I realized only very vaguely what a commitment to fieldwork and writing about fieldwork meant." Her academic prepration under Boaz was all theoretical and insufficient for the tasks he had assigned to her. "There was, in fact, no *how* in our education. What we learned was *what* to look for. . . . No body really asked what were the young fieldworker's skills and aptitudes—whether he had, for instance, the ability to observe and record accurately or the intellectual discipline to keep at the job, day after day, when there was no one to supervise, no one to compare notes with, to confess delinquencies to, or even to boast to on an especially successful day." It was in her letters that Mead filled some of these gaps in her preparation and adjusted to her new circumstances.

It is no surprise then that the letters from the small island of Tau, where Mead did the fieldwork for *Coming of Age in Samoa* from the fall of 1925 to early spring of the following year, contain the excitement of discovery, and evidence of growing confidence and increasing capability in building an ethological and anthropological method. Pride in her acceptance by the Samoans and rapid sophistication as a fieldworker is not, however, diminished by recognition of the persistent "curiosities" of participant observation.

It was a curious scene there at midnight on the edge of a fretting sea, raining a little, at times a sickly moon, the sand sticky and yielding under foot, tiny chilren escaped from home scurrying here and there, adults with blackened faces in strangely cohesive groups that scattered when anyone approached, shrinking indecisively behind the bordering cocunut palms. I had to skip, an unknown accomplishment in Samoa, to the tune of the deafening tin cans on the pulpy sand, and then of course, there were hundreds of salutations, some respectful and some not, it being New Year's Eve. The cut of my dress betrayed my identity, even at midnight. (1/10/25)

It is curious to see these two (household helpers) and half a dozen other boys, clad only in lavalavas (cloth wraps) with hibiscus behind their ears or a graceful fillet of leaves on their hair, sitting on the floor of my room, tremendously at ease amid its various sophistications. The Santa Claus which is weighted at the bottom so that it always stands upright is their favorite plaything or they musingly turn over pages of a *Dial* or a *Mercury* with an air of detached tolerance. But when one of them discovered a letter of Louise Bogan's about the style of Henry James, all neatly typewritten and legible, he admitted himself stumped. (1/16/25)

Such anomalies are, as Mead of course knew, more than mere curiosities. They are suggestive of the cultural differences her interest in which motivated fieldwork in the first place.

Mead sought in her fieldwork an epistolary style that would accomodate the curiosities, relieve the intellectual and emotional pressures associated with the demanding settings, and convey as much as possible of the total character of the native population and her own relation to it. "Gradually I am becoming part of the community" she reported from Samoa after she had been there several months and her longer letters from the island and subsequent fieldwork locations convey not only the details of this achievement but a certain structure and coherence which make them small essays. They display many of the tools of prose artistry: narrative, figurative language, dramatization, and management of tone and point of view. Even as a schoolgirl Mead wanted to be a writer; she wrote poems and stories through her college years. When she undertook original research as a professional anthropologist she no doubt hoped for an influential place in the scientific community, yet her literary interests required that she develop a style which was not simply part of her fieldwork method but actually represented her unique combination of scientific vigor, imaginative sympathy for foreign cultures, and ambitions as a writer.

A letter from Alitoa, near Mt. Arapesh in New Guinea, for instance, displays these virtues while it provides, together with other letters from this mountain community, an informal ethnographic record supporting the formal findings of *Growing Up in New Guinea* (1930). The letter (4/20/32) begins with the admission that Mead and her husband and co-fieldworker, Reo Fortune, faced a very basic methodological problem indeed: "We have still not decided what to call this mountain people for they have no name for themselves, just friendly little nicknames or names for sections of the community, like man-o-bush or "poisonous snakes!" A remark then on the weather—that classic epistolary gambit—becomes a comment on Arapesh supernaturalism.

The weather has continued glorious, although now that the northwest monsoon is dying there are bad storms which make the thatch stand up like fur on the back of an angry cat and knock down the more superannuated houses of the village. All wind and rain come from supernatural creatures called *walin*, who inflict storms on the entire community whenever unwanted people from another clan invade their domain or when members of the proper clan come and do not speak politely, reminding them of the relationship. . . . These people have made the man-o-bush into the devil, the man who traffics in the temporary angers of his nice neighbors, the professional sorcerer. The ghosts they have localized under the care of the *walin* of each clan and you do not have to encounter them if you go hunting elsewhere and are careful where you get your firewood.

Conscious of the highly charged atmosphere in which the Arapesh live, Mead portrays ordinary village life with some irony.

So in the village you are free to have a good time—to smoke and chew and yawn and hum little songs under your breath and repeat the name of the nicest baby over and over or sing the baby to sleep by reciting the names of your favorite pig—or if you haven't any baby, a puppy or better still a little pig will do. If you are feeling gay, you can put flowers in your hair and red and white paint on your face; or if you like, you can put the paint on the baby or the pig. If you are feeling cross, you put the black paint of war on the forehead of the ten-year-old. If you have a headache, you tie a piece of bark around your head and go and sit in the *place clear* so that everyone will know how miserable you feel. If your mind runs on feasts, you can get out the hand drum and thump it happily all by yourself. If your pig dies, you can fasten a set of spears in a piece of bark and tie a yam to the bundle and set it in front of your wife's doorway, just to show her what you think of the way she looks after the pigs, and then *she* can take a long bright leaf and tie it into a knot and hang it over the door, just to say that she won't cook any more food for the people whose jealous talk made her pig die until they give her something nice for a present. If you have something important to say, you stalk through the village and everybody knows by your shoulders that something is up and trails along to see what it is.

"For all that," Mead acknowledges "life is complicated at times" and in a well-timed dramatic detail she suggests something of her own domestic arrangements, again with some of the irony which is part of her method.

The village is dark, only an occasional flicker of fire shows through the eyelets in the bark walls of the houses. A tense nervous boy appears by the entry to the housecook and stands there staring. We know that he has something important to say and wait. Is the sago bad, or has there been a fight, or has someone run away? He explains: "Gerud would like to work tonight after dinner. Myelahai has lost a big knife and wants Gerud to tell him where it is." Gerud is assistant cook-boy and the only diviner in the village. We assent. Gerud's divining always brings us a fine lot of ethnological detail.

He eats a little bone-scraping from the skull of an ancestor mixed with a little ginger. Then he dashes madly about in the dark, plunging up and down the steep slopes at either end of the village until he unearths a bit of bamboo filled with rubbish, which he can allege is a bit of the physical essence of someone which has been placed in a wild taro root to cause a sore. Then he falls flat on the ground, arms outflung in a crucified position, and answers questions and also makes startling remarks about usually unmentionable things and throws in a few dark hints about future disasters.

Gerud's divining turns out to be, in this instance at least, harmless, so Mead turns to the difficulties of maintaining a satisfactory food supply and then to the problems of storing a growing collection of Arapesh ceremonial artifacts. "While they are being carried," Mead notes, "I hid in a native house with a woman who spent her time showing me an abortive drug and commenting sharply that men could not see the drug, that they could not even hear the name of it. Thus feminine self-esteem was avenged."

Mead's laconic and rather surprising judgment at midpoint in this representative letter is "And so it goes." She adds: "A mad world where little bits of taro and little bits of yam are each bought separately for a separately served spoonful of beads or matches, where every misfortune is magically determined and where one sits ready to pounce on the significance of a plate of croquettes being carried by the door." Her detachment, even bemusement, is balance, however, by the letter's closing sections which reaffirm the centrality of taboos and sorcery in Arapesh culture. Gender separation, as is evident from the above, is the most common theme. It is rendered in this passage in the kind of detail and tone Mead reserved for her letters.

Then there was the night last week when Amito'a and I dyed skirts. This is one of the occasions when the women get back at the men. No men or children can come near, no smell of meat cooking, no knife which has touched meat, no feather headdresses can come near. The very sound of men's voices will spoil the dye, just as the sound of women's voices will anger the Tambaran and as the touch of a woman's hand may spoil hunting gear. We squatted in a windswept little leaf shelter and watched the great pot, its top covered with pads of big green leaves, boil over with a bubbling fluid which gradually turned blood red. And once some boys talked, and the skein of sago threads which was being put into the pot caught fire. And Amito'a's husband stayed with Reo until midnight and just to reassert his masculine superiority told Reo all about the nice brain soup which the warriors used to drink, brewed from the scooped-out brains of the enemy, although up to now they had been denying any touch of cannibalism. So Baimal danced about the room, illustrating the savage delight of war, for Baimal is always light and airy even when his talk is of death. And Amito'a and her sister-in-law, Ilautoa, squatted by the watched pot and said: "We feed pigs, we make grass skirts, we dance, two by two we go for firewood, two by two we bring up water, two by two we dye our grass skirts." The wind howled and ruffled the thatch, and I enjoyed it in spite of the smoke in my eyes.

And after noting Reo's determination to pursue his data on language whatever the obstacles—he even spoils some of Mead's own research based on doll play to check a small point of pronunciation —Mead closes this letter with a quick glance at the outside world. "Our knowledge of it is fragmentary," she says, and copies of American magazines are "manna in the wilderness." There is a final dramatized comment about the relationship of ethnology to its informants and the relative merits of anthropological research and native wisdom.

On the veranda Reo is doing legend texts and the old men passing by ask: "What are you doing?" "Legends." "Child's play," they snort and pass by. Legends are only for children, you tell them to your children and then heave a sigh of relief and forget the nonsense so that you are free to concentrate on important things like charms, which are just (as it were)

"Tweedledum and Tweedledee, Rumptydum and Rumpty-dee," male and female. Of one thing these people are very sure and that is "Male and female created he them." But at that, even those who are sophisticated about white people sometimes slip up in talking to me.

Reo, to be sure, produced authoritative accounts of Arapesh language and custom but Mead's triumph, as is often revealed in her letters as well as in her books and essays, is what might be called her methodological equilibrium. She recognized from the beginning of her career that the relation of subject to object, researcher to researched is fluid and imprecise, requiring, in addition to descriptive and analytic rigor, the use of stylistic devices more characteristic of art than science. The artistry of Mead's letters is in her careful integration of setting, incident, and judgment with sufficient variety in diction, syntax, and tone to establish a genuine epistolary voice.

The best letters include a mix of devices and intentions but even those which are less complete and ambitious contain pointed psychological and cultural and colorful passages of description. In a letter accounting for some of the "transparent social processes" among New Guineans, she offered with her own bracketed glosses an incisive cross cultural analysis of incest taboos. "The saying goes: 'Other women, other pigs, other yams, you can eat. [This is literal.] Your own sister, your own mother, your own pigs, your own yams which you have piled up [indicating a surplus], these you cannot eat.' Seen in this light, incest prohibitions can be understood not as some obscure psychological process in the mind of the individual, but as necessary to social cooperation in societies which operate at the kinship level of integration." (8/ 10/32) And Mead also included in her letters, as she did only occasionally in her scholarship, elegant descriptions of scenes of great natural beauty.

The lake to which we came, through a *baret*, was all black, polished like a mirror, with faraway mountains ringing it all about and on its shining surface floated pink and white lotuses, lying in patches of thousands, their pads still and fixed on the black water, while among them stood, as if posed for a portrait, white ospreys and blue herons. It is all as ordered, as simple in its few contrasting themes, as a Japanese print, and the lack of miscellaneous, only half-congruent notes makes it seem unreal. It was before sunrise when we slid into the center of the lake and the black irregular arms of water stretched away among further and further patches of lotuses, seeming almost to meet the mountains, and there was no human thing there except ourselves. It is the best this country has to offer and very, very good. (2/1/33)

Like Darwin and Thoreau, Mead often depended on such scenic pleasure to fortify her analytic interests.

In her later letters, especially those following WWII when she had the opportunity to look back at the development of her method, Mead recognized that her younger contemporaries faced critical artistic dilemmas which reflected the complexity of modern anthropological methods.

Writing from New Guinea again in 1965, she offers a compact explanation of the relation of the scientific imagination—those resources for hypotheses building and the reporting of experimental results—to the data on which it must ultimately depend.

Today we give the fieldworker a whole battery of methods, techniques, tools and theories from which to choose—more than anyone can use, just as the vivid, ongoing life of a people is more than anyone can possibly cover in the same detail, with the same vigilance, with the same attention. So the fieldworker must choose, shape, prune, discard this and collect finer detail on that, much as a novelist works who finds some minor character is threatening to swallow up the major theme or that the hero is fast taking him out of his depth. But unlike the novelist . . . the fieldworker is wholly and helplessly dependent on what happens—on the births, deaths, marriages, quarrels, entanglements and reconciliations, depressions and elations of the one small community. . . . One must be continually prepared for anything, everything and—perhaps most devasting—for nothing.

According to Mead, good fieldworkers inevitably find themselves in the artistic situation, dependent finally on intensely creative resources to reveal the meaning of facts as artists do of images and imagined events. For "there are rewards for the individual who likes to work alone, just one mind required to take in a culture that has been hundreds, perhaps thousands of years in the making. . . . All the skills he can employ as a scientist and all the skills he can draw on as an artist are needed here, and he is accountable to no one except to the actuality before him." While the anthropologist is one in a "series of minds" who have come before and will come after, he is also, Mead insists, part of the "orchestral realization" of the themes of scientific fieldwork expressed in artistically satisfying ways.

Deborah J. Robbins

WHATEVER HAPPENED TO REALISM:
JOHN BARTH'S *LETTERS*

*Man is that alien presence with whom the forces of egoism must
come to terms, through whom the ego is crucified and resurrected,
and in whose image society is to be reformed.*

Joseph Campbell—*The Hero With a
Thousand Faces*

John Barth's *Letters* is his most ambitious, possibly his best,
novel to date. In spite of his use of one of the novel's earliest and
most restrictive forms, the resurrection of characters from earlier
works and the almost overwhelming mass of material, *Letters*
makes strange and delightful reading. Barth plays with the traditions of the epistolary novel (as well as what we think of as those
of the realistic novel) without ever losing control of the form or
indulging in those weaknesses which led to its fall from popularity. The characters are strong and varied, the episodes fascinating
and realistically believable (in typical Barthian fashion) and the
thematic concerns serious enough to satisfy even the crankiest of
readers. *Letters* may not revive the epistolary novel as a viable
form, but there's absolutely no reason why it should.

As a form, the novel-in-letters was one of the early steps toward
realism in fiction, but its basic strengths became flaws as realistic
technique broadened and developed beyond gimmickry. In contemporary fiction the letter has most often made its appearance
as a fictive element, or device, rather than as a controlling or
shaping form. Its use as a form has been most effective in poetry,
where its strong, exclusively first person narrative and episodic,
often meditative, presentation can be desirable qualities without
recalling an awkward, often embarrassing, tradition of sentimentality. In poetry the letter-as-form has been one method for eliminating some of the same excesses which characterized it in fiction.

One of the basic strengths of epistolary form is its effectiveness as a realistic method of indirect, non-descriptive character development. In only first person narrative the speaker moves, uninterrupted, through whatever sequence of events he or she has chosen to reveal—editing, commenting and reflecting upon the material as the narrative progresses. The narrator, as character speaking, has complete control over the presentation (unless the author makes the mistake of injecting extraneous comment or information) and unconsciously reveals his/her own character in the process. First person narrative in letter form has the added complications of its *written* presentation (as opposed to speech or thought) and its mode of address. The narrative is both considered and slanted. The narrator, because he/she writes, deals most dramatically with events which have been completed and become part of the larger sequence of episodes which will comprise the whole of the novel. The letter writer has time, writing after the fact, to choose and compose an effective description of the event. While this does provide an "I was there" realistic basis for the narration, the fact of the narrator's survival to tell whatever happened, at leisure, erodes any atmosphere of suspense which may have been building. Because the letter writer addresses someone *in particular*, in contrast to journal and stream-of-consciousness formats where the character speaks to him or herself, or to no one, the narrative also filters through whatever relationship the writer and addressee have developed. This relationship will obviously affect which events are selected for the telling, how the letter writer presents the material and the reactions he/she passes along to the addressee. The reader's conclusion will be directed by those of the letter writer.

The reader of the novel-in-letters must maintain at least three separate perspectives at any given moment—the letter writer's, that of the character addressed and his or her own—in order to evaluate what the author is, or isn't, accomplishing in terms of the novel's progress. The narrator's version of events is always open to interpretation on several scores. Character must be continually reevaluated in relation to the specific letter being presented, the character addressed, and its position in the novel as a whole. Motives are always questionable.

This letter writing character developed serious problems, many arising from the reading habits of the public as the form developed. The epistolary novel most often detailed a romantic involvement or functioned as a type of travel journal for assorted purposes (i.e. relation of strange adventures, sights, reinforcement of social opinions, the display of a certain character-type, etc.). Romantic involvements were by far the most common, and the form became known for its sentimentality, seduction scenes, happy (if dull and protracted) endings and non-endings and melodramatic predictability. The form became identified more often with the Gothic tradition and its excesses than with the realistic, serious mainstream whose readers grew more sophisticated and critical of technique. The first person narrator could easily become so ego-bound as to be completely uninteresting or silly. Events could be so slanted or over-described that they were boring at best—a catalog of furnishings, cast list and stage directions with running commentary. Plot could be reduced to an endless gush of description and interpretation, totally lacking in suspense or narrative thrust. Instead of a continuous rise to a specific climax, the plot often represented a series of neap and ebb tides, as the narrator described the scenes and their consequences, with no concern for anything but their personal implications.

Part of this problem can be traced to the time, and timing, of the presentation. Any novel-in-letters deals with three separate time references—the narrator's past, in which the events took place, the narrator's present, in which the letter itself is written and the events described, and the narrator's future, in which the addressee reads the letter and reacts to it, along with the reader, and often in the light of information the letter writer did not possess. These overlapping time frames can be valuable as the characters interact to accomplish the novel's resolution, but the reader can't help but become aware of the maneuvering involved. There can be no disputing the dramatic problems involved in a novel in which all real action takes place in the past and is described and reflected upon at relative leisure. While gimmicks can be utilized to combat this effect (posthumous letters, unfinished letters, letters never mailed, forgeries), such are recognizable as tricks, plot devices, and are only useful within realistic boundaries a limited number of times.

As a form, the epistolary novel lost popularity because its operations became painfully, ludicrously obvious and artificial. Its strengths could be utilized to better advantage without accepting the crippling problems inherent in the form. Mechanical devices, architecture of this type, had no place in the realistic novel.

Or so it seemed. The obvious question, since John Barth has now written a novel in letters, is whether or not he has succeeded in accomplishing something which probably has not been done since the 1700's—that is, make it work.

According to the title page, *Letters* is "An Old Time Epistolary Novel by Several Fictitious Drolls and Dreamers Each of Which Imagines Himself Actual." The reader had best keep this statement in mind. The world of this novel is, at least in large part, a literary one. In this context, Barth's revival of his own past creations is more than justified, where it could otherwise be merely self-indulgent. What writer doesn't want another try at their old creations? The world system of *Letters* partakes of "real" history as the reader might recognize it as a part of his/her own experience (the late 1960's and assorted earlier eras), Barth's own literary universe, with which a reader may or may not be familiar, and a literary/mythical universe which the reader may or may not share. The reader has the option of doing research to fill in the blank spaces where experience and prior knowledge do not overlap. While this may make the reading more rich, it isn't absolutely necessary. As the Author-character makes clear, when he discusses time and reading as opposed to writing, nothing (or everything) *may* be taken for granted, but it is risky to do so. Barth acknowledges that the reader's time frame is not fixed. Since the reader's experience is always a variable, one which can't really be controlled or taken accurately into account, Barth allows himself all of time and space and imagination as his proper range of experience for literary purposes. There is no reason why he shouldn't. The reader is not allowed to forget for any length of time that this is a novel and these are characters. Realism can only go so far.

Though the individual letters which comprise the novel are not necessarily what a reader might expect to find in the mailbox, Barth is consistent in terms of format and character throughout. The letters are presented in seven blocks, according to the month in which they were written. Each block contains letters written by seven letter-writers, who always "speak" in the same order—Lady Amherst, Todd Andrews, Jacob Horner, A. B. Cook (either the fourth or the sixth), Jerome Bray, Ambrose Mensch and the Author (not necessarily to be construed as Mr. Barth, though there may be similarities). The Author discusses a projected work, describing the characters as "seven correspondents; one from each of my previous books (or their present-day descendants or counterparts, in the case of the fabulous works), plus one invented specifically for *this* work, plus—I blush to report, it goes so contrary to my literary principles—the Author, who had better be telling stories than chattering about them." (The Author to A. B. Cook IV, p. 431.) The Author discusses his projected novel with most of the other correspondents as the novel progresses, asks them to participate as characters in it (then uses them whether they consent or not, incidentally) and to contribute their own ideas to its development. In fact, Ambrose Mensch, in his last letter, almost the final letter presented, suggests exactly the structuring used for *Letters*, complete with a cryptic diagram in seven parts. The reader has already seen this model without calendar overlay on the title page, was referred to it in the Author's letter to "To Whom It May Concern" in the first section and one block at a time at the beginning of each section. The diagram gives the reader the order of the letters, their authors and calendar dates within each month, at a glance. So, the letters are organized according to the month in which they were written (though not necessarily the year), and then chronologically within the month according to who wrote them. Simple. It's a completely arbitrary and mechanical arrangement, but it organizes things. The Author says, "Their several narratives will become one; like waves of a rising tide, the plot will surge forward, recede, surge farther forward, recede less far, et cetera to its climax and denouement" (p. 40). All as it should be. Each of the letter writers has, by this time, been introduced, or re-introduced if the reader is familiar with their past "lives," their voices established, their separate narratives begun. And a lovelier group of eccentrics could scarcely be gathered, outside of one's own acquaintence.

The reader first meets Germaine Pitt, Lady Amherst. She and Ambrose Mensch will represent the more traditional romantic involvement. She writes, quite intimately, to the Author, whom she has never met or even spoken with directly. She is that one character created specifically for this novel, and incidentally its heroine. She does have some connection with characters present in previous books—Joe Morgan, the cuckholded husband in *The End of the Road*, hires her to teach at Marshyhope State University where she meets Ambrose. Todd Andrews, the next writer, addresses his dead father almost exclusively, in a continuation or echoing of his actions and concerns in *The Floating Opera*. Jacob

Horner, the sometime-immobilized narrator of *The End of the Road*, writes letters to himself. His involvement with Marsha Blank (Ambrose's ex-wife) provides part of the non-traditional romantic balance. A. B. Cook, IV and VI, are both descendants of the hero of *The Sotweed Factor* (both Ebenezer Cooke and and Henry Burlingame, take your choice), and fancy themselves masters of "the Game of History." They address themselves, for the most part to their own offspring, in the hopes that past generational rebellions can be averted for the good of their cause, their Second Revolution. Jerome Bray is a real oddity, seen by some of the novel's inhabitants as other than human. He writes his letters via a computer of his own devising, named LILY-VAC. LILYVAC also edits. He is a descendant of Harold Bray, the false Grand Tutor of *Giles Goat-Boy*, and also figures in *Chimera*, as do others among the *Letters* cast, in a strange hypothetical sense—as verbal incarnations of the shape-changer Poleidus, in his document phase. Ambrose Mensch, of *Lost in the Funhouse*, is still addressing letters to Yours Truly and mailing them in bottles dropped into various bodies of water. The Author corresponds with all and sundry, including the reader.

Obviously Barth has evaded the problem of address, or relationship between letter writer and addressee. With these characters, the addressee is non-existing, non-participating in the novel's main events, has almost no relationship at all to the letter writer, or *is* the letter writer. So much for slanted or filtered narratives which might impede the novel's progress. For the most part, the correspondents here are writing for the sake of recording, reporting or reflecting upon their experience. They have little or no hope that what they write can influence the outcome of the sequence of events they describe.

The characters do believe themselves actual; there's no point if they don't believe in themselves. They are also aware of their literary lives as part of the Author's body of work, and comment or complain of their treatment therein. They have been misrepresented or maligned, their ideas have been stolen or perverted, or they couldn't care less. The reader is made aware that the characters have originated elsewhere, but that it is of minimal importance to the events described here. The reader need not be familiar with these past lives because they were fictional, inaccurate. The letter writers say so, and they should know, since they are the original models. The "characters" have moved beyond past literary concerns and their present lives and futures are what is important to them.

In terms of the plot the letter writers are all gathered together in the performance of two artistic endeavors. One, which provides the backdrop and occasion for much of the action, is the filming by an almost totally non-verbal, even anti-verbal, character named Reg Prinz of one, or all, of the Author's works—he hasn't read them. The other gathering of characters is the totally verbal construct, entitled *Letters*. These two "events" provide the only active connections between all of the characters, other than their geographic proximity. Few of the letters, other than those written for business purposes (e.g. Germaine's initial letter inviting the Author to accept an honorary doctorate at Marshyhope State University) ever play any part in the development or resolution of the plot. They exist, as documents, a part of history. In this sense they truly are several narratives which become one, and serve no other purpose.

By eliminating address of the letters as a problem, Barth allows his letter writers to be as free and open, as cranky and idiosyncratic with their narration as they wish. Another problem with the intimate first person voice of the epistolary novel has been its tendency toward ego-centricity and self-indulgence on the part of the characters. Barth has actually eliminated the difficulty by indulging it. These characters are not overly sentimental types. When they wax self-indulgent some of the most interesting ideas pop up, and readers familiar with Barth's other work will recognize them. They discuss history, revolution, re-enactment and the cyclical or non-cyclical nature of life, heroism, their own lives and deaths. They are strong-thinking individuals, whether or not they are able to find anyone in agreement with their particular positions on the issues. As they present themselves, as they act out their parts in the events described—playing various roles as the situation demands, they achieve an equilibrium as characters, a balance which gives the novel depth and breadth.

As mentioned earlier, the Ambrose Mensch/Germaine Pitt and Jacob Horner/Marsha Blank love affairs contrast each other, and the tradition of the novel in letters. Ambrose and Germaine, rather than acting as if their relationship were the only one ever, re-enact his earlier love affairs, with the added difference that Germaine plays all the major women's roles. Ambrose feels doomed to re-cycle through his life, seeking some resolution and never finding it. Germaine finds herself most often in Todd Andews' "left-hand column, doing everything for the first time." They do, through the course of the novel and as related by Germaine to the Author, manage to work things out or through to some resolution. Whether this is the start of another cycle or a release to begin something totally other is a matter for conjecture, but this goes beyond the bounds of the novel. Jacob Horner and Marsha Blank (a.k.a. Pocahontas) are both residents of the Remobilization Farm. They come together as a result of a strange re-enactment of the events of *The End of the Road* at the demand of Joe Morgan, who also insists that Horner produce his wife Rennie, alive rather than tragically dead, at the completion of the series of scenes. Odd, but people do come together for strange reasons, and by the end of the novel these two are as likely candidates for success and some measure of happiness as any others. Two love affairs, two resolutions, two new beginnings presented in the Romantic tradition. Sort of.

Todd Andrews and Joe Morgan are also involved in the re-enactment of their lives' earlier halves. Andrews draws up charts, observes correspondences between events in his life, as if he could be objective about the whole thing. He expects the darker portions of his history will certainly recur, only hopes that the happier moments will do the same. He is a surprising gentleman, wonderfully human and involved in life. Joe Morgan, on the other hand, is not a nice man, though he is a sad one. He forces others to take part in the repetition of his life's major cataclysm—the death of his wife. His focus is unhealthy, malicious, destructive. He is certainly doomed, and our main concern is how many of the others he will drag down with him. This pair of characters represent rational and irrational perspectives on one's own life and those events which make people what they are and shape their interactions with others.

Another of *Letters* major themes, as opposed to re-enactment, is revolution. Two of the "speaking" characters concern themselves almost exclusively with this idea, though other concerns creep into their discussions. Both A. B. Cook IV and his descendant A. B. Cook VI present their family's struggle to achieve what they call the Second Revolution. If you can't discern what, exactly, they mean by this, you're not alone. Over the course of the family history they describe involvements in everything from the writing of the Star Spangled Banner to Benedict Arnold's attempted surrender of Annapolis to the British to the rescue of Napoleon from Elba to . . . it never ends, and probably never will. Family duplicity is legendary, particularly within the family. No one knows what, or who to believe. Documents may be forged and have been, people lie or tell the truth for motives all their own. These two concern themselves mainly with relating the family history for the express purpose of convincing their offspring that they are sincere. They wish to further the Second Revolution by discouraging their children from setting back the great work in futile personal rebellions. How is the Second Revolution ever to be accomplished if each generation insists on recreating the first, that of the child against the parent? Jerome Bray is also concerned with the success of a Second American Revolution. His revolution is to be accomplished in some mystic fashion with the completion of his computer project—a revolutionary novel composed by LILYVAC. This novel, "as the 1st genuinely scientific model of the genre . . . will of necessity contain *nothing original whatever*, but be the quintessence, the absolute type, as it were the Platonic Form expressed." Bray's revolution also involves, presumably, the creation of a new race, via some sort of insemination of selected females, by himself or LILYVAC. Here is an echo of *Giles Goat-Boy* and related identity and parental mix-ups. Bray addresses, at times, his ancestors. Since he is an orphan, they cannot help him. Cook addresses his child, but past patterns would indicate that they will not cooperate. Both characters are a lot of fun, with their plots and counterplots, their mysterious revolutions, their downright craziness. The ideas they discuss are obviously not so light, but they provide the novel with a unique sense of history, as well as a rather personalized and open-ended view of the world itself.

If the artist's proper concern, at least in part, is art—and consequently, reality—*Letters* is filled with discussion of the subject. All of its characters participate in the filming of the Author's books, with the exception of the Author. This is a strange filming, since its prime mover, one Reg Prinz, believes the written word to be *so* dead that he has refused to either read the books or use a script prepared from them. Prinz, totally wrapped up in his non-verbal and sometimes non-art stance, is naturally a non-speaking character. He writes no letters, and in fact scarcely opens his mouth. He and Ambrose Mensch, who is a writer, carry on a running battle— some of which deals with the proper nature of art, some of which deals with more mundane issues such as their competition for the same woman. The Author makes little or no comment on this whole process. He merely sits back, collects letters and presents them for the reader's viewing. He does ask for advice, contributions to his novel-in-progress, at times tells the other characters that their participation is no longer necessary or desirable, then includes them anyway, as the reader may witness since he or she has the novel in hand. Several aspects of the question of art's proper position, purpose and method are presented. Nothing is decided, as, of course, it never will be. Reg Prinz represents the non-verbal, the Author and Ambrose Mensch represent, for the most part, the verbal (though Ambrose toys with the Prinz position and finds it attractive at times—he is an experimenting writer) and Jerome Bray with his Revolutionary Novel (RN, finally *Numbers*) comes up with something that would seem totally alien to the discussion. These are, after all, verbal constructs, characters in *Letters*. They need reach no ultimate, and perfect solutions. No one else ever has.

Discussions of character, theme, plot all lead back to the original questions. Why a novel-in-letters and does it work? Formally, it does work. It is consistent with the form as established. The voices are clear and distinct. The events progress and converge at some point (whether the reader finds these resolutions satisfactory or not). As an *epistolary* novel it is a step forward, though a very individualized one, not to be duplicated or copied to any effect. Its themes are "serious" and well displayed.

The obvious difficulty in writing realistically is reality, which may be slippery, dull, even unbelievable. There are as many opinions on its nature as there are voices to speak. Is the realistic novel dead? Can it be revived? All a matter of opinion.

Sam Hamill

EPISTOLARY POETRY
The Poem as Letter; the Letter as Poem

Several years ago in Missoula, at the customary after-the-reading bash, I was approached by a young grad school poet.

"I didn't realize that you were a former student of Richard Hugo's," he said.

"I'm not."

"But you write letter poems," he declared, "and that's an invention of Dick's."

With all the specializing and pigeon-holing done by scholars, it has always astonished me that no one (to my knowledge) has written on epistolary poetry as a genre. The poem as letter has been with us for nearly as long as we have had written poetry. In the Western tradition, the honor of inventing the genre is generally bestowed upon Quintus Horatius Flaccus, a Latin poet who preceded Hugo by roughly two thousand years. And ever since Horace, the letter poem has been prominently evident, especially during the 17th and 18th Centuries when English poets were much taken with imitations of the Horatian epistle. In 1804, Wordsworth wrote "To a Young Lady Who Had Been Reproached for Taking Long Walks in the Country;"

> Dear Child of Nature, let them rail!
> —There is a nest in a green dale,
> A harbour and a hold;
> Where thou, a Wife and Friend, shalt see
> Thy own heart-stirring days, and be
> A light to you and old.
>
> There, healthy as a shepherd boy,
> And treading among flowers of joy
> Which at no season fade,
> Thou, while thy babes around thee cling,

Shalt show us how divine a thing
A Woman may be made.

Thy thoughts and feelings shall not die,
Nor leave thee, when grey hairs are nigh,
A melancholy slave;
But an old age serene and bright,
And lovely as a Lapland night,
Shall lead thee to thy grave.

A thousand years before Wordsworth, the great masters of T'ang poetry, Li Po and Tu Fu, were writing copiously in the same genre. Pound has translated Li Po's "The River Merchant's Wife: A Letter," and "Exile's Letter." Shigeyoshi Obata translated "Addressed Humorously to Tu Fu" with the following footnote: "In contrast with Li Po, who depended largely on inspiration, Tu Fu was a painstaking artist careful of the minutest details." The poem is a marvelous example of just why the genre is so universally appealing:

Here! is this you on the top of Fan-ko Mountain,
Wearing a huge hat in the noon-day sun?
How thin, how wretchedly thin, you have grown!
You must have been suffering from poetry again.

Much of the charm of the letter poem lies in its "inside" information. Without Obata's footnote, we could not possibly gain the insight into the difference between these two poets and their respective approach to craft, and yet even without the footnote, there is a certain appeal, even at a single reading. The poem as letter allows a privacy of speech, and a certain confidentiality of tone that other genres tend to repell. Epistolary poetry may be said to be the first expression of the "confessional school" since its tendency is to include and/or refer to autobiographical and biographical detail not generally known to the public. However, in order to establish a certain degree of accessability in the poem, these details must reveal their own significance somehow without the context of the poem. Obata's footnote is unnecessary.

Many years later, Tu Fu would write a letter poem "To Li Po on a Spring Day:"

Po, the poet unrivaled,
In fancy's realm you soar along.

> Yours is the delicacy of Yui,
> And Poa's rare virility.
> Now on the north of the Wei River
> I see the trees under the vernal sky
> While you wander beneath the sunset clouds
> Far down in Chiang-tung.
> When shall we by a cask of wine once more
> Argue minutely on versification?

While the reader need not know that Yui Hsin and Pao Chao were probably as well known during the early T'ang as were Li Po and his correspondent, it requires little imagination on the part of the reader to sort out the details. Similarly, the last line requires no explication nor exegesis.

East or West, the letter poem is a fundamental concern. Shelley's wonderful longish "Letter to Maria Gisborne," all the Romantic poems beginning with "To . . . ," these form the tradition of the genre on which all the modern and contemporary poets draw. In the Eastern tradition, there is so much epistolary poetry that it seems silly to mention a few of better-known: Li Ch'ing-chao, Po Chü-i (see Waley's Po Chü-i's "The Letter," Ch'in Chia's "To His Wife" and "Ch'in Chia's Wife's Reply") and others.

Whether we prefer to trace the origins of the letter poem back to Horace, or whether we take it back beyond him to some anonymous poet of the *Shih Ching* (assembled roughly 600 B.C.), we shall soon see that it has become a mainstay since the advent of Modernism.

Although there is nothing in the title to designate it as such, William Carlos Williams wrote one of the Modern epistolary classics, "Asphodel, That Greeny Flower:"

> Of asphodel, that greeny flower,
>
>   like a buttercup
>   upon its branching stem—
> save that it's green and wooden—
>
>   I come, my sweet,
>   to sing to you.
>
> . . .

This poem, with its personal, confidential tone, its private revery, and its declarative structure make it, undeniably, a poem directly out of the epistolary genre. Williams wrote many such poems, although he did not bother with the formality of calling them "letter poems" in his titles.

Nor has the letter poem in its Modernist application been a pure product of America; nor, for that matter, of the English-speaking world. While his finest translators, Edmund Keeley and Philip Sherrard, note his preeminent "Greekness," George Seferis was at times fond of taking events that might seem, superficially at least, to be only of local and passing significance, and of transforming such events into a kind of universal understanding. This kind of poem is very much epistolary, drawing on the confidential tradition. Seferis spoke, Keeley and Sherrard remark, of the "Waste Land feeling," and a great many, most, of his poems draw on Greek custom and history, place-names and events. But in poems such as "Letter of Mathios Paskalis," and "Last Stop," and especially "An Old Man on the River Bank," Seferis becomes an epistolary poet of the first order, working within a well-developed, well-defined genre.

Likewise, we have Octavio Paz writing a "Carta a León Felipe" in a private and calm voice that refers to philosophy, literature, and politics, that calls back a letter of Felipe's, bringing in more and more as it turns through its syntactic labyrinths. And Borges, of course, writes across the centuries "To a Saxon Poet:"

> The snowfalls of Northumbria have known
> And have forgotten the imprint of your feet,
> And numberless are the suns that now have set
> Between your time and mine, my ghostly kinsman . . .

as though the dead poet might receive his mail as promptly as the living. Borges, Seferis, and the others invite us into their studies as they write. We read their mail before it's sent.

It is not in the least surprising that so many poets find the confidential style of the epistle attractive. Whether it is written in English iambic pentameter or in the classical literary Mandarin of the T'ang (usually in a five-character line), or whether, with the contemporary hand, it is composed in organic form, the letter poem rhymes across the centuries; it permits an intimacy which no other genre admits; it is almost always "occasional" in the best sense. From Allen Tate ("To a Romantic") writing to Robert Penn Warren, from Yvor Winters writing "To Emily Dickinson," poets of conservative literary persuasion, to the slightly less formal Lowell of *Life Studies* ("To Delmore Schwartz") and Elizabeth Bishop's "Invitation to Marianne Moore" ("but please/ please come flying," the poet begs), and "letter to N.Y." in which she says, "In your next letter I wish you'd say/where you are going and what you are doing;/how are the plays, and after the plays/ what other pleasures you're pursuing:/ . . ." the letter allows us to enter the poem in the *midst*, most often, of its occasion.

Sometimes the letter poem arrives inside a larger format, as with Robert Penn Warren's "The Letter About Money, Love, or Other Comfort, if Any," which serves as the second section of the longer "Garland for You." Likewise, in the fourth of ten sections in *The Book of Nightmares*, Galway Kinnell continues a previously established epistolary tone with "Dear Stranger Extant in Memory by the Blue Juniata." In the second movement of this section, he carries the letter poem another step by including a letter addressed "Dear Galway," and concluding with, "Yours, faithless to this life, Virginia."

Continuing to explore letter poems in organic forms, we find John Logan's "Letter to a Young Father in Exile," his "Lines to His Son on Reaching Adolescence," and even "Heart to Heart Talk with My Liver," each of these falling clearly into the epistolary tradition. Other poets have freely modified the tradition to include the "postcard" poem, a brief letter, such as Denise Levertov's "Postcard" in *Life in the Forest*; she is also author of "Letter" (from the same book), in which she says, ". . .And I in my house/of smaller plants, many books, colored rugs,/my typewriter silent,/have been searching out for you. . . ."

Levertov is working well within the genre, using, marrying, the discriptive and the declarative, allowing a smooth discursive element into the informal appearance or realization of the poem. William Stafford does the same kind of thing in "A Poet to a Novelist," and then returns to the simpler "Letter from Oregon," addressing his mother directly:

> "Mother, even home was doubtful;
> many slip into the sea and are gone for years,
> just as I boarded the six-fifteen there.
> Over the bar I have leaped outward.
> . . .

There seems to be hardly a contemporary poet who does not make use of the epistolary tradition, whether s/he grounds the poem with the moniker "Letter" or not. The style and tone declare the genre as certainly as fourteen lines of rhymed, five-syllable-stresses declares itself a "form."

I shall close these comments with a few words of reference to certain epistolary poems of recent years that seem to me high points, not only of a genre, but of poetry in our time in general. Among "younger" poets, I recommend Robert Hass's rhythmical tour-de-force, "Not Going to New York: A Letter:"

> Dear Dan—
>   This is a letter of apology, unrhymed.
> Rhyme belongs to the dazzling couplets of arrival.
> Survival is the art around here. It rhymes by accident
> with the rhythm of days which arrive like crows in a field
> of stubble corn in upstate New York in February.
>   . . .

Hass has the ability to carry four pages of discursive, intuitive poem by ear alone. It is a fine poem that expands the epistolary genre, reinvigorates it, and very nearly redefines it in strong narrow terms.

But there remain two absolute masters of the epistolary poem in our time. The younger, Thomas McGrath, has totally re-visioned all epistolary writing in poetry that I know of—and he's done it by adapting the genre as a form for his long poem, *Letter to an Imaginary Friend*:

> —"From here it is necessary to ship all bodies east."
> I am in Los Angeles, at 2714 Marsh Street,
> Writing, rolling east with the earth, drifting toward Scorpio,
>   thinking, . . .

and so on, presently nearly 300 pages and as yet unfinished. But McGrath's contribution to the letter poem is not limited to his neglected and unfinished masterpiece. In his collected shorter poems, *Movie At the End of the World,* there are short lyric letter poems of a very high order: "Postcard *Amchitka, 1943*," and "A Letter for Marian" which opens:

> I sit musing, ten minutes from the Jap,
> Six hours by sun from where my heart is,

> Forty-three years into the hangman's century,
> Half of them signed with the difficult homage
> Of personal existence.
>
> . . .

The letter poem is, for the poet, "the difficult homage of personal existence," as all being is first personal, then universal. It's declarative nature premits the poet a freedom of commitment and subjective experience utterly alien to other genres. At its most fully realized and most lyrical, at its most intense occasion, the letter poem expresses emotion more *purely* than any other. And here I shall close with a few references to the poetry of Kenneth Rexroth: the elegies for Delia and Andree Rexroth, poems like "For a Masseuse and Prostitute," and "The Signature of All Things," and even the longer "The Heart's Garden, the Garden's Heart," poems that bring together the epistolary tradition of East and West as perhaps no other poet has done. A great deal of the shorter poetry of Rexroth is very clearly within this tradition. That he is not universally recognized for the master he is, that he, like McGrath, is almost a neglected poet, is nearly incomprehensible. As Rexroth says at the close of "A Letter to William Carlos Williams:"

> And that is what a poet
> Is, children, one who creates
> Sacramental relationships
> That last always.

The letter poem will remain with us for as long as we write poems. There was nothing I could say to the young man in Missoula but to go home and read the classics, both ancient and modern.

Hank Lazer

THE LETTER-POEM

The epistolary poem today is oddly attractive. Our age, at least in terms of poetic temperament, distrusts didacticism. But I think that, secretly, the poet would very much like to give in and say what he has to say straight out. His hope would be that the statement, like the image, would have its own attractiveness. As in Robert Hass's "Letter to a Poet" in *Field Guide*, the words of the statement do battle, unlike prose, with the sharp, short line breaks:

> John, I am dull from
> thinking of your pain,
> this mimic world
>
> which makes us stupid
> with the totem griefs
> we hope will give us
>
> power to look at trees,
> at stones, one brute to another
> like poems on a page.

Even a direct statement has suspense.

But the sustaining example for the contemporary epistolary poem isn't a poem. It is Rilke's *Letters to a Young Poet*, as widely read, I would guess, As *The Duino Elegies* or *The Sonnets to Orpheus*. Rilke gives us in the *Letters* even more than a spiritual guide to the experience of being a poet. He reassures us: letters have dignity. In the eighth letter, Rilke explains,

Only those sadnesses are dangerous and bad which one carries about among people in order to drown them out; like sicknesses that are superficially and foolishly treated they simply withdraw and after a little pause break out again the more dreadfully; and accumulate within one and are life, are unlived, spurned, lost life, of which one may die.

The letter, and the letter-poem, attempt a healthy "carrying about among people." The attempt in the letter-poem is to share feelings. As Rilke explores the nature of fulfilled human love in the seventh letter, he writes of "the love that consists in this, that two solitudes protect and border and salute each other." The letter-poem must acknowledge the solitude of writer and reader. But at its best, the letter-poem can "protect and border and salute."

The letter-poem immediately provides a great solution to a problem that any poet faces, the problem of address. The very form, the salutation, helps to shape the poem. Private reference and gossip may follow. And so the poet, after the poem is done, must wonder if the poem speaks to more than one person. The letter-poem, from the first line, acknowledges that it speaks clearly and specially to one person. But all poems have a boundary of particulars and special references to get beyond if they are to speak to many.

So when we pluck up the courage to buck the current image-based trend in American poetry, some bold statements get made in a seemingly offhanded form, in that hybrid, the letter-poem. Robert Hass is one of my favorites at handling the letter-poem. In Hass's poem, "Letter," which appears in *Field Guide*, we begin with a common feature of the letter-poem, an extremely specific description of place:

> I had wanted to begin
> by telling you I saw another
> tanager below the pond
> where I had sat for half an hour
> feeding on wild berries
> in the little clearing near the pines
> that hide the lower field
> and then looked up from the red berries
> to the quick red bird brilliant
> in the light.

But Hass's description is more than the standard "here's where I'm writing this letter." And Hass's letter-poem is more than a snapshot and more than literal observation. His poem is about two loves: the love of naming and the love for the woman, his wife, whom he addresses in the poem. The description of the natural world, where naming takes place, gives way:

> But I had the odd
> feeling, walking to the house
> to write this down, that I had left
> the birds and flowers in the field,
> rooted or feeding. They are not in my
> head, are not now on this page.
> It was very strange to me, but I think
> their loss was your absence.

The key declaration in the poem is the simple, tender phrase, "It's you I love." Hass's letter-poem is the field wherein the poetic world—the world of plants, birds, naming, and words—and the world of real human relations confront one another. In this poem the poet chooses the world of the actual woman over the world of poetry:

> I have believed so long
> in the magic of names and poems.
> I hadn't thought them bodiless
> at all. Tall Buttercup. Wild Vetch.
> "Often I am permitted to return
> to a meadow." It all seemed real to me
> last week. Words. You are the body
> of my world, root and flower, the
> brightness and surprise of birds.
> I miss you, love Tell Leif
> you're the names of things.

The poem is not a rejection of poetic activity. Instead, the letter-poem insists that poetic activity, naming, be related to real bodies, an actual woman, a son, Leif, and not merely take place in the abstract meadow of literary cross-reference. In fact, the real world of love does not compete with the world of poetry; the real world of love sustains the world of poetry and gives the latter body and shape. The two worlds become one with the realization that "You are the body/ of my world, root and flower, the/ brightness and surprise of birds."

In *Praise* Hass includes "Not Going to New York: A Letter," in which various narratives are allowed to intersect. The letter-poem never really accomplishes its task—an apology to Dan (Halpern) for not flying to New York. Instead, the letter-poem becomes a field for memory—late winter in upstate New York, the poet's grandmother growing old and dying in San Francisco—

and a place to explain the present, December in California in a
room where the poet's children,

> Kristin and Luke are bent to a puzzle, some allegory
> of the quattrocento cut in a thousand small uneven pieces
> which, on the floor, they recompose with rapt,
> leisurely attention. Kristin asks, searching
> for a piece round at one end, fluted at the other,
> "Do you know what a shepherd is?" and Luke, looking for
> a square edge with a sprig of Italian olive in it,
> makes a guess. "Somebody who hurts sheep."

What the letter-poem becomes for Hass is an act of recomposition
"with rapt, leisurely attention." At the heart of the wandering
letter-poem is the clear memory of the poet's grandmother:

> Luke watched her wide-eyed, with a mingled look of wonder
> and religious dread she seemed so old. And once,
> when he reached up involuntarily to touch her withered cheek,
> she looked at him awhile and patted his cheek back and winked
> and said to me, askance: "Old age ain't for sissies."

That is one reason why the letter-poem is to be valued. In its in-
directness, its casual allowance for prosaic incidents and small
stories, the letter-poem provides an occasion and a place for a
memory that, otherwise, might not have come back.

When we point to the informality of the letter-poem, and the
possible bonuses that result from that informality, we must also
acknowledge that style itself is an issue in the letter-poem. The
letter-poem, because, after all, it is only a letter, not exactly a
"poem," ought to be informal. A conversational tone is alright,
even expected. And it is this conversational tone that allows direct
statements to get made. The poet's usual approach of speaking
through his images, the "no ideas but in things" approach, the
preference for showing over telling, the poem which "should not
mean but be," is altered by the demands of the letter. And of all
contemporary letter-poets, Richard Hugo knows best how to take
advantage of the seeming informality of the letter-poem.

In *31 Letters and 13 Dreams* Hugo exploits beautifully the
allowed directness and informality of the letter-poem. When we
say that style itself is an issue in the letter-poem, part of what we
mean is that there is a peculiar demand on the letter-poem for a
kind of fidelity that the non-letter-poem does not have. In the

letter-poem, the poet must convince the reader that the poet is genuinely addressing someone, Dear X, as well as addressing, almost by unwilled coincidence, the reader. Otherwise, one of two failures takes place: the letter-poem becomes just a letter or just a poem. Here is where contemporary poets will differ a great deal. Hugo, for example, seems to have the specific person to whom he writes the letter-poem in mind at all times. Hass, on the other hand, is more willing to jump to a greater level of generality. Hugo's letter-poems lean closer to the letter, Hass's to the poem.

What Hass and Hugo do share is a willingness to let the letter-poem, in its rambling, duplicate the mind's own wandering. Hugo, in "Letter to Kizer from Seattle," even apologizes, "Sorry to be so rambling." But, in "Letter to Matthews from Barton Street Flats," Hugo is also willing to ramble and explore the memories that come up:

> Why do I think
> of this today? Why, faced with this supermarket parking lot
> filled with gleaming new cars, people shopping unaware
> a creek runs under them, do I think back thirty some years
> to that time all change began, never to stop, not even
> slow down one moment for us to study our loss, to recall
> the Japanese farmers bent deep to the soil? Hell, Bill,
> I don't know. You know the mind, how it comes on the scene again
> and makes tiny histories of things. And the imagination
> how it wants everything back one more time, how it detests
> all progress but its own, all war but the one it fights over
> and over, the one no one dares win.

Hugo's letter-poems don't quote well because the thoughts do ramble on. And that's what is so unusual, and unfashionable, about Hugo's letter-poems: they're full of thoughts. They give up the tangible and the palpable and step forward, momentarily unadorned, with truths. For example, in writing to Charles Simic in "Letter to Simic from Boulder," Hugo risks the kind of big statement that would probably be too direct and abstract to survive in a "regular" poem:

> I don't apologize for the war, or what I was. I was
> willingly confused by the times. I think I even believed
> in heroics (for others, not for me). I believed the necessity
> of that suffering world, hoping it would learn not to do
> it again. But I was young. The world never learns. History

has a way of making the past palatable, the dead
a dream.

Hugo employs a host of abstractions—the times, heroics, the
world, history, the past, the dead—in the space of a few lines.
Such writing would not survive a creative writing workshop, probably not even one of Hugo's own.

But this poetry of statement, as Hugo shows in "Letter to Gold-
barth from Big Fork," makes the letter-poem an ideal place for
an informal poetics. Hugo explains that poems are "the warm
ways/ we search each other for help in a bewildering world,"
and that poems are not "the world photoed and analyzed, only one
felt." In "Letter to Birch from Deer Lodge," Hugo, refining the
poet-prisoner analogy, writes of poets,

> We find secret ways to play. No one
> except poets know what gains we make in isolation.
> We create our prison and we earn parole each poem.

In *31 Letters and 13 Dreams* many of Hugo's poems tell stories
about the desolate places of Montana. What is interesting is the
way Hugo's stories about Montana merge with his love of poems.
In "Letter to Oberg from Pony," Hugo writes,

> I love Pony like I love
> maybe fifty poems, the ones I return to again
> and again knowing my attention can't destroy what's there.

Even though Hugo can employ the letter-poem as a vehicle for
a poetics, the main issue that the letter-poem best addresses is
not so abstract a subject. As in "Letter to Gale from Ovando," the
subject best addressed by the letter-poem is loneliness:

> How scattered we become. How wrong we end finally alone,
> seeing each other seldom, hearing the wind in our teeth.
> Roethke himself knew and hated to know the lonely roads
> we take to poems. Mirian Patchen was right in her speech
> in Portland: it's a one man route and sad. No help. No friend
> along the way, standing beside the road with trillium.

The letter-poem is a gesture and an attempt to defeat the poet's
isolation. As Hugo concludes in "Letter to Gale from Ovando,"
the letter-poem is more than a pro forma reliance on a salutation

and a sincerely yours:

> Think of poems as arms and know from this town I am writing
> whatever words might find a road across the mountains. Dick.

But Hugo's letter-poems come full circle. Beginning as a gesture to another, the letter-poem returns to the act of self-definition and self-acceptance, as Hugo acknowledges in "Letter to Blessing from Missoula,"

> Do not depend on others for sympathy.
> When you need sympathy, you'll find it only in yourself.

A peculiar feature of the letter-poem, then, is that the letter-poem, despite its address to another, is ultimately an exercise in autobiography. Addressed to an intimate friend, the letter-poem can be used by the poet to tear away layers of self-delusion. To fellow poet and fellow "problem drinker," John Logan, in "Letter to Logan from Milltown," Hugo writes,

> Now no bourbon to dissolve the tension,
> to find self-love in blurred fantasies, to find the charm
> to ask a woman home. What happens to us, John?
> We are older than our scars. We have outlasted and survived
> our wars and it turns out we're not as bad as we thought.
> And that's really sad.

But Hugo's acts of self-definition, the autobiographical elements in his letter-poems, are achieved without ignoring the person to whom the letter-poem is addressed.

Aside from the beauty of rhetoric and the beauty of Hugo's well-tuned American sounds, what makes his truths register so strongly is the degree of emotion that he commits to the page. Sometimes with other letter-poets we feel that the letter convention is being used as an excuse or a prop. With Hugo, the letter-poems are as warm, intimate, and personal as the letters (that never claim to be "poems") that we get from friends in the mail. The most moving example in *31 Letters and 13 Dreams* is the "Letter to Annick from Boulder," which begins,

> Dear An: This will be your first widow Christmas. Such a young
> death, Dave's. A rotten cheat. The thirty or forty years
> he had coming torn way. I couldn't say at his grave where

we stood bowed, ignored by the freeway above us how
unlucky he was that he couldn't poke the corners of his life
and have fun. It was too grim, that's all. Too something damaged
to be anything but run from. To law. To literature. To film.
And he ran beautiful but not far enough. Forget that.
The beautiful never go far.

In this letter-poem Hugo's writing is personal and compassionate.
My own terms for his poem are vague, evaluative, judgmental,
and inadequate. He ends the letter-poem with more truth:

And it makes no matter whether we cringe
inside or roar defiance at stars. We touch each other
and ourselves no special day, no designated season,
just now and then, in a just poem under an unjust sky.
God, I get windy. This poem any season, for you always. Dick.

It should be noted, however, that the style of Hugo's letter-
poems is not so different from his other poems. For example, in
"Letter to Hill from St. Ignatius," Hugo writes,

I resent you once told me how I'd never know
what being Indian was like. All poets do. Including
the blacks. It is knowing whatever bond we find we find
in strange tongues.

Later in the same poem, Hugo tells Hill, "You're gaining/ the
hurt world worth having." The style is the same in Hugo's earlier
writing: the love of simple words, especially one syllable words,
the repetition of words and vowel sounds, and the clotted, compact
sentence structure verging on the awkward and the ungrammatical.
Even the attitudes that emerge from Hugo's letter-poems are
the same ones that crop up in his earlier poems. In "Letter to
Mantsch from Havre," Hugo notes that "So few of us are good
at what we do, and what we do,/ well done or not, seems futile."
The gray defeatism, the loneliness, and the self-mockery of Hugo's
letter-poems are no departure from his earlier writing. But in the
letter-poems Hugo works more and more with disarming directness. We aren't as aware of style and stance straining to become
content. Hugo seems able in the letter-poems to get to direct saying
any time he wants. Or, as Hugo writes to his home-run-hitting
friend, Mike Mantsch,

> when that style, the graceful compact swing
> leaves the home crowd hearing its blood and the ball roars off
> in night like determined moon, it is our pleasure
> to care about something well done.

Hugo continues and makes the connection more direct: "I want my poems to jump/ like that." His poems do "jump/ like that" because, at their best, the casual intersects something larger, as in "Letter to Sister Madeline from Iowa City," where the weather approaching flat Iowa speaks as well of a kind of personal vulnerability:

> No complaints except for weather. In the west
> where we have mountains, we can always assume that hidden
> from us but coming is something better. Here, no illusion.

Taken together, Hugo's letter-poems have a cumulative effect. The incidents add up. We learn the vicissitudes of an attractive character, the comical heroic Dick. The end effect is close to what Hugo himself says, in "Letter to Haislip from Hot Springs," about reading a novel:

> I know why I always feel sad when I finish a novel.
> Sometimes cry at just the idea that so much has happened.
> But then, I'm simply a slob. This is no town for young men.
> It sets back off the highway two miles and the streets stand bare.
> When I drive in, I feel I'm an intrusion. When I leave,
> I feel I'm deserting my past. I feel the same sadness
> I feel at the end of a novel. A terrible lot has happened
> and is done.

As a final example of the letter-poem, Pablo Neruda's "Letter to Miguel Otero Silva," translated by Robert Bly, contains some valuable general remarks. This particular letter-poem cannot become too specific in its description of setting because Neruda is in hiding. So, Neruda, sarcastically, gives "only details useful to the State." Though I would not call this letter-poem abstract, because what dominates is the poet's love for and gratitude to Miguel Otero Silva, Neruda does allow himself to talk about the nature of letters and poems. Early in the letter-poem he explains, "Writing poetry, we live among the wild beasts." Later, he writes,

> Have you ever spent a whole day close to sea birds,

> watching how they fly? They seem
> to be carrying the letters of the world to their destinations.

Letter and poem share in a universal circulation. They carry the news, the emotional and spiritual news we live by.

Consistent with the element of autobiography that we have already noted as a feature of the letter-poem, in this letter-poem Neruda describes his own poetic history. He used to be a spectacular poet of depression and metaphysics, the Neruda, especially, of *Residence on Earth*. In this poem he speaks of a turning point in his writing and of a time when "I didn't continue to be occupied exclusively with metaphysical subjects." Neruda's letter-poem is instructive not simply as literary autobiography. What is of interest to all of us is what happens when he gives up depression and metaphysics:

> But I had brought joy over to my side.
> From then on I started getting up to read the letters
> the sea birds bring from so far away,
> letters that arrive moist, messages I translate
> phrase by phrase, slowly and confidently.

In writing a letter, or a letter-poem, a strange transparency ocurs. So often the poet is willing to, or must, reveal the exact situation of his act of composition. Neruda, as the letter-writing poet, describes his actions this way:

> All at once I go to the window. It is a square
> of pure light, there is a clear horizon
> of grasses and crags, and I go on working here
> among the things I love: waves, rocks, wasps,
> with an oceanic and drunken happiness.

Neruda, after talking about an incident when a poem by Miguel Otero Silva lifted Neruda out of depression, writes about how, thus far, he had resisted writing to Otero Silva. Finally, Neruda finds himself coaxed into writing the letter:

> But today has been too much for me: not only one sea bird
> but thousands have gone past my window,
> and I have picked up the letters no one reads, letters they take along
> to all the shores of the world until they lose them.
> Then in each of those letters I read words of yours,

and they resemble the words I write, and dream of, and put in poems,
and so I decided to send this letter to you, which I end here,
so I can watch through the window the world that is ours.

The letter-poet is strangely egoless. Even though he writes to one person, his words, his letter, enter into a universal circulation. The letter is a kind of window through which we watch "the world that is ours." And a letter, in its essence, involves two actions: sending and receiving. The scope of the letter-poem depends on what we put in it. Neruda urges a passionate commitment to basics:

Life is like the sky, Miguel, when we put
loving and fighting in it, words that are bread and wine,
words they have not been able to degrade even now,
because we walk out in the streets with poems and guns.

Finally, I would argue that the letter-poem draws the best out of a poet. I would even go so far as to argue that Ezra Pound's greatest poem is his translation of a letter-poem, "The River-Merchant's Wife: A Letter." What is wonderful about the letter-poem is that it has an immediate appearance of utility. The poet's service is doubled: he writes in service of "the poem " and he writes to a good friend. And because it's only a letter he writes, he approaches the double obligation relaxed and ready to give.

Warren Slesinger

OTHER VOICES THAN THEIR OWN

Letters from Vicksburg, Gary Gildner, Unicorn Press, 1978, 29 pages, $10.00 hardcover, $4.00 paperback.

Letters from Lee's Army, Angela Peckenpaugh, Morgan Press, 1979, 44 pages, $7.50 paperback.

Compliments are due these two poets and their publishers for recognizing the potential for poetry in these letters, and for providing the kind of format that makes the excellence of the small presses more evident than ever. First, the poets restructured the sentences of the letters to clarify and intensify the voices of the individuals who wrote them; second, the presses reproduced the photographs of family members and field hospitals, wagon trains, and skirmish lines to enhance the effect of the letters now rewritten in the guise of poems, and to recreate the context of their time.

Of course, the connected series of events on which the general interest depends is the Civil War. In these letters we glimpse the War through the eyes of two soldiers on opposite sides: a Union soldier from Iowa and a Confederate soldier from Virginia who are writing from the midst of the action fighting for their lives.

By all accounts, the John Blood of *Letters from Vicksburg* could be considered more typical than the Ham Chamberlayne of *Letters from Lee's Army*. The average Civil War soldier was a farmer who possessed little formal education or military training. He was between 18 and 30 years of age. More of a fighter than a soldier, he scoffed at rank and military discipline. Even though the offer of a "bounty" might have enticed him to enlist, he was more likely to have volunteered out of loyalty to the region from which he came, and the idea that he could identify himself, if he supported a particular cause. At first, so many were so eager to join that the states produced more recruits than could be accomodated or equipped, but soon the Confederacy, and then the Union had to resort to military drafts that proved to be extremely unpopular. It was the provision that permitted the employment of substitutes that provoked the saying in the North that the war was fought with "rich men's money and poor men's blood."

In camp and field the Union soldier was better cared for then the Confederate. Still, it is difficult to tell how many died from diseases like typhoid fever and small pox—not to mention dysentary, dehydration, and starvation in overcrowded jails. According to the records that exist, 7 out of 10 deaths were due to illness. Worse were the weapons and the methods of early modern warfare: the rifled barrel, and then, the rifle loaded from the breech. Medical skills and facilities were so inadequate that the chances of surviving a wound were no more than 7 to 1.

Yet the basic strategy seldom changed. One side would gather itself together, then move toward a bridge, a railroad terminal or a supply post usually located inside a city; the other side would position itself to defend it, and open battle would take place. But owing to troop exhaustion, commanders could seldom follow up their victories. After the battle, both sides would disengage, reorganize, and reposition themselves for battle again. During a campaign, either army could be decimated, but it seemed that the essential conflict could not be resolved at all. Toward the end, a sense of stasis brought about an extraordinary boredom with the war.

The "pointlessness" of an event that becomes totally detached from its purpose is nowhere more evident than in the letters of lesser men who are destined to remain more anonymous than John Blood or Ham Chamberlayne. For the sake of comparison, I read a private collection of Civil War letters, and found the following:

"I ofen think this War will never be over it seames to
mee as if it for nothing only but to get poore men
killed."

"I hope to god thay will draft some of them dam loafers
about that town thay have pretty good time of it. . . if
could have my Way i would put them at head of battle
kill them off like dogs."

"It aint like it was last summer now and then thare
was some excitement but now thare is not any."

Peevish, vengeful, and truculent, they remind us how minor a
role in history can be. If they seem insensitive to their own experience, it is because they have neither John Blood's power of observation nor Ham Chamberlayne's faculty for forming a sentence.

Gildner's John Blood of *Letters from Vicksburg* is a Union soldier who, though barely literate, is bright and eager to report on a
recent march into enemy territory, if only to express the sense of
his own presence at these events:

> Dear woman I was glat to hear from you
> yours of Aprile 29 and glat
> to hear that you was well and Edward to
> we hav hat hart fighting sins we crost
> the Missippi   many maimed and lost
> a plan to martch was met by Rebels near
> Port Gibson   they was in a canebrake ther
> we hat to drive them out with beyonet
> witch we don with fulsom sped and got them
> on the open field wher we shot them
> down by hundrets but they stot thair ground til
> noon   they tried retreat   we charged and killed
> til sunset   Captain Staley lost his sord
> and I my cap for witch I thank the Lord

Spelling by ear, often employing a "t" for a "d" or an "s," he
gets by with bad grammar and occasional spacing for punctuation.
He is too intent on a clear account of himself to be diverted from
his purpose. For all the crude mannerisms of the man, the letters
are written with a remarkable sensibility, and the poems do more
to reenforce his feelings and perceptions than to refine them.
Their unpretentiousness is retained in the rhymes that tie the lines
together like knots in a cord. It is to Gildner's credit that he uses
the structure of the sonnet more for the effect of the form on the
material than a literary device that virtually guarantees that it is
poetry. The success of the poems in *Letters from Vicksburg* de-

pends on the semblance of awkward sentences, and they are faithful to their source. Gildner responds to the impulse of the speaker without asserting his authority as a poet to speak through him or for him. In spite of the apparent struggle with the wording, and unaware of the semantic ironies, John Blood makes sense.

Yet Gildner is sensitive to subtle changes in the syntax that indicates the growth and development of an individual who becomes increasingly conscious of his stature as a man:

> Dear wife and friend I dozed but now will try
> to finish this   I wondered in the thick
> until my hart sloed down   I hat to ty
> my foot   for I hat looked and seen the slick
> colecting ther along my boot   they shot
> my big toe off   also I was struck
> with grape against the neas   my pants wer cut
> by glancing balls witch left me welds on both
> my angels   God hat bilt me tal enough
> I gues   I herd a halt   to my surprise
> General Logan and his forse of seven
> thousand stot beyond the treas   O Heaven
> help the Rebels now   I hureyed up to him
> and said our men wer going down like flys

Of course, John Blood tells us more about himself than the events that he describes. In his effort to communicate, he indicates that while he is brave enough to be a soldier, he is not so sure of himself as a Christian or, indeed, as a husband, not to need a sign of reassurance from his wife:

> I have not hat a singel letter from you
> for a month   o you don't know how anctious
> I can feal

At times, it is his own loneliness that cries out; more often, it is empathy for others that he expresses:

> I hat seen hart sites
> befor I ever saw a battel
> field   at Edwarts station hospital
> I fount out what it was to see a hert
> the one that makes me dry hat lost his tong
> the ball past thro his teeth and cut it off
> and made his eyes and everything look wrong

All in all, the voice of John Blood is resoundingly American in the popular understanding of the term:

> Dear Cecelia we hav hat some warm times
> in the Company sins I last wrote to you
> on Monday the Lutenant died   and Sims
> first Corprel died of feaver   and a slew
> of other vakancys ar coming up
> as officers receive paroll   the way
> we fil them is by vote   well the question
> of Lutenant laid between Lon Baily
> and myself   only Colonel Connell hat
> promised Baily and he found out if he
> left it to the vote whi I would get three
> forth   so he sent rite strate for Bailys bars
> now he wants to make me sargent   well heres
> what I want   nothing   if it aint by vote

With no real notion of democracy, he supports the principles of popular vote without questioning the legal or cultural implications of the war. He prides himself on his place, as though to belong to a group were more important than the sense of his own identity.

In contrast, the Ham Chamberlayne of *Letters from Lee's Army* is a Confederate soldier who is just as committed to a cause, but he does not relish the reality of war. In his correspondence with family members and others, he tries to keep something in himself separate from events as though to protect his own poetic temperament:

> Now, you may imagine
> what time it is.
> The great round moon
> has just risen
> to give its light
> mellow, palpable,
> fit to bathe in.
>
> Moonlight is too fine
> a thing to waste in camp
> among idle soldiers.
>
> I don't need more than one
> moonbeam to ride off

to home and friends
back to when war was unknown
and to the future when war
will be forgot.

At times, the poetic impulse results in so much rhythmic movement that the sentences are easily divided into lines, and we are
aware of their "literary" quality. Angela Peckenpaugh is sensitive to Ham Chamberlayne's striving for a higher form of self-
expression. The problem is that the use of free verse is apt to
suggest a languorous ineptness at moments of extreme self-con-
sciousness. This is more a measure of the man who wrote the
letters than the poet who responded to his moods and mannerisms.
Ham Chamberlayne could conceive of himself as quite a romantic figure, and strike a pose to impress a young woman:

So I still chirp here
as you there
and tho the country
is for a time enslaved
tho friends are dead and exiled
tho I have not a dollar
nor any property
but one pair of top boots
(with spurs attached)
still I can laugh.

In working with the original material, Peckenpaugh is careful to
retain the tone that indicates the nature of the relationship between
Ham Chamberlayne and the person addressed in the poem. With
his sister, he is far more forthright, and honest to the point of self-
criticism:

Dullness has wrapped me
round like a blanket.
All things stupify in stillness.
Ex Nihilo Nihil. My head
could not be emptier
than a glass bell
over an exhausting air pump.

.   .   .   .   .

Conceive a ragged, half-demolishd mill.
Busy clack of clapper

replaced by weary whistling.
Me seated on a mud bounded shore
filled with a pine forest
rotting slowly in sadness.

It is characteristic of him to end as often as he can on a note of interest, creativity, or humor whenever he writes to a woman. However, his letters to his mother are the most direct and free of affectation. Implicit is their mutual respect and understanding. Consequently, he is less courtly and more open; he makes no attempt to protect her from the impact of an incident:

Today somebody kicked
up a red fox,
an old big fellow
in the grass.

There were some
11,000 men camped round
in a circle.
The country was open,
men shouting as so many children.
The fox doubled and twisted.
All his doublings
served but to increase
his pursuers.
Some one among the lousy crew
caught him.

An army is such a monstrous sight
the brute beasts stand aghast
at it and instinct falls.

Squirrels, hares and partridges
are easy prey and here
an "old red" succombed.

Generally he selects an incident that he can handle intellectually, if only to indicate that he can learn from his experience even in the midst of a war. It could be that he is too concerned with propriety and deportment in front of the women, but Ham Chamberlayne is a gentleman, and his courteous regard for them is genuine. His code of conduct requires the same restraint and self-control in his letters to other men. His southern gentility is nowhere more pronounced than in his sense of history:

When by accident I
see Gen. Lee there looms up
some king-of-men.

Was it King Henry whose son
was lost at sea,
whereafter he never smiled.

In weight he carried
to suppress all joy
he was but a fool to Lee.

When you and I are whitehaired
and tell huge stories of these times
then the shadow of Lee, lengthening
will mark a continent with giant form.

In these two collections of letters, one finds the kind of "material culture" that tells us more about the Civil War than the names, dates and geographic locations that abound in school books. I doubt that either John Blood or Ham Chamberlayne thought that he was making a public statement while he was writing. In the hope that their letters were only worth keeping, the claims that they made on posterity were modest indeed. But now they are no longer isolated in their time. Gary Gildner and Angela Packenpaugh have rescued them for us; these poets have spoken with other voices than their own.

Greg Simon

SEEKING KINDNESS FROM THE DUST
Chinese Letter Poems

... Read in the records, from earliest times,
How hard it is to be a great artist.
—Tu Fu

Few of us who live in a society decidedly indifferent to poetry
can appreciate what a necessity the ability to write rhythmic literature was for conscientious and ambitious citizens of the T'ang
Dynasty (A.D. 618-906). The invincible political and military
skills of T'ai-tsung, the first great T'ang Emperor, had filled the
broad tree-lined avenues of his capital with the negotiable asset
of absolute power. The entire government of the Chinese empire
was centered in Ch'ang-an under the direct control of the Emperors, supervised by men who were chosen, in part, by literary
examinations sponsored by the court. Competition for the relatively few comfortable positions near the reigning Emperor was
intense. A T'ang citizen had to be a beautiful woman, a eunuch,
a successful general, or a master of literary arts to even see an
Emperor in person.

The timeless poets of the dynasty, whose epistolary writings
are to be examined here, were nearly all members of families that
could afford to have them educated in provincial centers of Confucian studies. Scholarly success brought young poets to the attention of the Emperors, and their attention brought the poets positions at court, income from tax monies, and estates near the centers of power and intrigue in the Imperial capitals of Ch'ang-an
and Lo-yang.[1]

Emperors and commoners alike in T'ang China remained at
the relative mercy of the elements throughout their lives. Floods
and famines devastated the crowded mud-packed cities. Both
royal capitals were inundated by dissident tribes of Mongols and

Turks whose bloody invasions and revolts kept the empire in constant military turmoil, and dependent on the abilities of its generals. If this was not inducement enough for a wise and peaceful man to acquire literary prowess and, through judicial use of it, attain a position within the hierarchy, we could add the fluctuating nature of personal power in an empire surrounded by walls, and ruled by the whims of a single man who believed himself to be the son of god.

Entrance into the civil service was not, in itself, a guarantee of success in T'ang China. However difficult the years of intense study and testing that went into achieving positions at court, it was just as difficult to maintain such positions amid the uneasy alliances of military, administrative and financial advisers who ruled much of the known world in the Emperor's name. First-time appointees, for example, were usually sent to the troublesome and less civilized provinces of the empire. China's vast topographical expanse meant that travellers would be well separated from family and friends, and from their peers at court. More often than not, court intrigue based on the rigid factionalism of the government ministries resulted in banishment to such forsaken provinces for even the highest ranking ministers. The majority of the literate social class of Chinese scholars who comprised the court bureaucracy were uncertain from day to day if they would be spending their next few years in luxury at one of the capitals, or in poverty and duress in a distant village.

There exists in English translation[2] a poem presented as a letter to a friend by Han Yü (A.D. 768-823) which explains in almost oppressive detail the position of an official who was banished from Ch'ang-an:

> At a ten to one risk of death, I have reached my official post,
> Where lonely I live and hushed, as though I were in hiding.
> I leave my bed, afraid of snakes; I eat, fearing poisons;
> The air of the lake is putrid, breathing its evil odours . . .
> Yesterday, by the district office, the great drum was announcing
> The crowning of an emperor, a change in the realm.
> The edict granting pardons runs three hundred miles a day,
> All those who were to die have had their sentences commuted,
> Corruptions are abolished, clean officers appointed.
> My superior sent my name in, but the governor would not listen
> And has only transferred me to this barbaric place.[3]

Another such disappointed official is now famous *only* for the letters he wrote complaining of the unfairness with which he had been treated. In Jên Hua's letter to Tu Fu (written about 761) he asks:

Why is it that I no longer soar or sing? I am still waiting for someone at Court to recognize me. I have read countless books and one or two of my verses have made a certain impression. But looking at them now I see that they are poor, profitless things, and cannot bring myself again to pester the town with them. For the present I support myself by working on the land . . . . I am utterly desolate and alone. No one understands me.[4]

Regardless of rank, all excellent citizens soon succumbed to a need to maintain contact with each other, and to make their insecure lives more meaningful with an immense outpouring of written words. An anthology of T'ang poetry, compiled by a Manchu Emperor in 1707, contains 48,900 compositions arranged in nine hundred books. In spite of this largess, it is feared by scholars that countless works by even the greatest writers have been irretrievably lost.

Responsibility for introducing an English-reading audience to Chinese poetry lies with Ezra Pound and Arthur Waley. The immediate and sensational impression that Pound's *Cathay* (1915) and Waley's *Chinese Poems* (1916) had on writers and readers of poetry in England and America has been attributed to the general effort being made at that time to liberate poetry from the restrictions of rhyme and meter. But we must also take into account a remark made by Witter Bynner on the nature of Chinese poetry: "Because of the absence of tenses, of personal pronouns and of connectives generally, the translator of Chinese poetry, like the Chinese reader himself, has considerable leeway as to interpretation."[5]

Chinese poems are difficult to bring into English. Their spare and simple forms mock the awkward and wordy shapes into which they are forced in English.[6] Donald Davie has pointed out that Chinese poems from the T'ang Dynasty are not anything we can recognize from our familiarity with English verse forms.[7] They are not ballads, not odes, not madrigals; they are not even sonnets, although this is perhaps the closest form to which they can be compared. They are the results of literary traditions which are uniquely Oriental, coming from a place far beyond the youthful boundaries of English literature.

During World War I, Arthur Waley was working quietly on the immense holdings of Chinese literary antiquities in the British Museum. Ezra Pound had been contacted by the widow of Ernest Fenallosa, who had in her possession an essay and many unfinished manuscripts dealing with Chinese poetry and medieval Japanese drama. These she turned over to Pound for examination, completion, and possible publication. I can imagine Pound's joy now as he sifted for months through the material given to him by Mrs. Fenallosa and tried to make sense of the bewildering columns of Chinese characters and finally realized, one day, well, two of them, at least, are *letters*!

Despite the relative haste with which Pound finished Fenallosa's work and moved on to other projects, he did very well. A few errors crept in, but the shorter of the two letter-poems by Li Po (Rihaku, in Japanese, A.D. 699-762) which Pound first published in *Cathay*, "The River-merchant's Wife: A Letter" ("Song of Ch'ang-kan"), eventually found its way into Yeats's memory, and then into the *Oxford Book of Modern Verse*.

This poem is a letter, an autobiographical monologue literally stripped of non-essentials. It is also a lament, a record of interior as well as exterior growth, and the declaration of the life-giving dependence and love of a girl who has grown through sadness and joy to be a woman. The spines of the poem are the flat declarative statements she virtually throws in the face of her husband's absence, and which Pound has translated with utter brilliance:

> I never laughed, being bashful. . .
> At fifteen I stopped scowling . . .
> Why should I climb the look out? . . .
> They hurt me. I grow older. . .
> And I will come out to meet you . . .

There is no mystery or nostalgia or undue sentimentality in the wife's letter. She quietly imparts her confidence in her ability to endure on the strength of her desire alone. This is the poem that was on the minds of those students who sought Pound out in London, clutching already worn copies of *Cathay*, having heard a voice in that book that was so old, so free from the technical encumbrances of English poetry, that it seemed to be absolutely new:

While my hair was still cut straight across my forehead
I played about the front gate, pulling flowers.
You came by on bamboo stilts, playing horse,
You walked about my seat, playing with blue plums.
And we went on living in the village of Chokan:
Two small people, without dislike or suspicion.

At fourteen I married My Lord you.
I never laughed, being bashful.
Lowering my head, I looked at the wall.
Called to, a thousand times, I never looked back.
At fifteen I stopped scowling,
I desired my dust to be mingled with yours
For ever and for ever and for ever.
Why should I climb the look out?

At sixteen you departed,
You went into far Ku-to-yen, by the river of swirling eddies,
And you have been gone five months.
The monkeys make sorrowful noise overhead.

You dragged your feet when you went out.
By the gate now, the moss is grown, the different mosses,
Too deep to clear them away!
The leaves fall early this autumn, in wind.

The paired butterfiies are already yellow with August
Over the grass in the West garden;
They hurt me. I grow older.
If you are coming down through the narrows of the river Kiang,
Please let me know beforehand,
And I will come out to meet you
                    As far as Cho-fu-sa.

*

   Li Po was an extraordinary exile who, when sober, believed
himself to be a banished immortal, a "Minister on Distant Service
of Celestial Principalities." He led a charmed life, surviving several undisciplined years in northeastern China as a swordsman-
for-hire. He was eventually brought to the attention of the court
because of his brilliant lyrical abilities, his facility with languages, and his love of the high style of Imperial life. But Li Po's
habitual drunkeness and impropriety gradually placed him in
disfavor with the Emperor's inner circle of wives, eunuchs, and
ministers. Li Po wrote a friend from his inevitable exile:

Yesterday, clad in a brocade robe, I poured
    the costly wine,
Today, sore afflicted, I am dumb like
    the speechless trees.
Once I rode on horseback in the great
    imperial park;
Now I jog about slowly from house to house
    of mandarins.[8]

Ezra Pound translated another poem by Li Po in *Cathay*, which he called "Exile's Letter." This poem is a record of the meetings and separations of Li Po and an otherwise unidentified friend named So-kin. Their meetings are usually accompanied by much feasting and drinking; a strong bond grows between the two men in the midst of all the revelry. In different parts of the long poem Li Po reminds his friend of scenes like these:

The foreman of Kan Chu, drunk, danced because
    his long sleeves wouldn't keep still
With that music playing
And I, wrapped in brocade, went to sleep
    with my head in his lap,
And my spirit so high it was all over
    the heavens.

. . .

And the vermillioned girls getting drunk about sunset,
And the water, a hundred feet deep, reflecting green eyebrows
—Eyebrows painted green are a fine sight in young moonlight,
Gracefully painted—
And the girls singing back at each other,
Dancing in transparent brocade,
And the wind lifting the song and interrupting it,
Tossing it up under the clouds.

If we had no other surviving poems from the T'ang Dynasty than these two of Li Po's, we could still count ourselves fortunate. The two poems are opposite, but complimentary. "Wife" reveals the narrative gifts of Li Po; his deep interest in common life. Li Po was a poet who drew deeply from the traditional aspects of Chinese literature, and who, according to Waley, "almost alone among the better-known writers of the day remained throughout his life a pu-i, 'a person in plain clothes . . . .'"[9]

In "Exile's Letter" Li Po's own voice dominates throughout. He is not overwhelmed by longing for a return to the high life in the capital which we are accustomed to seeing in poems of this nature,[10] but instead celebrates his rare friendship with another man which survived all hardships and lifted him above the bitter disappointments of his official career. In "Exile's Letter" Li Po chastises his society for a crime much more serious than banishing him to the life of a wanderer: that of being indifferent to the glow of human warmth and gaiety.

*

Wang Wei (A.D. 701-761) was an accomplished poet, landscape painter, and administrator who early in his forty years at court aligned himself with the literary faction of the government, head by Chang Chiu-ling. The mercurial career of Chang made it necessary for his followers to possess the means of disappearing from court on short notice. A victim of personal tragedies, Wang sought religious solace in Buddhism. The poet satisfied those two needs rather nicely by purchasing an estate in the rugged Chung-nan hills southeast of Ch'ang-an, and establishing a retreat there.

The hills around Lan T'ien were sparsely inhabited by farms, jade mines, small villages and monasteries. Wang and his frequent guest P'ai Ti jointly composed one of the loveliest sequences in T'ang poetry about the estate and landscape around it.[11] The following passage is from a letter to P'ai Ti in which Wang describes a long walk into the hills surrounding his bungalow:

> Going northwards, I crossed the Yuan-pa, over whose waters the un-clouded moon shone with dazzling rim. When night was far advanced, I mounted Hua-tzu's Hill and saw the moonlight tossed up and thrown down by the jostling waves of Wang River. On the wintry mountain distant lights twinkled and vanished; in some deep lane beyond the forest a dog barked at the cold, with a cry as fierce as a wolf's. The sound of villagers grinding their corn at night filled the gaps between the slow chiming of a distant bell.[12]

It is child's play to separate the stiff and ornate poetry Wang composed for official occasions from the spare and passionate letter-poems he sent from Lan T'ien. Wang makes very clear the kind of solace he sought at his refuge in the folowing lines from a letter-poem sent in 737 to his patron in exile, Chang Chiu-ling:

> I mean soon to belong to the country, and sow
> And plant things, and grow old in my refuge.
> I watch the wild geese southwards out of sight
> And think how I may send a word to you.[13]

Wang Wei believed in the power of landscape, at least of one's personal landscape, to provide a man with something close to paradise on earth. A letter-poem exists in which Wang examines, somewhat indirectly, the way in which a landscape can nurture a man, and provide solace for him in times of disappointment. "To Chi-wu Ch'ien Bound Home After Failing In An Examination" is a poem which includes almost all of the elements of T'ang society which came directly to bear on the great poets: the influence of Confucian and Taoist optimism, heartbreaking failure, return in exile to the provinces, and expression of love and friendship:

> In a happy reign there should be no hermits;
> The wise and able should consult together . . . .
> So you, a man of the eastern mountains,
> Gave up your life of picking herbs
> And came all the way to the Gate of Gold—
> But you found your devotion unavailing.
> . . . To spend the Day of No Fire on one of the southern rivers,
> You have mended your spring clothes here in these northern cities.
> I pour you the farewell wine as you set out from the capital—
> Soon I shall be left behind here by my bosom-friend.
> In your sail-boat of sweet cinnamon-wood
> You will float again toward your own thatch door,
> Led along by distant trees
> To a sunset shining on a far-away town.
> . . . What though your purpose happened to fail,
> Doubt not that some of us can hear high music.[14]

This delight in the way the world moves "led along by distant trees" is inherent in all of Wang's work. His heart was engaged by the poetry of his peers, the closeness of a few friends, and above all by the sensation that his hours in the deep lanes of Chung-nan were speaking to him of home:

> (To Chang Shao-fu)

> In life's evening I love only quiet;

Things of the world no longer concern me.
Having no plan to lean on,
I yearn in vain to return to the old forest.
The pine wind blows as I disrobe;
The mountain moon shines as I play my lute.
You want to know about failure and success?
The fisherman's songs are penetrating deep into the other bank of
the river.[15]

When Wang Wei returned to Ch'ang-an from captivity at the court of the renegade Emperor An Lu-shan in 758, one of the official letter-poems which greeted him had been composed by Tu Fu:

Mr. Wang's high reputation is of long standing.
Recently, he has been deep in trouble.
We hear of the arrest of the fine scholar who has returned from
among the rebels;
We rejoice to know it has not been made a case of literary treason.
Your illness was entirely due to your longing for Their Majesties;
And for three years, your heart remained as stout as ever.
You must have written songs of loyalty in distress,
Please read us some of them.[16]

In fact Wang Wei had composed two tiny letter-poems against the rebels during his captivity; they saved his life. These two quatrains were not only dedicated to his faithful friend P'ai Ti, but were actually whispered to P'ai in a corner of An Lu-shan's quasi-imperial gardens, in what was surely one of the most unique and dangerous moments in the postal history of China.

The considerable sympathy Tu Fu (A.D. 712-770) felt for Wang Wei was undoubtedly derived from his own adversities during the rebellion. Tu Fu had been captured and interred in Ch'ang-an in 756, cut off from his large family and from the patrons he depended upon for income. After about a year in captivity, Tu Fu took advantage of a lull in the savage fighting and walked 100 miles east from Ch'ang-an to join the T'ang court in exile. This act of loyalty and courage was rewarded by a position of consequence in the administration.

*

The unsuccessful rebellion of An Lu-shan was the turning point in Tu Fu's poetical life, much more so than in the lives of the older Li Po or Wang Wei. Hardships suffered and atrocities witnessed by Tu Fu during the rebellion never again allowed him to gloss over the obvious inequality of life in the empire, nor to fully harmonize with the other official voices. His experiences at this time extinguished in him any desire for complete solitude and retirement, although the life of a hermit at one time had greatly attracted him. Inspired to boldness by the political unrest of the times, Tu Fu bombarded the court and the officials he knew with lines such as these:

At court they are distributing rolls of silk,
Which the women of the poor have woven.
To extort it from them and offer it to the emperor their husbands have
    been beaten with rods.
Moreover I have heard it said that all the gold plates in the imperial palace
Have passed, one by one, into the hands of the family of the favorite.
In the palace there is such abundance that meat is allowed to go bad and
    wine to turn sour,
While in the streets, people die from poverty and cold.[17]

During the rebellion another friend of Tu Fu's found himself in deep trouble. Li Po had been caught up in the ill-advised campaign of a prince trying to take advantage of the disorganization of the T'ang empire. The unfortunate Li Po, who had been born in the northwest found himself drafted, embattled, imprisoned, and exiled at various locations on the Yang-tsze River, a region in the south of China noted for its humid and malarial weather. In "Twenty Rhymes Sent to Li Po," Tu Fu offered the following summary of Li Po's life as condolence to his troubled friend:

You had great talents but you wanted no political success.
Holding aloof from the world, you lived alone in retirement.
Though you were a private individual recognized for unusual ability,
You were also a scholar content to remain in extreme poverty.
When a hungry man had a few grains of Job's tears,
How the slanderers made them into ill-gotten pearls!
The climate of the southwestern corner of the empire is hot and unhealthy,
And you were exiled there as if you were a wicked rebel!
How long can you stave off a visit by the bird of death?

And in a letter-poem composed a year earlier, he wrote Li Po:

Who says that the heavenly law is merciful;
Here is an aging man with his freedom lost.
A fame that is to last thousands of years
Will rise after an unappreciated life is past.

It is not surprising that the author of such uncompromising lines would find popularity among his peers and the common people, even become a legend, but bring his official career to a complete standstill. "Have we forgotten," he wrote, "that wealth and prominence are less stable than dew in the grass?" After his banishment in 758, and his voluntary retirement from a post near Lo-yang that did not suit him in 759, Tu Fu occasionally served the empire as a military adviser in the southwestern provinces, and also became a small land-owner and farmer. A letter-poem sent to his cousin Tu Tso in 759 concerns an overdue shipment of grain:

The millet was harvested early in September,
You had promised to share it with me.
It must have been ground very fine;
I feel it has been somewhat delayed in reaching me.

A later letter, written in 763 to his brother Tu Chan, shows his deep concern for a small house he had long considered his home:

Be sure to count the ducks and geese every evening;
And do not forget to shut the wooden gate.
The shade of the bamboo grove on the east is too thin;
Plant more, even though the year is late.

Tu Fu spent the final years of his life exploring the Yang-tsze River and its tributaries, causing general consternation to the poor souls who had to row his boat. His final composition, written on the shore of Lake Po-yang, was a long and rambling letter-poem to his family which does not easily lend itself to partial quotation. But with his usual foresight, Tu Fu had presented his biographers with a perfect and compact summary of his life in a letter he wrote to the Emperor's favorite nephew, the Prince of Ju-yang, in 749:

I have been a hermit possessing half a gourd for a drinking cup,
And living in a shut-in dwelling high up among the cliffs.
Now I presume to face your largeness as a little shell might measure

an ocean,
Not to say your generous wine is as plenty as the water of the Sheng!
Are the secrets of everlasting life forever hidden?
There must be steps that will lead to them.
So long as the immortal prince will keep his friend,
He will never need to suffer the lack of friendly advice.

*

The blunt and self-confident Po Chü-i (A.D. 772-846) wrote letters to all kinds of high T'ang officials, introducing himself or his travelling friends in the hope of obtaining patronage, remonstrating against corruption or inactivity in high places, and even in one case explaining his own actions to the Emperor. Po's outspokenness, like that of Tu Fu, brought him early recognition at court, but also created enemies among his peers, and led to his eventual banishment from court due to their intrigue against him.

Po was 28 years old when he passed his first examination at Ch'ang-an, and began his life-long friendship with Yüan Chên, "the most memorable relationship in the literary history of China."[18] Po lived to be 74; he was proud of his age and of the prolific literary activity with which he relentlessly filled his days. Among the many letters which he sent to Yüan Chên (who was an exile from the capital for much of his official career), none is more interesting to modern readers than the quite lengthy one in which Po outlined the important aspects and discoveries of his poetic career. One section of the letter, written in 815, reads:

By the time I became a Collator, I had written three or four hundred poems . . . but in reality I had not yet discovered the true domain of poetic creation. The change began after I got a post at Court. I was getting older and more experienced; in conversation I always tried to pick up information about current problems, and in reading histories and other books I always tried to discover the principles underlying good government. It was then that I reached this conclusion: the duty of literature is to be of service to the writer's generation; that of poetry to influence public affairs.[19]

The evidence of the genuine nature of the relationship between Po and Yüan Chên lies in the early letter-poems which the two poets exchanged after Yüan Chên's first exile from Ch'ang-an in 805. In the following excerpt, Po, immersed in the long dream of his life, transmits to his friend the awesome responsibility of providing him with happiness on earth:

The flower of the pear-tree gathers and turns to fruit;
The swallows' eggs have hatched into young birds.
When the Seasons' changes thus confront the mind
What comfort can the Doctrine of Tao give?
It will teach me to watch the days and months fly
Without grieving that Youth slips away;
If the Fleeting World is but a long dream,
It does not matter whether one is young or old.
But ever since the day that my friend left my side
And has lived an exile in the City of Chiang-ling,
There is one wish I cannot quite destroy:
That from time to time we may chance to meet again.

Po's friendship with Yüan Chên was conducted almost entirely on paper and in their minds. Arthur Waley has translated letter-poems detailing Po's numerous meetings with Yüan in dreams, and outlining Po's responses to Yüan's poetry, and Yüan's responses to Po's popular poetry which he found, among other places during his travels, on the wall of a country-inn and on the lips of a courtesan. One of Po's poems is entitled "The Letter," and is the account of the arrival of a traveller at Po's house bearing precious mail from the absent Yüan:

They came and told me a messenger from Shang-chou
Had brought a letter,—a single scroll from you!
Up from my pillow I suddenly sprang out of bed,
And threw on my clothes, all topsy-turvy.
I undid the knot and saw the letter within;
A single sheet with thirteen lines of writing.
At the top it told the sorrows of an exile's heart;
At the bottom it described the pains of separation.
The sorrows and pains took up so much space
There was no room left to talk about the weather!

One of the all too brief and infrequent meetings in the flesh between the poets is altogether unforgettable. Yüan Chên had been recalled to Ch'ang-an from his exile on the upper Yang-tsze River. Po Chü-i was transferred from Chiang-chou on the lower Yang-tsze to be governor of Chung-chou on the upper Yang-tsze. "They met," according to Waley, "the one coming downstream and the other going up, near I-Ch'ang . . . ." Po Chü-i, presumably in a letter, now takes up the story: "Next day Yüan turned his boat and came upstream with me as far as the Hsia-lao garrison post. We intended to part on the twelfth; but when the time came, we could not bear to do so, and kept on being hauled upstream and then turning round and going downstream again."

In the final pages of Arthur Waley's magnificent collection of Chinese translations is a long story in prose, about 3,000 words, by Po Chü-i's friend Yüan Chên (A.D. 799-831). "The Story of Ying-ying" is by far Yüan's most famous work, having gone through numerous retellings in many different forms not only in China, but world-wide.

Yüan's prose romance is the story of a young scholar Chang who meets and falls in love with a cousin Ying-ying while the two of them are temporarily residing in a monastery at Pu-chou. Although the woman is very shy, the two are soon exchanging poetry. "Then came the sharing of pillow and mat, the time of perfect loyalty and deepest tenderness." Chang is called to the capital for his examinations; Ying-ying, who entered into the relationship without illusions, remained in Pu-chou and realized that she had lost her love: "Ch'ang-an is a city of pleasure where there are many snares to catch a young man's heart. How can I hope that you will not forget one so sequestered and insignificant as I?"

Ying-ying's letter to Chang, which she sent accompanied by a jade ring she had possessed since her childhood, then continues on to offer him an open look into the depths of her heart:

The good man uses his heart; and if by chance his gaze has fallen on the humble and insignificant, till the day of his death, he continues the affections of his life. The cynic cares nothing for people's feelings. He will discard the small to follow the great, look upon a former mistress merely as an accomplice in sin, and hold that the most solemn vows are made only to be broken. He will reverse all natural laws—as though Nature should suddenly let bone dissolve, while cinnabar resisted the fire. The dew that the wind has shaken from the tree still looks for kindness from the dust; and such, too, is the sum of *my* hopes and fears.

Yüan Chên's image persists. Although it has been years now since I first made the acquaintance of the exiled poets—Li Po, Wang Wei, Tu Fu, Po Chü-i—I now see them fallen like dew from the glittering tree of Ch'ang-an, seeking kindness from the dust.

NOTES AND REFERENCES

1. Ch'ang-an, now called Sian, lies on the alluvial plain of Kuan-chung in west-central China. It's population at one time during the T'ang Dynasty was over one million, making it the largest city in the world. Lo-yang, a much smaller city, was the eastern or social capital of the empire.

2. David Hawkes, in his excellent book on Tu Fu, identifies two distinct types of letter-poems: those presented to the dedicatee by the poet himself, and those sent through the mail. The published English translations I have chosen to examine in this article are those which I believe impart a strong sense of meaning and structure to a reader who may not be familiar with the Chinese originals, and which do so without the aid of lengthy notes.

3. Translation by Witter Bynner & Kiang Kang-hu in *The Jade Mountain*, New York, 1929. See also the excellent version by Kenneth O. Hanson in *Growing Old Alive*, Port Townsend, 1978, pp. 25-27.

4. Translation by Arthur Waley.

5. From Bynner's Introduction to *Jade Mountain*.

6. Many of the letter-poems examined in this article are, in Chinese, a series of hierographic monosyllabic characters, printed five or seven to a line in sixteen lines. The variations possible on this form involve the number of syllables per line, and the number of lines per poem. Poems of this time were usually rhymed at the end of even-numbered lines. Thus a poem entitled "Twenty-two Rhymes" would be forty-four lines long.

7. Donald Davie, *Ezra Pound: Poet as Sculptor*, N.Y., 1964.

8. From Li Po's "To His Friend at Chiang-hsia." Translation by Shigeyoshi Obata.

9. Arthur Waley, *The Poetry and Career of Li Po*, London, 1950.

10. Longing for a return to the capital permeates another much longer autobiographical letter-poem by Li Po, translated in the Obata volume, and written to a certain Governor Wei.

11. See Jerome Ch'en & Michael Bullock, *Poems of Solitude*, New York, 1960, pp. 47-75.

12. Translation by Arthur Waley. This letter has also been translated in full by Wai-lim Yip (1972), G. W. Robinson (1973), & H. C. Chang (1977).

13. Translation by G. W. Robinson.

14. Translation by Bynner & Kiang.

15. Translation by Shou-yi Ch'en in *Chinese Literature*, New York, 1961.

16. All translations of Tu Fu, unless otherwise noted, by William Hung.

17. Translation by Rene Grousset, Anthony Watson-Gandy, & Terence Gordon in *The Rise and Splendour of the Chinese Empire*, Berkeley, 1953.

18. Angela C. Y. Jung Palandri, *Yüan Chên*, Boston, 1977.

[19.] All translations of Po Chü-i by Arthur Waley.

Three other books were particularly helpful to me:

China, by C. P. Fitzgerald, New York, 1938.

Cold Mountain: 100 Poems by the T'ang Poet Han-Shan, Translated by Burton Watson, New York, 1962.

The Sui Dynasty: The Unification of China, A.D. 581-617, by Arthur F. Wright, New York, 1978.

CONTRIBUTOR'S NOTES

HAROLD ADLER is a graphic designer with the motion picture industry. His wife, Helen, the recipient of these letters, is a weaver whose workshops and exhibitions require her to travel widely.

JODY ALIESAN is the author of *Soul Claiming* (Mulch Press, 1975), and *as if it will matter* (The Seal Press, 1978), and was a 1978 recipient of a grant from the National Endowment for the Arts.

LESLIE-BETH BERGER is a clinical psychotherapist and co-editor of a small poetry press in Baltimore.

AUDREY BORENSTEIN's stories and essays appear widely in such magazines as the *North American Review*, the *Antioch Review* and the *Georgia Review*. Columbia University Press published her *Redeeming the Sin: Social Science and Literature*, in 1978.

REGINA DECORMIER-SHEKERJIAN has recent work appearing in *Porch*, *Willow Springs*, and *The Smith/News-art* magazines.

JACK DRISCOLL's *The Language of Bone* appeared from Spring Valley Press in 1979. Recent issues of *New York Quarterly*, *Poetry Northwest*, and *Beloit Poetry Journal* include his work.

PAUL GENEGA recently won the Lucille Medwick Award of the *New York Quarterly*. He teaches at Jersey City State College.

GARY GILDNER's latest collection, *The Runner*, is available from University of Pittsburgh Press, 1978. He received the Theodore Roethke and Helen Bullis prizes from *Poetry Northwest*, and publishes his short stories in the *Georgia Review*, *Kansas Quarterly*, and elsewhere.

PATRICIA GOEDICKE is on the guest faculty at Sarah Lawrence, where she teaches poetry. Her fourth and fifth books were published this year: *The Dog that was Barking Yesterday*, from Lynx House Press, and *Crossing the Same River*, from the University of Massachusetts Press.

MORRIS GRAVES is one of the outstanding artists of our time.

JOHN HAINES will have a book of his essays published next year by Michigan University Press. Also next year, Wesleyan University Press will publish his *Selected Poems*.

SAM HAMILL's book of essays, *At Home in the World*, to be published in January by Jawbone Press, will include "Epistolary Poetry." *Animae*, his most recent volume of poems, is available from Copper Canyon Press.

CARLA HOFFMAN is a graduate student in English literature at the University of Notre Dame; her recent work appears in *Poetry Now*, and elsewhere.

HAROLD LELAND JOHNSON is the author of *Cities of the Blue Distance*, published recently by Hearthstone Press. He is at work on a book on the Northwest United States between 1908 and 1928.

ROSE KAMEL is an assistant professor at the Philadelphia College of Pharmacy and Science, and is the recipient of two NEH grants. Her essays appear in *Modern Poetry Studies*, and other journals.

PHYLLIS KOESTENBAUM teaches creative writing at San Francisco State University. Her books include *Hunger/Food* (Jungle Garden Press, 1980), and *oh I can't she says* (Christopher's Books, 1980).

HANK LAZER's poems appear in the *Virginia Quarterly Review*, *Poetry Now*, and *The Nation*. He teaches at the University of Alabama.

CHARLES LEVENDOSKY is poet-in-residence for the Wyoming Council on the Arts. Wesleyan University Press published his *perimeters*, in 1970, and Point Riders Press brought out *aspects of the vertical*, in 1978.

LYN LYFSHIN is the author of eleven books of poems. She recently edited *Tangled Vines: a Collection of Mother and Daughter Poems*, published by Beacon Press.

ROBERT LOUTHAN has published poems, criticism and interviews in a number of magazines, including the *Paris Review* and the *New Republic*. His first book of poems, *Shrunken Planets*, was released by Alicejamesbooks, in 1980.

KEVIN MCILVOY is a frequent contributor to *Northwest Review*. The selections here are from his forthcoming novel *The Shakino Gang*.

GERARD MALANGA's latest book of poems, *This Will Kill That*, will be published by Black Sparrow Press in the fall, 1980.

WILLIAM MEISSNER is widely published; his work appears in magazines such as *Field*, *Poetry Northwest*, and *Chelsea*. *Learning to Breathe Underwater*, his first book of poems, is available from Ohio University Press.

DON MILLER teaches with the art department at the University of Wisconsin at River Falls. These postcards were sent from Eugene, Oregon to a postal art exhibit in River Falls.

ANGELA PECKENPAUGH's poem here, from her chapbook *Letters from Lee's Army*, (reviewed in this issue by Warren Slesinger), is an adaptation of a letter from her great grandfather to his son, her great uncle. Her work has appeared in the *Virginia Quarterly Review*, and *Southern Poetry Review*.

JOHN QUINN is an assistant professor at the Daido Institute of Technology in Nagoya, Japan. Abattoir Editions, of the University of Nebraska, brought out his first book, *The Wolf Last Seen*, recently.

JOAN RETALLACK chairs a seminar on the "Irrational" for the Forum on the Humanities at the Washington School of Psychiatry. Her poems, fiction and articles have appeared in *London Magazine*, *Massachusetts Review*, *Epoch*, *and* elsewhere.

DEBORAH ROBBINS is a former member of the *Northwest Review* fiction staff. She received her MFA in fiction at the University of Oregon.

LEN ROBERTS teaches at Northampton Community College, in Pennsylvania. His poems have appeared recently in *The Smith*, *Colorado-North Review*, and elsewhere.

GREG SIMON has published homages to Osip Mandelstam and Elizabeth Bishop in recent issues of the *New Yorker* and the *New Republic*. An essay on Norman Dubie will appear soon in the *Sonora Review*.

WARREN SLESINGER is the editor and marketing manager of the University of Pennsylvania Press. He has published in the *American Poetry Review*, the *Georgia Review*, and the *Northwest Review*, and received an Ingram Merril Foundation grant in 1974.

JULIA THACKER has published poems in *Antaeus*, *Mademoiselle*, *Ms.*, the *North American Review*, and the *Massachusetts Review*. This is her first published fiction.

DAVID WALKER's books of poetry are *Moving Out*, and *Fathers*. Recent work of his appears in *Poetry*, the *Georgia Review*, the *New England Review*, the *Antioch Review*, and the *Yearbook of American Poetry, 1980*.

STEVEN WEILAND is Executive Director of the Federation of Public Programs in the Humanities, in Minneapolis. His articles have appeared in the *Iowa Review*, the *Michigan Quarterly Review*, and *Kansas Quarterly*, among others.

ROBERT WEXELBLATT teaches literature and philosophy at Boston University. His stories, poems, and essays have appeared recently in the *Massachusetts Review*, the *Denver Quarterly*, and the *Literary Review*.

ROBERT WRIGLEY's book of poems, *The Sinking of Clay City*, was published in 1979 by Copper Canyon Press. He received a National Endowment for the Arts fellowship in 1978.

Northwest Review is deeply grateful to the following individuals and institutions for their generous support.

Patrons
($100 or more per year)

The Autzen Foundation
The Coordinating Council of
    Literary Magazines
Robert D. Clark
Mrs. Virginia Haseltine
Ken & Faye Kesey
Albert R. Kitzhaber
The Jackson Foundation
Glen Love
Mr. & Mrs. Carlisle Moore
Chris Mumford
The Oregon Arts Commission
Southwest Forest Industries
George Wickes

Donors
($25 per year)

Mr. and Mrs. Roland Bartel
Mr. and Mrs. Edwin Bingham
Mr. and Mrs. Robert A. Eisen
Alice Henson Ernst
Mr. and Mrs. Otto J. Frohnmayer
Walter Havighurst
James L. Henry
Stanley Maveety
Waldo F. McNeir
Carolyn and Ernest Moll
Clarence W. Schminke
Jordan D. Schnitzer
John C. Sherwood
Jim Sullivan
Janet Witte Tanner

Contributions are tax-deductible, and may be sent to the University of Oregon Development Fund, designated for **Northwest Review.**

NORTHWEST REVIEW

EDITOR

John Witte

FICTION & ART EDITOR   **POETRY EDITOR**

Deb Casey   John Addiego

ASSISTANT EDITORS

IN FICTION

J. D. Brown
Robin Leigh
Chris McCarthy
Jim McGuire
Maxine Scates
Robert Ward
Danna Wilner

IN POETRY

Cecelia Hagen
Jonathan Monroe
Rodger Moody
Frank Rossini
Anne Sheffield
Mark Thalman

ADVISORY EDITORS

Kenneth O. Hanson
William Stafford
George Wickes

BUSINESS MANAGER

Faye A. Darnall

Northwest Review is published three times yearly. All correspondence should be addressed to Northwest Review, 369 PLC, University of Oregon, Eugene, Oregon 97403. Submissions of poetry and fiction are welcomed. Submissions of book reviews, essays and artwork should be preceeded by a query. Unsolicited manuscripts cannot be returned unless accompanied by a stamped, self-addressed envelope. The sole criterion for acceptance of material for publication in **Northwest Review** is that of excellence.
Copyright ©1981 by **Northwest Review.** ISSN 0029 3423. Member CCLM.

Northwest Review is indexed in the **American Humanities Index**, the **Index of American Periodical Verse**, and the **Index to Periodical Fiction.** Back issues of **Northwest Review** are available on microfilm from University Microfilm, Inc.

Subscriptions: One year at $6.00; two years at $11.00; three years at $16.00. Student subscriptions: One year at $5.00; two years at $10.00.